"How Did You Get This Job?"

Four Hueys leave Phuoc Vinh POL (fuel) point. Of course, it's raining.

"How Did You Get This Job?"

The Daily Journal of a
1st Air Cavalry Combat Photographer
in Vietnam

Terry A. Moon

© Terry A. Moon 2017 All Rights Reserved

This book is dedicated to all of those Americans who served in Vietnam, not necessarily by choice, and did the best job they could. They were part of a team whose bonds of brotherhood remain today. Upon their return, they were threatened by hateful antiwar protesters, driven by biased, ratings driven media. These misguided activists insulted, spat upon and even violently attacked the very military members that had defended their rights of free speech.

Welcome home, Brother.

A Chinook brings in a sling out load of ammo to LZ White late in the afternoon.

Table of Contents

Preface		ix
Key to 1st Cav Unit Designations		xi
Maps of 1st Cav Area of Operations 1969		xii & xiii
Chapter One	Into the Unknown	1
Chapter Two	A Surprise New Job at the Photo Lab	15
Chapter Three	I Will be a Photographer After All, But Where?	25
Chapter Four	From FNG to Photo Coordinator	45
Chapter Five	A Different Job Every Day	67
Chapter Six	A New Information Officer	83
Chapter Seven	A New Commanding General	101
Chapter Eight	One Job that Changes Everything	113
Chapter Nine	Great Response to My Combat Assault Photos	127
Chapter Ten	I Go to the Field with 2nd Brigade	145
Chapter Eleven	They Call Me Back Early as Photo Coordinator	179
Chapter Twelve	Short Timer Paranoia, Leaving with a Flourish	193
Epilogues		219
Acknowledgements		231
Bibliography		233
Glossary		235

PREFACE

As a photographer, like many of the 150,000 men who served with the 1st Air Cavalry Division in Vietnam, I had a supporting job. I was very proud to be a part of such a great tradition, and was motivated to do the best job possible in support of the combat battalions.

I do not address the ugly upper level politics of why we were there, as I could do nothing about it. This is not a story about the horrors and brutality of war. There are plenty of those. My journal is about my daily experiences with the soldiers, not just the grunts, of the 1st Air Cavalry Division. It is about teamwork and cooperation. It is about the guys I photographed daily who kept everything moving, the unsung heroes, artillery, engineers, medics, maintenance, logistics, signal, and all the support guys. I also salute the grunts. We know they had by far the toughest job. It took everyone performing together to make it work. None of us wanted to be there, but we tried to make the most of it, and did the best job we could, as part of the team.

My story is about what I saw every day in my travels around the 1st Cav's area of operations. It is about my experiences, many ordinary, many interesting, and some scary. It is filled with stories of the daily cooperation I saw in the members of the 1st Cav as they did their jobs, and the help from them that I personally received to take photos showing the world what the 1st Air Cavalry Division was about.

I was privileged and proud to photograph most of the varied activities of the 1st Air Cavalry Division, from my job as photo coordinator for the 1st Cav Information Office at Phuoc Vinh from November 1968 to November 1969. I saw first hand the great team spirit, and the intense pride. I found this pride with wounded skytroopers in hospitals, when I visited them with the commanding general. It was at the base camps, the fire support bases, and with the helicopter pilots and crews. Of course, it was with the grunts in the field.

At a time of race-related unrest in the USA, I saw several racially-mixed crews function as well-oiled machines. Wherever I went, it was apparent that a huge majority had bought into the team concept. Most of the people went out of their way to help me with transportation to places I needed to go. Others helped me with the photo assignments.

I worked several times with the South Vietnamese Army (ARVN) and local police personnel in the villages. Some of the locals had relocated from North Vietnam where Catholics were brutally persecuted by the Communist government. Thousands fled to the South. Most of the Vietnamese people in our area were cooperative and friendly to us.

Nothing meant more to me than when a dirty, tired grunt at a fire support base or in the field would see my camera and name tag, smile, and say, "I liked your pictures in the paper."

I have over 400 photos to illustrate my daily journal. Most of the photos in this book were taken with my own camera and my own film. I always shot my Army assignments first with the Army camera. I don't have any of those thousands of negatives. They were either buried in some archive that no one had been able to find, or they never made it out of Vietnam.

My information was gleaned from the two hundred and fifty-seven letters that I sent home. They gave me hard dates on events and specific details, but there were incidents I didn't tell my family. I also had other items that I had saved, including forty-seven different copies of our 1st Cavalry Division weekly newspaper, the *Cavalair*. Reading those letters released a barrage of memories that were my inspiration for this journal.

During my tour, I received marvelous support through the mail from my girlfriend, family and friends. It took four or five days for a letter from the USA to arrive in Vietnam. Our link with home was so important. I wrote letters almost every day, and that might be difficult for people to understand in today's age of instant communications.

A hostile media ignored some facts, and fabricated stories to feed the antiwar sentiment in the USA. This was the first television war. It wasn't the news on TV anymore, it was a ratings game. They weren't interested in our civilian medical and engineer aid projects, our heroic acts in battle, or our noble cause. I remember one particularly galling statement made by an Australian member of a TV network news team. I asked if the team would like to cover one of our medical aid projects at a local village. He answered, "I don't give a shit about your aid projects, show me dead Americans."

The media created a criminal image for us to face when we returned. That was never the case with the 1st Cav. Few incidents of civilian abuse of any kind were reported concerning 1st Cav personnel for the seven years they were there.

I had to deal with misdirected, hateful, angry antiwar people when I went to my next duty station in Washington D.C. Like many others in uniform, I was insulted, spit on, and had rocks and bottles thrown at me. The intense hatred from these incidents continues to haunt me to this day, more so than anything from the war.

In the last two decades there has been a change in the public perception of Americans that fought in the Vietnam War. Today, when I wear my hat with the 1st Cav pin, people recognize it and thank me for my service.

KEY TO 1ST AIR CAVALRY DIVISION UNIT DESIGNATIONS

Infantry (Grunt) unit example C 1/5 is Company C, 1st Battalion, 5th Cavalry

The nine 1st Cav Grunt Battalions were 1/5, 2/5, 1/7, 2/7, 5/7, 1/8, 2/8, 1/12, and 2/12

Division Artillery known as DIVARTY

Artillery unit example: B 1/30 is Battery B, 1st Battalion, 30th Artillery (Artillery Companies are called Batteries)

The four 1st Cav tube artillery units were 1/30 (155mm), 2/19 (105mm), 1/21 (105mm), 1/77 (105mm).

Division Artillery also had a Cobra Gunship Battalion, 2nd Battalion 20th Aerial Rocket Artillery,

and an air support battery (Hueys and LOHs) E Battery, 82nd Artillery.

Aviation unit example D 227th AHB was Company D 227th Assault Helicopter Battalion

Division Aviation 11th Aviation Group

227th AHB - Hueys, LOHs and Cobras

228th AHB - Chinooks

229th AHB - Hueys, LOHs, and Cobras

1st Squadron, 9th Cavalry, a Battalion sized unit, the Divisions Reconnaissance unit with Hueys, LOHs and Cobras.

Units attached to the 1st Cavalry Division

273rd Aviation Company (Heavy Helicopter) Skycranes

Parts of the 11th Armored Cavalry Regiment: Tanks, Armored Personnel Carriers, and self propelled Artillery

6th Battalion, 27th Artillery 175mm howitzers

Division General Staff breakdown

G1 Personnel
G2 Intelligence
G3 Operations/Training
G4 Logistics
G5 Civil Affairs/Psychological Operations

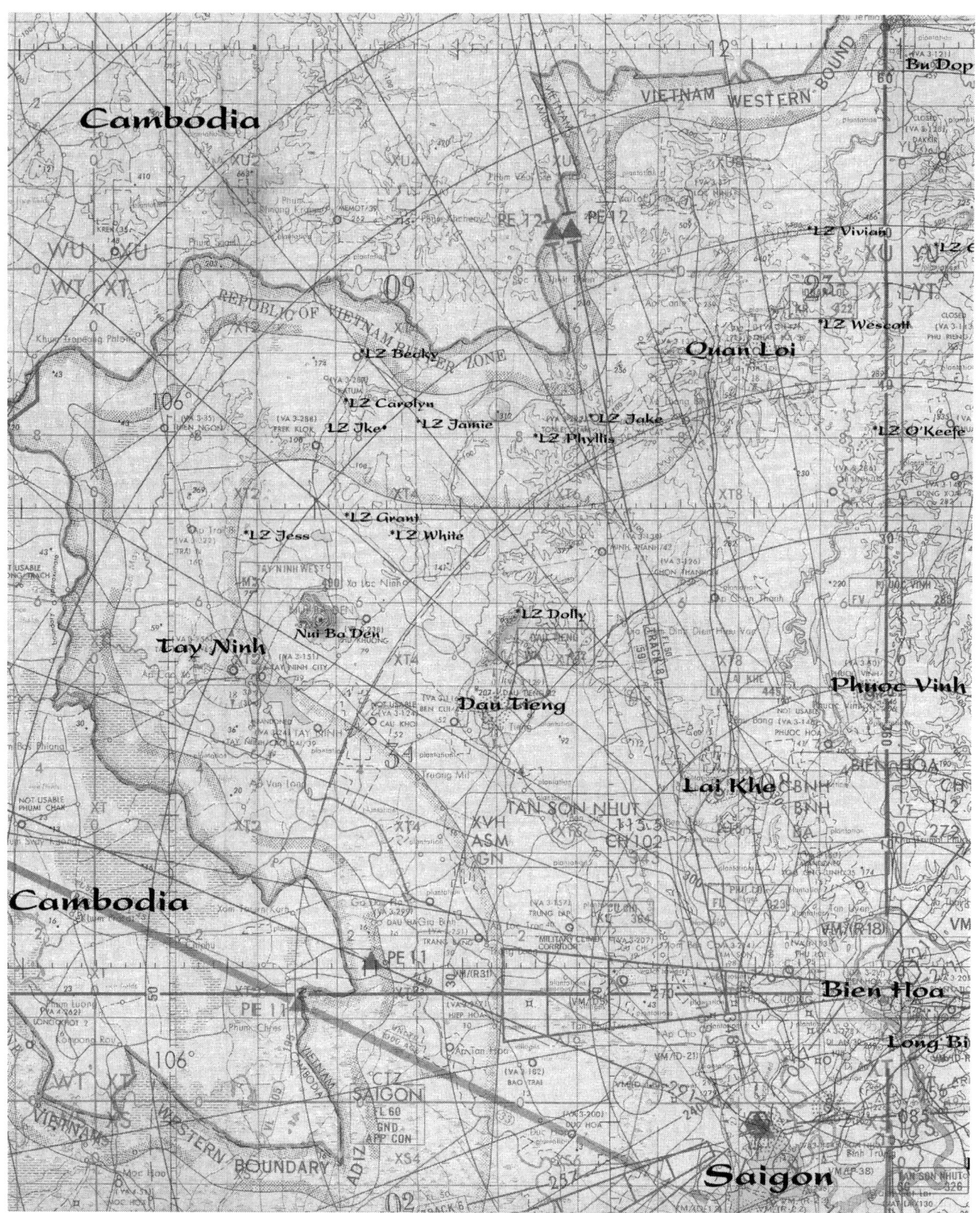

1st Cav Area of Operations Westside Map

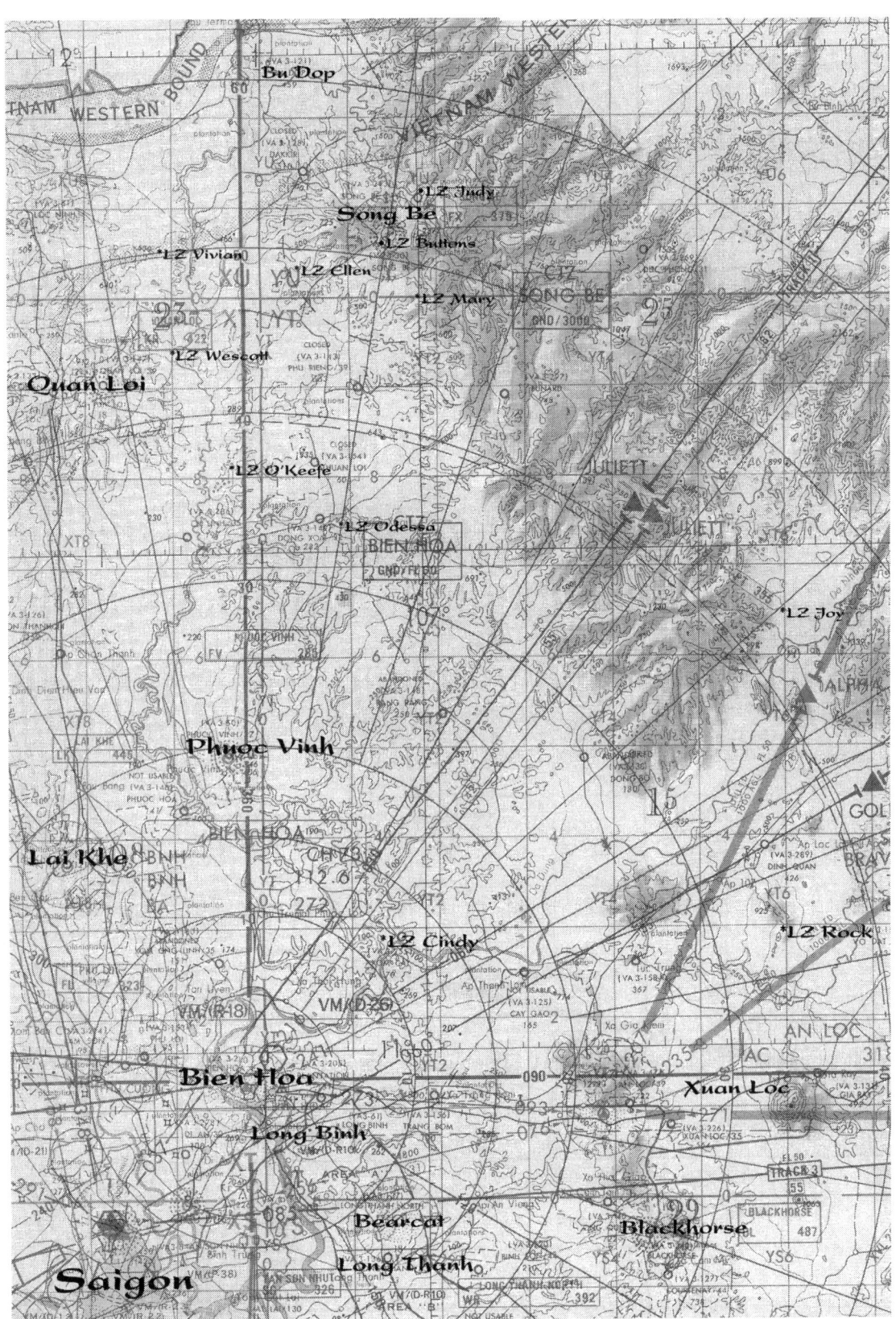

1st Cav Area of Operations Eastside Map

"How did you get this job?"

Grunts, artillerymen and even REMFs asked me this question countless times.

My answer:

I planned by enlisting for Army photo school.

Working hard, I finished first in my class.

Subsequently, I was chosen to serve as an information office photographer with

the legendary 1st Air Cavalry Division, the elite Army unit in Vietnam.

Furthermore:

It was late 1968, VC and NVA forces had been soundly defeated In the Tet Offensive.

The 1st Cav saw no local Viet Cong, only NVA invaders in their area between Saigon and Cambodia,

the Vietnamese civilians there, many of them Catholics, supported us.

Just as I finished my time in Vietnam, the American troop withdrawal began, and morale deteriorated.

Without a doubt, if I had to go to Vietnam,

I had the right job, in the right place, at the right time.

Chapter One Into the Unknown

The front gate at Fort Monmouth, New Jersey   *Photo by Allan Douglass*

"Whoever ranks number one, when this class graduates, will earn an instructor assignment to the Army Photography School here at Fort Monmouth, New Jersey," announced lead instructor, Sergeant First Class William Rosenmund. He spoke to the top five students in a class of twenty that included two Marines, slated to graduate October 18, 1968. "Only one thing can prevent the number one ranked graduate from joining our staff. This would be if everyone in the class receives orders for Vietnam. That has never happened."

Every week, Sgt. 1st Class Rosenmund posted the top five students on the board. However, he never displayed the point totals from our weekly assignment performance and quality, so I didn't know how close to me the others were. I had held the top position since the first standings were announced. Jerry Born, upstate New York, was second followed by Pete Sommers, Daytona Beach, Florida, Rick Keller, Anchorage, Alaska, and Greg Michaud, St. Louis, Missouri. At 21, I was the oldest.

On two of our assignments, we had to use antique Speed Graphic cameras, a big problem for everyone but me. When I worked as a photographer for the *Vista Press* Newspaper in 1967, editor Russ Dietrich had shown me how to use one. With it, I had photographed an awards ceremony because he bet me I couldn't. In the photo to the right, I was in the classroom with the Speed Graphic camera.

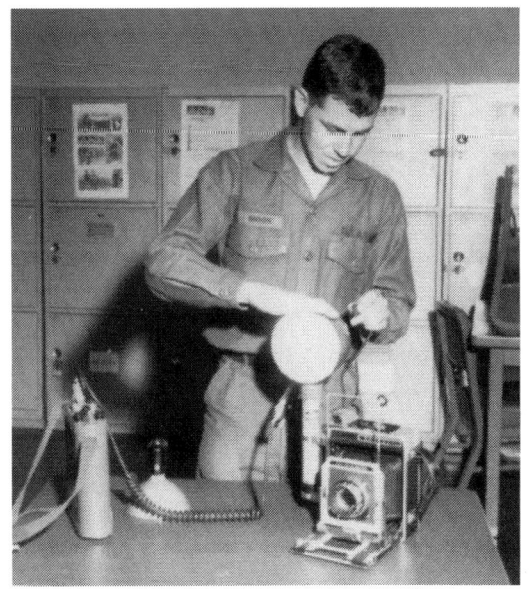

Traveling by bus to Lakehurst Naval Air Station for two aerial photo training assignments, where we flew in an ancient Sikorsky H-34 helicopter. All of us wore harnesses, a wise move as one student fell out and dangled precariously until we pulled him back in. I thoroughly enjoyed my two days flying in the helicopter.

Four more weeks remained of pressure packed assignments. The last lessons were far more difficult. Some evenings, the five of us would cruise Asbury Park together in my car with the prestigious California plates and once, we drove to Atlantic City. We had fun together, but were fiercely competitive during class, the instructorship was a valued prize.

Finally, after building suspense, Sgt. 1st. Class Rosenmund announced that I had finished first and would become an instructor. Jerry Born was second.

Great! I won. Now I will be an instructor here.

Sgt. 1st Class Rosenmund took me on a tour to introduce me to the Photo School staff.

Not so fast grasshopper! The unimaginable had happened. Our entire class received orders to Vietnam. It was a crushing blow, when I thought I would be an instructor and escape the war.

"I never believed an entire class would go to Vietnam." Sgt. 1st Class Rosenmund mumbled as he shook his head. According to him, we were one of the best classes he had ever taught.

Learning our fate, we formed an instant bond. The war was ramping up and we anticipated this could happen. We cringed at the Country Joe and the Fish song, "I Feel Like I'm Fixin' to Die," a morbid antiwar song that ended with the line, "Be the first one on your block to have your boy come home in a box." That could happen to any of us.

We graduated with the job title, or Military Occupational Specialty (MOS) 84B, Still Photographer, with the rank of Specialist Four. The five of us had skipped over PFC. My graduation day photo to the right. Our orders were all the same, we would meet again in Oakland on Veteran's Day for our flight to Vietnam.

Rick Keller helped drive my car to St. Louis, with only one "nap" stop. There, he caught a flight to his home in Anchorage, Alaska. My dad flew into the St. Louis airport and we drove my 1957 Ford Fairlane hardtop back to California with one overnight stop in Flagstaff, Arizona.

The day after arriving home, I visited with my numerous local relatives. One of my childhood friends, Jerry Miner called to set up a visit for me to meet his wife. He said one of her friends would really like to meet me. The next afternoon when they arrived, watching them get out of the car, I thought Jerry sure had a beautiful wife. *What! That wasn't his wife, it was my date, Sally.*

They looked at some of my photos and visited with my family, then the four of us went to dinner. It was a great evening and Sally agreed to another date. I ended up seeing her almost every day of the three weeks before I had to leave for Vietnam. We quickly built a strong relationship. My brother, Dennis, took the picture of us to the right with my C-33 twin-lens press camera that he would use while I was away.

Jerry Born flew out to visit a few days before we needed to report to Oakland. We went to the beach and cruised around with Sally. I wanted to repay Jerry for visiting his family. The two of us drove my car to his home in upstate New York during a weekend pass from Fort Monmouth.

Nov 10 - After painful, tearful farewells to Sally and my family, I flew to Oakland with Jerry on Pacific Southwest Airlines and we shuttled to the Army facility. After a brief search, the other three guys from our photo school group reunited with us.

Nov 11 - Veterans' Day - We joined approximately 160 military personnel aboard a Northwest Orient 707 to depart from nearby Travis Air Force Base (AFB) for Vietnam. (See my baggage tag to the left.)

Stopping for fuel near Seattle, we then headed across the Pacific. The plane experienced a problem, and the crew changed course to Anchorage, Alaska. This resulted in a delay of several hours. We deplaned in our short sleeve khaki uniforms and shivered our way across the tarmac in the 20 degree weather. A few lucky guys were given blankets. Most of us were trembling as we entered the terminal and were given hot drinks.

Later, we took off over the Pacific, heading to Japan. For hours, only ocean was visible in all directions. The seemingly infinite lights of Tokyo appeared as we approached. The 707 landed at nearby Yakota Air Force Base. It was still dark as we shuffled off the plane. Staying there a while, my mind was in chaos, worrying about the future. I had no perception of time passing.

Meanwhile we lost a day crossing the international date line.

Nov 13 - We reassembled and boarded the plane to leave Japan for the six hour flight to Vietnam. I could see the sun rising on Mt. Fuji.

It was the dawning of my great adventure.

Bien Hoa Air Force Base, just northeast of Saigon

Our plane landed at Bien Hoa (pronounced Ben Wah) Air Force Base, (photo above) near Saigon, in the early afternoon. The heat was stifling. We deplaned, picked up our bags and gathered on the tarmac near a small platform. Here, we would receive orders informing us of our new units and where we would spend the next year. My name was the first one called from the large group that exited the plane. The captain who announced the names added, "Congratulations man, you're going to the Cav." I was assigned to the 1st Air Cavalry Division, the Army's elite airmobile unit. *Was this an omen? Why was I first? Unsettling!* Sadly, I said goodbye and good luck to my friends. At least they knew I was headed to a good unit. I hoped they would contact me in the future.

4   Into the Unknown

With my new orders, I walked to the "terminal" in the steaming heat to wait for our flight on a four engine C-130 cargo plane to the 1st Cav Replacement Center at An Khe, located in the central highlands. Arrivals from previous flights were already waiting. Fortunately, we were in the shade. After a few hours, we hauled our heavy loads through the heat and humidity to a C-130. Struggling up the loading ramp, we entered the giant oven-like plane and found there were no seats inside, just ropes across the cargo bay for us to hold onto as we sat on the floor with our bags. Fortunately, it was a smooth flight. Part of the way, the droning engines lulled me to sleep as I leaned against my duffle bag. We landed in An Khe with quite a jolt, when the C-130 reversed its engines to land on a shorter airstrip, similar to slamming on the brakes. Some of the guys were tossed around, one guy rolled over the guy next to me and landed on the guy in front of him. As the back ramp of the plane opened, we welcomed a blast of cooler air. We had arrived in the central highlands, quite a change from the oppressive heat of Bien Hoa.

Nov 14 - In the early morning, an orientation was presented to new arrivals. The crusty sergeant addressed us as "fucking new guys," but only gave us humdrum information on when and where we would eat, sleep, piss and shit.

I made a friend, Mark Orthman from Indiana. Both of us realized the authorities didn't really know who was present, as there was no roster or roll call. We were able to avoid the menial work details of filling sandbags and building bunkers.

Various 1st Cav units were still finishing the move south from Hue and the DMZ to a wide area between Saigon and Cambodia. The massive move started on October 27. There were 20,000 troops in the 1st Cav that moved south. Some flew in C-130s, and some arrived by ship. The new base camp would be at Phuoc Vinh (50 km north of Saigon), a former 1st Infantry Division Brigade base. Some units had recently arrived and were not yet ready to receive new people.

They issued us jungle fatigue uniforms, and changed our real money (US currency) for military payment certificates (MPC). The bills were small, similar to monopoly money with paper nickels and dimes. A grunt in the field didn't want change jingling in his pocket. Mark took a picture of me (at right) in my brand new uniform.

Nov 15 - Mark and I continued to be successful in avoiding dirty and sweaty work details. We found books to read and in the evening saw two movies.

There were several incoming mortar explosions during the night. They didn't sound close, but I couldn't tell. It was unnerving, a wakeup call to reality. Someone out there was shooting at us.

Nov 17 - What a surprise! As Mark and I were loitering by the PX, I ran into Jerry Born, my best friend from Army photo school. He was already working in An Khe at the photo lab of the 173rd Airborne Brigade. We had arrived on the same C-130 from Bien Hoa and didn't know it. He gave me his address. I would send him mine when I received it.

Nov 18 - At 6 a.m., we had actual orientation classes and demonstrations. They issued us our M16 rifles and in a classroom we had detailed instruction on its care and maintenance. I had a different, heavier M14 rifle in basic training, so close attention was necessary. Two hours later, they marched us out a couple of miles past the greenline (base perimeter defense zone) through tall, thick elephant grass. Loud demonstrations followed of artillery, mortars, a recoilless rifle, and a Claymore mine.

A Claymore was a directional command detonated anti-personnel mine. It shot a 60 degree pattern of steel balls like a giant shotgun with a kill zone of up to 100 meters. The demo shredded a 55 gallon drum from more than sixty feet away.

There was strong pride among the guys as many had volunteered for the Cav. They said it was the best unit in Vietnam. We should be proud as this elite unit had first choice of all the skilled personnel arriving in Vietnam. *So we were chosen to be here.*

Later, at the rifle range, Mark and I zeroed in our M16s, adjusting the sights until we hit dead center on the target. They gave me two extra magazines since I had previously only shot an M14. I yelled at Mark, "This is great! I can actually hit stuff with this rifle." *With my job as a photographer, I doubted that I would have to shoot anyone.* We threw some grenades creating big explosions, and were pelted with debris. Exciting. Next, they sent us to greenline guard duty on a bunker. I was sunburned and then soaked as it rained intensely for a short while. We walked over five miles today and my new jungle boots were comfortable. Throughout the night, outgoing artillery awakened me. Adapting to this new environment would be tough. We hadn't learned to tell the incoming from the outgoing.

Nov 19 - Earlier, they had a roll call with our names on it, so we could no longer escape the work details. We were stuck most of the day with the dirty, sweaty job of filling sandbags and building bunkers.

Nov 20 - The clerks were confused, but they finally figured out that I was assigned to the information office at Phuoc Vinh. My orders said that. Mark's unit was 15th Supply & Service, the 1st Cav's logistics battalion.

There were no flights scheduled during the day. In the evening, we had guard duty with one other guy at the helicopter pad. All night, two hours on, four hours off. With no idea of what we were supposed to do, we were totally clueless. It was damn scary.

Nov 22 - To add to my heavy load, they gave me a whole bunch more. Now my duffel bag, and newly acquired field equipment bag, weighed 150 pounds. I tied them together and hung them over my shoulder. I also had my aluminum camera case, my M16, the pistol belt with all its pouches, and I was wearing my flak vest. *I hope I don't have to carry all this stuff too far.*

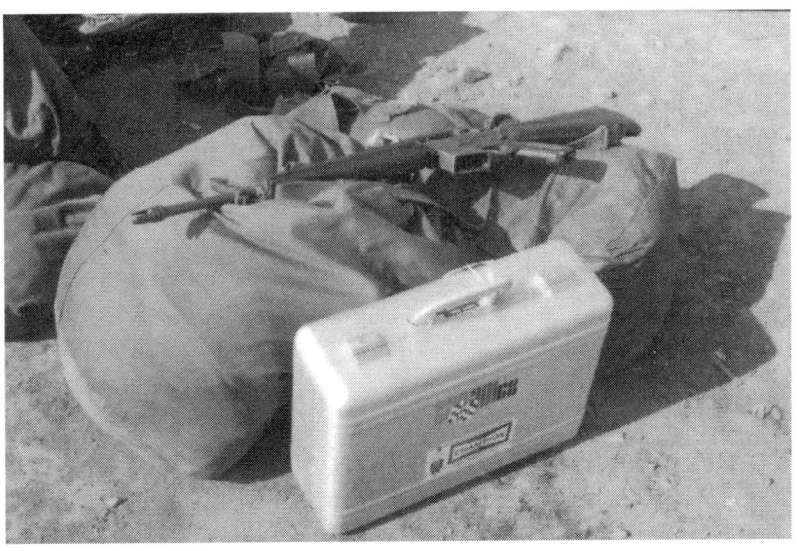

FNGs ('Funny' New Guys) board a C130 at An Khe to fly to 1st Cav base camp at Phuoc Vinh

Nov 23 - At 8 a.m., I finally boarded a C-130 to leave An Khe and fly to Phuoc Vinh. Many "fucking" new guys (FNGs) were struggling to carry heavy loads up the ramp into the loaded plane. It was like an oven and we were tightly packed. The ramp finally lifted in back, the engines roared, we rolled forward and headed for our new "home."

An aerial photo, through the haze, of 1st Cavalry Division base camp at Phuoc Vinh (PV), 50 km. north of Saigon.

We arrived at Phuoc Vinh (PV) at 9:30 a.m. Exiting the C-130, we trudged down the ramp onto the perforated steel decking (PSP) that made up the surface of the airstrip. As we waited in the blazing heat and steaming humidity, we noticed a fenced area a slight distance away, with no view inside, hiding something. One of the guys pointed and asked, "What is that?" Apparently his eyesight was weak, as I could clearly see the small sign on the fence, "GRAVES REGISTRATION."

"You don't want to know," I replied. I heard gasps and saw horrified expressions on the faces as each one saw the sign, and realized what it was. There were groans, and an "oh shit." This was an unwelcome reminder of our own mortality. Each one of us knew that he could return home in a body bag.

Later in the morning at the small area they called the processing center, most of the "fucking new guys" (FNGs) that were in larger units and all the grunts (Infantrymen MOS 11B) were given instructions, or were picked up by their respective units. My friend Mark left early with about ten other guys for 15th S&S, the large supply battalion. About 2:30 p.m., I remained with a few others assigned to smaller units.

A kindly water truck driver from the engineer battalion looked down from his cab as I sat on my duffle bag and asked me, "Where do you need to go?"

"The information office," I told him.

"That's part of 15th Admin Company, the office is in the rubber trees near the southeast greenline. I'm headed that way, throw your junk up here, hop in, let's go." I tossed my stuff behind the cab and jumped up onto the seat. "Welcome to the Cav, what is your MOS (job)?"

"I'm a photographer," I enthusiastically replied.

He smiled, "You will like it here."

The heavy truck rumbled to a few water stops at makeshift showers and drinking water tank trailers along the way.

BAM! BAM! We jumped into the ditch beside the road when incoming rockets hit nearby. I was stunned by how close the explosions were to us. It was over quickly, In denial, I couldn't believe it, I dusted myself off and we rumbled on. *Another reality check for me, there was a war going on.*

We entered the rubber trees, and stopped at the 15th Admin company mess hall and ate dinner. I felt welcome. *This small act of kindness was the first example of the many helpful attitudes I would experience daily during my year with the Cav.*

The helpful driver pointed out the information office across the street. I thanked him and walked over to the PIO building, (photo above from a rainy day). Eight or ten guys were lounging inside the office as I entered, someone yelled "FNG alert."

Another guy asked me, "What is your MOS?"

"I'm a photographer, 84 Bravo," I said.

They all groaned loudly. "We don't need another photographer right now," someone replied.

I didn't know what to think. They said I was the first FNG to arrive since before they came south. They told me about the recent attacks. The PX took a direct hit from a rocket a few nights ago, so now it was almost impossible to get a Coke, Pepsi, or a beer. Apparently, they liked to scare FNGs.

My deluxe sleeping accommodations at PIO in Phuoc Vinh, in the rubber trees a short distance from the greenline. The 55-gallon drum on the left is our shower.

Sergeant Frank Smart introduced himself as NCOIC (enlisted man-in-charge) and told me, "Take your bags to the tent at the end of the road and pick out an empty cot." It was about a fifty-yard walk from the office down a small road past a few other buildings, situated close to the greenline (base perimeter defense zone). I couldn't believe it, the old tent was so grubby, with a strange smell, perhaps mold, or, maybe it was the mangy dog one of the guys had in the tent. The two guys there were strange. Neither one told me his name. One just talked to the dog that he affectionately addressed as Myrtle. All the other guy said was, "If you see a rat, shoot it." Without hesitation, I took the cot by the front corner since those two were in the back. *Who were these guys? Had I been exiled with the misfits?*

Nearby, was our 55-gallon drum shower. A water truck would fill it daily. We also had our outhouse, a "four-holer" with a cutoff 55-gallon drum under each hole. An unfortunate guy had to take out each drum, pour in diesel fuel and burn it each day. This was the notorious "shit burning detail." The rumor was, the company first sergeant used this repulsive job as punishment.

Nov 24 - In the morning, when I arrived at the office, I was told to report to 1st Cav Information Officer Major Fox McCarthy. A small, pleasant man with a large forehead, he asked me numerous questions. The interview was more positive than the office entrance the previous day. It appeared that he already knew me. He liked my college background (journalism major, psychology minor and many photography classes), photo experience with my local newspaper, and the number one ranking in my Army photo school class.

"I also have photo lab skills." I added.

"If you do well, a lot of your pictures will be in print. The 1st Cav publishes a weekly newspaper and a quarterly magazine." He paused, and looked away, "I am disappointed with some of the seventeen photographers I have now," he said.

About two weeks ago, the information office staff arrived at Phuoc Vinh from Camp Evans, near Hue, in the far north of South Vietnam. They now had four photographers in Phuoc Vinh and four or five with each of the three combat brigades. The brigade photographers worked out of the base camps at Quan Loi, 92 km north of Saigon and Tay Ninh 100 km northwest of Saigon. They had assignments at fire support bases and out in the field with the grunts (infantry). The brigade base camps were only 15-20 km from Cambodia.

The major accompanied me to the back office building and introduced me to Press Officer, Captain Frank Carrara, and Photo Coordinator Spec. 5 Federico (Fred) Fiallos, a savvy veteran of the 1968 Tet Offensive in Hue and relief of the Marines from Khe Sanh. I was also introduced to the other photographers and writers, some of the same ones who had groaned when I arrived the day before. Staff artist, Larry Collins, a former grunt, had his drawing table next to Fred's desk in the press/photo office.

The major finished by telling me, "For a while, you will fit in where needed."

"Oh, oh!" I knew what that meant.

Sure enough, that afternoon, I had a grueling detail filling sandbags, and stringing barbed wire on the greenline. The humidity was worse than New Jersey in August, and it felt much hotter. Some of the guys told me to bring along a towel to keep the stinging sweat out of my eyes.

Attacks were expected soon and the greenline needed work. It consisted of three layers of nasty concertina wire, and regular barbed wire, that was solidly anchored to the ground so that the NVA couldn't crawl under it. Trip flares were set throughout the wire. Claymore mines, and chain link fencing to stop rocket propelled grenades, encircled the front of the bunkers. The detail guys told me stories about huge rats, snakes, and big, black scorpions. Everyone liked to scare FNGs, and they could sense one quickly.

Later, a CBS News team visited our office. The front guy was the only American. The other members were Japanese and Australian. Later some of the short-timers, veterans of the 68 Tet offensive and Khe Sanh, pulled me aside and told me they didn't trust the media. One guy said they lied to make us look bad.

About midnight, a short distance from us, we were startled by automatic weapons fire and several explosions on the greenline. We were under attack. We could see flashes and green tracers as they flew over our heads. It was deafening, and difficult to sleep because the NVA were right outside the wire. *Another "welcome to the war" reality check for me.*

Nov 25 - In the morning, I heard nothing about the previous night's attack, like it was no big deal. *Does this happen all the time?*

Fred, the photo coordinator, said I would work with him for a while. He explained some of the office procedures to me. Soon after, I went out on a photo assignment, just to watch. The Army cameras were the same as mine, 35 mm Pentax Spotmatics. I brought two with normal lenses, an 85-210 mm zoom lens, and a small electronic flash unit. It was a good thing, because now, no Army camera was available for me.

Returning from lunch, we walked through the front information office building. On a desk was a pile of 1st Cav Christmas card packets. They featured a big Cav patch on the front. Having just arrived, I grabbed two packs and planned to send a card to everyone I knew. Mail was so important to us, being our only connection with home.

All afternoon, I strung barbed wire on the greenline. It was hard work and difficult to avoid being scratched, and sweat only increased the pain. However, we were motivated to beef up the greenline to keep the bad guys out.

After dinner, I walked a half-mile with some of the guys to the service club and we watched *Wild, Wild West* and *The Glen Campbell Show* on TV. Later, when we returned to the office, automatic weapons' fire erupted nearby. Everyone grabbed their M16s, but it was only test firing on greenline bunker 35, about 100 feet behind the press/photo office.

Nov 26 - This morning, I had a brief two-hour work detail. I filled sandbags to raise the protective wall around one of our buildings. Later, Fred logged in film and wrote captions, while he explained to me the best way to do the job.

The VIP helicopter pad at Phuoc Vinh with the Hueys of the Commanding General and the two Assistant Division Commanders

In the afternoon, I toured the base with a couple of the guys and took photos of my "new home" to send to family and friends. We visited the VIP helicopter pad where the general's parked their Hueys, division headquarters, the busy airstrip, the APO (post office) and the small, recently repaired PX (photo at right).

An aerial photo of the greenline behind the information office.

In the evening, I had my first greenline guard duty at Phuoc Vinh. Two nights before, there had been an attack by North Vietnamese Army (NVA) units on the greenline less than 200 yards from our area. The guys had warned me about the mosquitos, so I tried to apply the repellent to all exposed skin. They told me mosquitos bite FNGs more than others.

Three of us staffed the bunker. We were on a slight corner, two bunkers down the line from the one behind the office. There was one every 60-90 yards. *The earlier attack might have been here.* We had floodlights on part of the wire, but there were areas that were pitch-black. We watched more than a hundred yards of greenline. Being the only FNG, I was stuck with the worst shift, midnight to 3 a.m. I sat on a folding chair on top of the bunker peering intently into the darkness. Frequently, the mosquitos required smacking. They sounded much larger here. A telephone was connected to the other bunkers in our sector and I had to check in every twenty or thirty minutes. All was quiet. It didn't seem so bad.

About 2 a.m., I saw a brilliant flash, and felt the force of the explosion. Leaning back in the chair, startled by the blast, I lost my balance, fell over backwards and tumbled down behind the bunker. Immediately, I felt another explosion close by. My ears were ringing. Several more followed. Debris rained on me as I crawled into the bunker. It was a mortar attack, the NVA must have focused on our bunker. *Incoming was terrifying, the next one could kill any of us.*

I gave the phone to the senior guy. He gave me a peculiar look and asked, "Are you okay?"

I could barely hear what he said, but replied, "I'm okay."

The plans came through on the phone as we prepared to defend the expected ground attack. The bunker to the right fired illumination flares so we could see beyond the wire. The senior guy asked me, "Do you know how to load an M60 machine gun?"

"No."

I received a brief, but intense lesson on loading an M-60. It was usually a two-man operation, requiring a loader and a shooter. We waited, during this extremely stressful time, always looking for movement and expecting to be shot at any moment. Several more illumination flares were fired, but no further attack occurred. The three of us stayed inside the bunker the rest of the night. I felt totally wired. It was impossible to sleep.

Close aerial of a greenline bunker near the Information Office.

So this is war, so random, the incoming either misses you or it doesn't. You do your best to stay safe and try not to let the fear get into your head.

12   Into the Unknown

At daylight, we saw that a mortar round had hit the sandbag wall on top of the front left side of our bunker. Much of the wall was gone. Many of the sandbags were torn from shrapnel. There were other craters close by. The senior guy was dumbfounded, "Holy shit! How did that miss you? Man, you are one lucky son-of-a-bitch."

In retrospect, I could see how fortunate I was not to have been hit by any shrapnel. My hearing was messed up, and I was covered with mosquito bites. The arrogant little buggers ignored the repellent.

I felt extremely lucky to have escaped my first close call, but I couldn't escape the mosquitoes.

A Huey helicopter takes off from Phuoc Vinh

Nov 27 - I had just collapsed on the cot after the terrible, sleepless night on greenline guard duty dodging incoming mortar rounds.

I was shaken awake by Sergeant Smart. "Moon, I have a job for you, *now*!"

"What?" I protested. "Don't I get to sleep?"

"We need you to shoot a big job, the 2nd Brigade Change of Command," he said. "You can sleep later."

"A *real* job?" I asked. "Yes, I would love to do something legitimate, taking pictures beats filling sandbags." My enthusiasm overpowered my fatigue. I hurried to find a clean shirt, picked up my camera, and almost forgot my M16, (you always had to have a weapon with you).

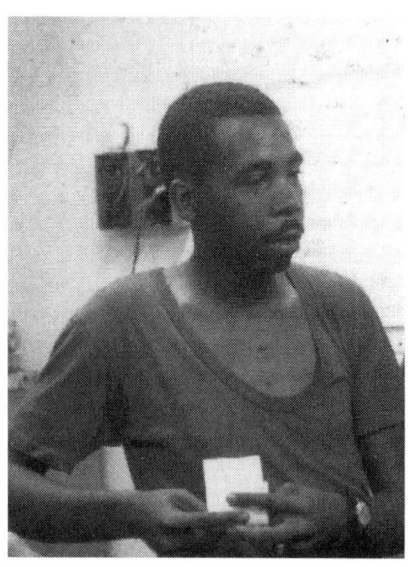

We flew a half hour north to Quan Loi, my first ride in a Huey helicopter. I accompanied senior photographer, and short-timer, Jim Caldwell (photo at left); he shot color and I shot black and white film. He had two weeks to go and I had fifty. I received a briefing from him on how the ceremony would unfold and the way he usually shot it. The band and flags made it a large, festive production. The 1st Cav Commanding General (CG) George Forsythe finally passed the "Blackhorse Brigade" colors to the new 2nd Brigade Commander, Colonel Conrad Stansberry. I wasn't exactly sure what they wanted, so in order to do the best job, I shot everything I could. *A photo from this job would run in the Cavalair, the 1st Cav's weekly 8-page newspaper.*

A quick Huey ride back to PV and we arrived in time for lunch. I gave my film and caption notes to Fred, then had the afternoon off because of guard duty the previous night. Returning to the tent, exhaustion hit me hard, as I collapsed on my cot and slept well into the evening. *The enormity of my close call on the greenline last night, never had a chance to sink in, I was too busy.*

Nov 28 - Thanksgiving Day. It felt like a real holiday. We had a delicious turkey dinner with all the trimmings in the mess hall, and thereafter, I enjoyed much-needed rest. Senior writer Don Lonsway interviewed me for a story he was writing on FNGs. I was the first one in more than a month for PIO. He told me that most FNGs didn't have so many sandbag details, but the information office didn't have a slot for me so I might be shoveling a few more. The timing of my arrival was poor, but some PIO photographers would leave soon, so there was hope. He heard about Sgt. Smart rousting me out of bed after guard duty for the job at Quan Loi. Jim Caldwell commented I had performed well there. Don told me PIO photographers were respected. If I did well, doors would open. The interview was fun. We laughed at the FNG culture, and he gave me helpful advice on what to expect.

Still unable to adjust, I was jolted awake during the night by our own outgoing artillery.

Nov 29 - Another all-day sandbag, barbed wire and bunker-building detail for me on the greenline. It was brutally hard work, steaming, hot, and dirty. Again, a towel was necessary; it was unbelievable how much I sweated. Some of the other guys on the detail said they only did this about once a week. My timing was not good. It was my third detail this week. My toughest day so far, building a bunker, each sandbag was heavier than the last. This was how I was "fitting in where needed." In bed early, I slept until awakened again by outgoing artillery.

Nov 30 - After a half-day sweat soaked, greenline sandbag detail, I returned to the tent, took a quick shower and changed clothes for a possible photo job later. Joining some of the guys for lunch, I was in line with them at the mess hall when the whole room started spinning. I saw pinpoint flashes of light as my vision darkened.

I collapsed as someone shouted, "FNG."

There were vague recollections of being carried by several guys. I regained consciousness a while later looking up at a gigantic IV bottle. I lay on a bed at the 15th Med facility surrounded by wounded guys. With no idea what had happened, I frantically checked to make sure my body was still intact.

"You were badly dehydrated," the medic told me, "You need to drink more water, and take salt pills every day. Always carry a canteen." After a pause, he added, "You still need more fluid. We have to watch you for a while longer." No one had told me about salt pills. It was so different here. A few hours later one of the PIO guys picked me up and drove me back to the office. *How embarrassing. Everyone will think I'm a wimp.*

Good-natured teasing from the guys greeted me when I returned to the office. Apparently, it had been a dramatic scene in the mess hall. The guys were concerned. They said I looked terrible crumpled on the floor. Five or six guys carried me out to a truck. Someone drove me to the 15th Med building, which was a giant emergency room.

1st Cav PIO Photo Coordinator Fred Fiallos

Dec 1 - I took the salt pills and drank more water, and I felt fine, although some of the guys still gave me peculiar looks. People I didn't know were asking me how I felt. Some of them said they thought I was treated unfairly, being given so many sandbag details during my first week. Being an FNG, I appreciated their concern. I thought they would think I was weak, but instead they had given me their respect, and I felt the strong camaraderie.

Fred went over photo lab paperwork with me in the morning. In the afternoon, I had a real photo assignment. Walking to the APO (post office), I took photos of hundreds of packages being sorted by the clerks for the upcoming *Cavalair* Christmas issue.

Fred's photo coordinator job was comprehensive. He was the head photographer, gave out photo assignments to the photographers at the Phuoc Vinh office. All film was logged in daily and sent on courier flights to the photo lab at Bien Hoa for processing. Proof sheets and prints from the lab came to him for distribution to writers, photographers and editors for selection. Final prints were distributed to the proper units. He would shoot some jobs himself, and caption his own photos.

14 Into the Unknown

We had to take two Malaria pills, a small white one daily, and a large orange one weekly to protect us from the two types of the disease. The orange one was huge, almost the size of a nickel. Some guys choked on it. These were necessary because no one could avoid the mosquitos.

Hooray! My first goodie package arrived today in the mail, a large coffee can full of brownies from my family. Coffee cans were the perfect durable lightweight packing containers. The brownies were extra good, a welcome touch of home.

That night, I nervously approached my second greenline guard duty. *It couldn't be as bad as the first one.* In the unmistakable FNG photo to the right, I was ready for guard duty except I would exchange the camera for a flak jacket. Bunker 35 was behind me.

During the night, several B-52 strikes hit nearby. These were spectacular, huge chains of brilliant flashes in the pitch-black night, appropriately called "arc lights." The closer ones felt like earthquakes. The time between the flashes and the sound was only 12 to 15 seconds, that made it about three miles away. *I can't imagine what it was like for the NVA troops who were really close to the explosions.*

I had the first shift tonight, but after that, remembering last time, I was unable to sleep in the bunker. The enormity of my previous close call sunk in here, but it was a peaceful night, and there was no attack.

Chapter Two A Surprise New Job at the Photo Lab

Dec. 2 - After an uneventful night on greenline guard duty, I slept until 11a.m. After I entered the office, Fred told me to report right away to Major McCarthy. I arrived at his office door and he motioned me in. "This is Lieutenant Tom Sheridan, Officer in Charge (OIC) of the 1st Cav Photo Lab at Bien Hoa." I shook the hand of a cheerful, freckled, red-haired officer. The Major smiled, "You are going to the photo lab for a week or so. They can use your help. Three photographers will be DEROSing (going home) in the next two weeks, so changes will occur at that time. Leave now with the Lieutenant and catch the 227th courier flight to Bien Hoa."

"Thank you, sir." *Terrific! He found a slot for me, even if it were only temporary.*

I eagerly packed my gear from the tent and picked up my camera case from the office. Fred gave the lieutenant the day's packet of film for the lab. The guys were smiling as I hauled my stuff out the door. A voice croaked from the back, "Have a nice vacation." Everyone laughed. My bags didn't feel heavy at all as I loaded them in a jeep and left the grubby tent behind. I hoped I wouldn't fill another sandbag for a very long time.

We caught a 227th Assault Helicopter Battalion courier Huey for the half-hour flight south. When we arrived at the Bien Hoa Army Base, (photo at right) the lieutenant helped me carry my gear up the hill to the photo lab. It was in a quonset hut, a building made of corrugated metal and had a semicircular design (see photo below).

Wow! They had air conditioning.

I guzzled my first cold Coke since arriving in Vietnam. Vastly improved sleeping quarters were in a real building next to the lab with lights and eight fans. I couldn't believe how much better conditions were here. We even saw a movie in the evening, *Blackbeard's Ghost*.

Major McCarthy must have been concerned when he heard that I had collapsed in the mess hall after those grueling, sweaty days on the greenline. He found a place where I might be able to fit in. Some of the guys who had been worried about me may have lobbied on my behalf. *They had my back.*

Dec. 3 - First thing in the morning, Lieutenant Sheridan interviewed me to find out what I knew about photo lab work and materials. I had previous lab experience in photography classes at Palomar College and as a photographer at the *Vista Press* newspaper.

When we finished, he told me, "You might be able to stay here for a while."

The 1st Cav Bien Hoa Photo Lab

16   A Surprise New Job at the Photo Lab

Later, I fixed two broken chemical mixing machines, as I looked for constructive things to do in the lab. It was pleasant working here, relatively speaking, almost comfortable. There were many fans throughout the lab and air conditioning in the two darkrooms.

I needed a haircut. It took the diminutive Vietnamese barber half an hour to cut my unruly hair, a bargain for 40-cents. One of the lab guys, Larry Staeb, was extra happy to see me. Now he was no longer the lab's FNG. In the photo to the right, I posed in front of the lab. We didn't even wear helmets. It was so different. Some of the lab guys had never experienced incoming.

Dec. 4 - However, as quiet as it was here, there was a war going on out there. The previous day, Company D, 2nd Battalion, 7th Cavalry (D, 2/7) was airlifted into an area of mostly elephant grass 15 km northeast of Quan Loi. After the entire company arrived, they were ambushed by a large, dug-in NVA (North Vietnamese Army) force. There were 27 KIA (killed in action), 51 WIA (wounded in action). *It was the worst 1st Cav casualty day during my time in Vietnam.* It was the topic of conversation everywhere. The enormity of this tragedy was overwhelming. It seemed so distant from us here at Bien Hoa.

Note: In 1971, Sergeant John Holcomb was awarded (Posthumously) the Congressional Medal of Honor for heroics during this battle. As a photographer at The Military District of Washington, I accompanied the Holcomb family during their two days touring Washington DC. They received The Medal of Honor from President Nixon on February 16.

Today, with Lt. Sheridan's assistance, I was able to make a Military Affiliate Radio Service (MARS) call to my girlfriend, Sally. I had to fill out a form and wait for them to call me back at the lab. The call was short and sweet. How wonderful to hear her voice. She was happy that I was at the photo lab, and said several letters were on the way. Hopefully, I would receive mail soon.

The MARS system transmitted the call to the USA using short wave radio. It was necessary to say, "over," each time you finished speaking. The system only worked when it was night between Vietnam and California and we were 14-hours ahead of the west coast.

Our Bien Hoa Mess Hall, below, and the MARS station to the right.

Later, I joined some of the guys for a trip to the huge local PX. The Phuoc Vinh PX was a mini-mart compared to this supermarket.

The food here was better. At dinner, our mess hall menu had roast beef with mashed potatoes, salmon salad, lettuce and tomato salad, several assorted vegetables and ice cream. The problem was getting enough on the small paper plate. It became a real science to efficiently stack food to maximize the limited area. They usually had apples that could be stashed in one of the many handy pockets of my jungle fatigues.

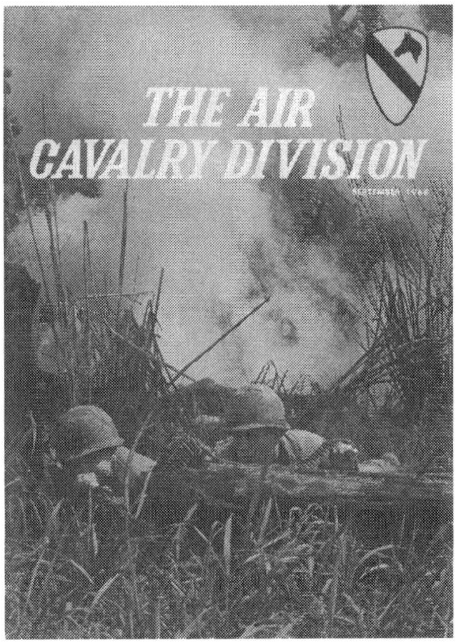

Dec. 5 - My FNG job today was cleaning and organizing store rooms. They had unusual chemicals and equipment they would never use, so I stashed them in the back. I found some old Air Cavalry Division magazines. How interesting! There were some excellent pictures from the 68 Tet offensive in Hue and the Khe Sanh operation where the Cav broke through to the besieged Marines. No individual photos were credited, just a general list of photographers on the inside back cover, so I couldn't tell if the guys I had met at Phuoc Vinh had taken any of those pictures. Artist Larry Collins had several paintings on the history of the Cav in the September 1968 issue (photo on the right).

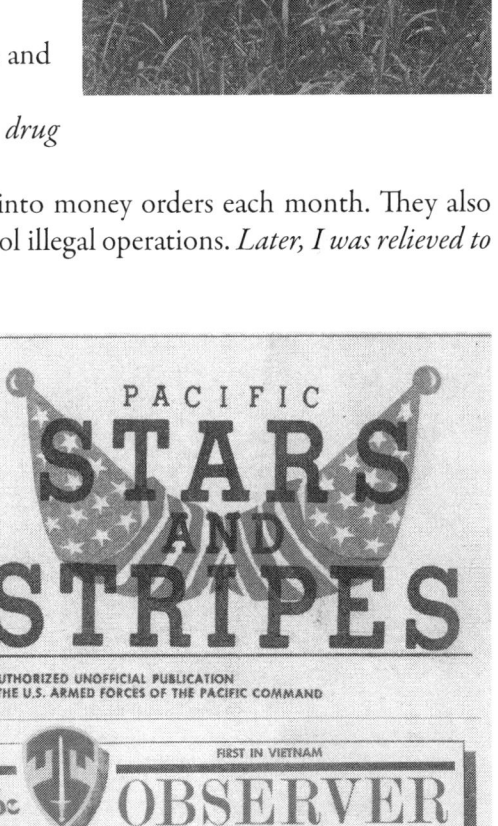

I was interrupted by two burly lab guys who approached and cornered me in the storeroom. After pointless small talk, they asked, "Will you buy two money orders for us." I had the uneasy feeling that I didn't have a choice.

Trying to be cool, I cheerfully replied, "Sure, no problem this time."

After I bought the money orders, they gave me several rolls of film and quietly cautioned me, "Don't tell anyone."

Great, I was minding my own business and now I'm laundering drug money.

There were limits on how much money an individual could turn into money orders each month. They also changed the Military Payment Certificates (MPC) every so often to control illegal operations. *Later, I was relieved to find out these guys were not drug dealers. They were black marketeers.*

I finagled another MARS call, this time to my mother. It was her birthday. I was almost finished when I noticed someone working on the pole outside the lab. He cut a wire and my call went dead. Lieutenant Sheridan, outside the open door, also saw him cut the wire. He heard my "Hello, Hello," turned bright red and yelled "You idiot, you just cut off someone's MARS call."

"I'm sorry, sir, we are replacing several lines here."

Immediately, the lieutenant sent me to the nearby MARS station. They were courteous and allowed me to set up another call. It was an enjoyable conversation with the family. I spoke briefly to everyone. Shocked when the line went dead, they were relieved that I called back quickly and were thankful that I was now at the photo lab.

Dec. 6 - We received three newspapers, the daily *Pacific Stars and Stripes,* a 24-page tabloid similar to a US newspaper. It was for all branches of the military in the Pacific Command. Weekly the *MACV Observer* from the Military Assistance Command, Vietnam, was twelve-pages for American units, all branches. Also weekly was the twelve-page tabloid, *The Army Reporter,* from U.S. Army, Vietnam (USARV), that went to all Army units. However, sometimes the papers were days late or failed to arrive at all.

We needed to copy color slides into black and white to make prints for the newspaper, but we didn't have fine-grain copy film. The negatives looked like hell on the high speed film the lab was using, and prints had no contrast. In the past, I had copied slides for the Vista Press. With all his connections in Bien Hoa and Long Binh, the lieutenant couldn't find any. The black marketeers weren't successful either. I wrote to my brother, Dennis, and asked him to immediately send me a 100-foot bulk roll of copy film. I made a deal for it with Lt. Sheridan. He would give me twenty rolls of color slide film in trade. It would allow me to shoot my own pictures.

18   A Surprise New Job at the Photo Lab

What! Tonight, here at Bien Hoa, we had incoming, and a ground attack on the greenline. They said it was the largest one in a long time, but only one building was hit. Although the incoming was not remotely close to us, fear gripped the lab guys. This was a new experience for them. Like my first incoming, they had no idea how nearby it was. I told them about my close call and the frequent incoming at Phuoc Vinh. Now they were afraid to travel there. A lab guy occasionally had to take the daily courier packet to PV, and might not find a ride back. God forbid, he would be stuck overnight and might experience incoming.

Dec. 8 - Hooray! Today, I finally received a stack of mail, a dozen letters, six from Sally, some of them weeks old. Elated, I read them all several times. My family sent me the November 29 *Vista Press* newspaper. Editor Russ Dietrich had quoted my Christmas card in his column.

More rumors surfaced that I would be sent to 2nd Brigade upon my return to PV. At the photo lab, I had easily become readjusted to flush toilets, hot showers, mirrors, cold beer and Pepsi, plus movies every night.

Dec. 9 - Today, my week was up, and I expected to return to Phuoc Vinh. Lt. Sheridan said he appreciated my work ethic and talked to Major McCarthy. They agreed I would stay a few more days. After cleaning and adjusting one of the D-2 enlargers, I made black and white prints for several hours. The air conditioning was fantastic in the printing, washing and drying rooms. However, it felt much hotter outside when I left the comfort of the AC.

Dec. 10 - One of the Phuoc Vinh photographers, Melvin Clarke, made the courier flight today with the film packet. With three weeks to go, he had an extreme case of short-timer paranoia. He smoked constantly. In the photo on the left, lab man Larry Polys (left) stood next to Melvin as he puffed away.

I received another goodie package containing dark chocolate brownies from my family. I gave a few to the guys and they loved them. We often shared homemade treats among our small group. We had an Australian photographer visiting with us briefly. He was interesting, at times difficult to understand, but loads of fun.

Dec. 11 - Today, the entire crew painted the photo lab two coats of tranquilizing "easy eye green." We also added insulation to keep the place cooler. It turned out to be a massive job. Everybody worked hard throughout the day. Melvin was happy to stay and help. *The paranoid short-timer wanted to stay here in Bien Hoa, where it was relatively safe.*

I received a load of mail today, again some of it was weeks old. Sally had slipped in a wallet-sized picture (photo at right) in one of the letters. I copied it with my camera and made a large print. All the guys liked it, and the short-timers wanted her phone number. Also, a goodie package arrived from Grandma Miller. She baked wonderful cookies.

Our Bien Hoa movie theater

Dec. 12 - A pleasant working routine, mostly printing, had developed for me each day. There were three Omega D-2 enlargers in the print darkroom. They were busy throughout the day. A large quantity of prints would be delivered to PV the following day for distribution. It was satisfying to be doing meaningful work.

The movie tonight was, *Custer of the West*. During the battle, the wisecracks were nonstop, "Send in the gunships. Where is the artillery? Call for an airstrike."

There was a huge amount of pride in the 1st Cavalry. Three battalions of Custer's 7th Cavalry were now in Quan Loi with 1st Cav's 3rd Brigade.

Dec. 13 - Today, Lt. Sheridan invited me to ride into Saigon with him to a media center for a print delivery. We left at 7:30 a.m. I stood in the bed of the 3/4-ton truck behind the topless cab. He wanted to show me the huge city since I was the FNG.

We traveled on a modern highway out of Bien Hoa, crossed the Dong Nai River and continued the fifteen or twenty miles into Saigon. As we approached the city, we ran into heavy traffic, mostly motor scooters and bicycles. Lt. Sheridan pointed out interesting sites, but most of the time I couldn't hear him over the city noise. I saw the Saigon USO, the US Embassy, the Presidential Palace and felt numerous potholes. For me, it was an amazing experience and definitely a sensory overload.

The lieutenant turned around, pointed and yelled, "Look over there!" I spun around and took a photo of two pretty girls walking along the street. He said something about an elite school nearby, but I couldn't hear him.

We made our routine delivery, headed back through miles of gridlock, and arrived at the photo lab about 4 p.m. The driver did an excellent job.

Although in a war zone, today I felt like a tourist. After this chaotic adventure, my body was humming from the bumping and the constant noise. No movie for me. I retired early. *Observing a part of Vietnam up close today, that I thought I would never have the opportunity to see. Priceless!*

20　A Surprise New Job at the Photo Lab

Downtown Saigon, I had no idea what this was, but it was typical.

Gridlock! It was a slow return trip.

More chaotic traffic and a gas station surrounded by concertina wire.

Dec. 14 - A former brigade photographer, Staff Sgt. Steve Robinson, passed through the lab on his way to process out for his return to the U.S. "I bet they will send you to 2nd brigade soon because they need a photographer at Quan Loi now," he said with a smile.

The power was off most of the morning, so I wrote letters. I made prints throughout the afternoon and into the evening to finish the jobs for the next day's print packet to Phuoc Vinh.

Dec. 15 - Today, Lt. Sheridan called a meeting and announced to the assembled lab crew. "Spec.4 Terry Moon is now a regular member of the photo lab dayshift. He fits in well here, and does good work. Major McCarthy approved it this morning." This surprised me. Army personnel were supposed to work in their designated MOS, and I was a photographer, not a lab specialist.

Of course, that called for a party. Later, the black market guys brought a cake, and a bottle of Bacardi to invigorate our Cokes. We didn't ask where the stuff came from, we just enjoyed it. They were my friends now, so resourceful, but I stayed away from their 'operations.' *I don't think the job here will last, but I will enjoy it while I can.*

Dec. 16 - I had asked Lt. Sheridan if I could take the courier packet to Phuoc Vinh. He scheduled me to go today, but something had happened at the office. Major McCarthy called the lieutenant early this morning, and told him to fly up for consultation on PIO personnel changes. *Have I already been shuffled, or will there be another move in store for me?*

Dec. 17 - I spent the entire day printing, developing, fixing, washing and drying black and white prints. It was cool in the print room. We enjoyed listening to AFVN radio while we worked, with only two choices, AM or FM (schedule at right from *Stars and Stripes*).

The movie this evening was *King Kong Escapes*, so I escaped back to the lab, wrote several letters and read an old *Psychology Today* magazine I had found earlier.

I bought a three-inch reel to reel tape recorder at the PX. Now I could record tapes to send home. My brother, Dennis had one at home so the family could send tapes to me. *Hearing their voices would help me feel closer to home.*

Dec. 18 - Seven of us moved a half-ton refrigeration unit into the photo lab. It was awkward and damn heavy. The lab chief decided to recruit a couple more guys from the next building to help and we finished the job quickly. One of them, Glen, had been in my basic training squad at Fort Ord. We were in many activities together there, always lined up in alphabetical order with him right in front of me.

It was great to see a familiar face from six months ago, but he had dramatically changed. He looked terrible, emaciated and nervous, with good reason. He told me his grunt unit, Delta Company, 2nd Battalion, 7th Cavalry had been ambushed by an NVA battalion sized force hidden in bunkers behind the tree line. The enemy waited until the entire company had been airlifted onto a flat area of elephant grass before they opened fire from three sides. The unfortunate company had mistakenly thought there was no resistance, and had relaxed. This occurred northeast of Quan Loi on December 3. The Americans took heavy casualties, one of the Cav's worst days in their entire time in Vietnam (27 KIA, 51 WIA). Only a few dozen grunts from his 116 man company escaped unhurt.

Glen had reenlisted to get out of the field because he couldn't take it anymore. Now, he was at Bien Hoa waiting for his permanent non-combat job assignment. Still badly shaken from his experience, he was trembling and sensitive to loud noises. My friend now referred to his old unit as "No DEROS Delta." DEROS was date eligible for return from overseas, meaning no one survived a year in his "cursed" company.

Vietnam AM

Monday, Dec. 16
6:00—News & Sports
6:30—Purple Grotto
7:05—Town & Country
8:05—Go
10:00—News & Sports
10:30—Tonight
10:55—World Of Money
11:05—John Doremus

Tuesday, Dec. 17
12:05—Roger Carrol
1:05—Orient Express
3:00—News
4:05—Herman Griffith
5:05—Joe Allison
6:15—Dawnbuster
7:00—News & Sports
7:10—Dawnbuster
9:05—Young Sounds
10:05—Mad Morning
12:00—News & Sports
12:30—USO Show Time
1:05—Gene Weed
3:00—News & Sports
3:10—Million Dollar Music
5:05—Chris Noel

Vietnam FM

Monday, Dec. 16
9:05—Tempo
11:05—Just Music
12:00—World News Roundup
1:05—Young Sounds
2:05—Golden Sound
5:05—Young Sounds
6:00—World News Roundup
6:15—Enchantment Of Music
7:05—Classical Side Of Nightfall
9:05—Golden Sound
10:00—World News Roundup
10:15—Golden Sound Of FM

Saigon TV

Monday, Dec. 16
2:28—What's Happening
2:30—Pro Football Scoreboard
2:52—Wild Wild West
7:30—Evening News
8:00—Bonanza
5:30—Survival
6:00—Daniel Boone
7:00—Animal Kingdom
9:00—Mission Impossible
10:00—News
10:05—Joey Bishop

22   A Surprise New Job at the Photo Lab

After we talked for a while about memorable events from basic training, he relaxed. Then he wanted to tell me about the battle. Glen spoke slowly, in amazing detail about the traumatic ambush. He witnessed horrible things. His best friend was blown away, along with several others, right before his eyes. He paused, looked away and almost whispered, "Why them and not me?" He mumbled something about blood all over him, but his voice faded, his eyes glazed. Unable to continue, he spoke no more. He left slowly a few moments later. I was shocked. I couldn't imagine a scene like that.

Glen had been an eyewitness to the worst horrors of war. This had crushed him and left him an empty shell. Extremely disturbing, this unexpected encounter haunted me for weeks. How can anyone recover from such extreme emotional trauma? This was PTSD at its worst. I hoped he would overcome this, but I doubted that he ever would.

Late in the afternoon, Lt. Sheridan finally returned. He called me into his office, smiled weakly, and said, "I'm sorry, but you have to go back to Phuoc Vinh. I had hoped you could stay here until the first of the year."

"Thank you sir, I appreciate your support and I thoroughly enjoyed my time here, but I am an 84B photographer," I said. *This was no real surprise to me. I knew this would happen eventually.*

Dec. 19 - I said goodbye to everyone. The black market guys told me if I ever needed anything to come see them. A couple of the others helped me take my stuff down to the Bien Hoa airport, the same place where I had arrived in Vietnam. My flight was supposed to be at 11 a.m., but it wasn't, so I waited. I had a boarding pass for the flight to Phuoc Vinh, whenever.

I saw a jet come in loaded with shiny-new FNGs, the poor souls moved around like zombies. I remembered well that overwhelming feeling, having arrived only five weeks before. Later, there was a 707 leaving with a laughing, animated group going home, a jubilant sight. *What an emotional contrast of guys arriving in and departing from Vietnam.*

I caught the regular 2 p.m. Carabou flight to Phuoc Vinh, a small twin-engine plane that carried nineteen passengers, (photo at right). When I arrived at PV, I started walking to the information office loaded down with my gear. A patrolling MP stopped his jeep and cheerfully gave me a ride, another example of the cooperative spirit here with the 1st Cav.

Sergeant Smart, enlisted man in charge (NCOIC) of PIO, greeted me as I entered the office. "Welcome back, Moon. How was your vacation with the REMFs?"

"REMFs?"

"Yeah, those rear echelon mother-fuckers at that cushy Bien Hoa photo lab!"

"It was cushy all right, but I'm not disappointed coming back here. It had to happen, I'm an 84B photographer."

"Good for you. Y'know, it's funny, the grunts call us REMFs."

It's all relative.

I would be assistant, for now, to photo coordinator Fred Fiallos in Phuoc Vinh. My brigade assignment could occur at anytime. Another PIO guy told me that during close incoming a few nights before, one of the guys in their hooch panicked and ran screaming out the back door. It was unsettling to everyone. "Welcome back to the war," he added.

While I was away, they made a huge 'Christmas Tree' out of beer cans in back of the press/photo office, now a festive place. I was back in the grubby tent again, definitely not so festive there. Fortunately, the strange guys and the mangy dog, Myrtle, who had been there before, were now gone. The tent, the sergeant told me, was the 15th Admin Company overflow "quarters." The PIO guys had their own building, but, there was still no room there for me.

I would certainly miss the copious comforts of Bien Hoa.

How Did You Get This Job? 23

Col. Stansberry Takes Command Of Division's 'Blackhorse' Brigade

QUAN LOI — A veteran of two previous wars who rose through the ranks to the grade of colonel assumed command of the 2nd Brigade of the 1st Air Cavalry Division in ceremonies here recently.

COL. Conrad L. Stansberry took command of the brigade from Colonel Robert N. Mackinnon. COL Mackinnon will assume COL Stansberry's former job, Division Chief of Staff.

COL Stansberry was inducted into the service as an enlisted man during World War II and later graduated from Officer Candidate School and was commissioned a Second Lieutenant of infantry.

During World War II COL Stansberry served with airborne units in the European Theater of Operations where he participated in five campaigns. During this period he made combat jumps into Nazi-occupied France. At the termination of the war he was a battalion commander.

During the Korean Conflict, he served as a battalion commander with the 32nd Infantry Regiment and later as Assistant Chief of Staff for Operations of the 7th Infantry Division. He participated in the famous battles of Triangle Hill, Old Baldy and Pork Chop Hill. Since graduation from flight training in May 1961, COL Stansberry has had numerous assignments dealing with the Army's aviation program, to include being assigned to the Office of the Director of Army Aviation at Department of the Army level, where he was the deputy director in 1964.

He was assigned to the FIRST TEAM in January, 1968.

COL Stansberry has been awarded the Distinguished Flying Cross, Legion of Merit with Oak Leaf Cluster, Bronze Star with two Oak Leaf Clusters, the Air Medal with six Clusters, the Combat Infantryman's Badge, Master Parachutist Badge and Army Aviation Badge.

After passing the colors from COL Mackinnon to COL Stansberry, the FIRST TEAM commander, Major General George I. Forsythe, presented the new Chief of Staff with the Silver Star for gallantry in action on June 28, during a combat mission near Binh An in the I Corps Tactical Zone.

In praising COL Mackinnon's job as brigade commander for the past six months, MG Forsythe said, "Bob Mackinnon's brilliant leadership and the standards he has set. His wisdom, practical judgement and (Continued on Back Page)

Cavalair

Vol. 2, No. 106   1st Air Cav Div   December 18, 1968

COL. Conrad L. Stansberry receives the colors of the Second Brigade from Major General George I. Forsythe, 1st Air Cav Commanding General. Also taking part in the ceremonies are COL Robert N. Mackinnon, the former Brigade commander (left) and CSM James Christensen.

Medevac System Reduces Number of War Casualties

PHUOC VINH — Deep in the elephant grass, the Skytrooper's boot touched a wire. There was a blast, a hiss of grenade fragments, and two members of the company fell wounded. Booby trap!

As the 2nd Battalion, 5th Cavalry's combat medics tended the wounded men, the call went out for MEDEVAC — the helicopter evacuation system that has given the U.S. Army in Vietnam the lowest ratio of fatal casualties in history.

An airborne ambulance, waiting at a nearby base camp, was on the way in two minutes. This time the landing would be routine, but countless times MEDEVAC pilots have brought their ships down through tangled jungle, into landing zones swept by enemy fire.

The UH-1B hovered in. The wounded, on stretchers, were slid into the chopper, where more trained medics were prepared for emergencies. A quick "thumbs-up" and the "Huey", rotors beating, was headed back to one of the 15th Medical Battalion's forward area hospitals.

Another landing, another quick transfer by stretcher, and the patients were being treated by skilled surgeons and nurses, using the most modern equipment in sanitary conditions.

Only 11 minutes had elapsed since one of the men had tripped the Viet Cong grenade.

Back in the field, the 2nd Bn, 5th Cav resumed its search for the enemy. The Skytroopers, though sobered by the incident, knew that if the worst came, another MEDEVAC team was standing by.

Tapped Wire Tunes In On Enemy

TAY NINH — Wire-tapping soldiers from the 1st Air Cavalry Division tuned in on an enemy commander and foiled his plans during a sweep near here.

The men from Company A, 1st Battalion, 8th Cavalry were on the move. The unit had split up into platoons, flanking each other as they moved through the thick jungle.

"We found a complex of 40 bunkers which showed recent use," recalled Sergeant Arnold M. Reyes, an artillery forward observer attached to the company, "so we moved out quickly, hoping to catch Charlie."

A short time later, two of the platoons found communication wire running along a jungle trail. The unit's Kit Carson scout went to work.

"He tapped the wire and listened for the enemy. Chuck was on the line, too," stated SGT Reyes. The enemy had spotted the troopers sweeping their way. They did not want to stay around.

"The Americans are in the area. Everyone move out at once, except for an element to make contact and slow them down," crackled the wire.

A few minutes later, the Skytroopers opened fire on a platoon-sized unit. The message had been right, but prearranged Aerial Rocket Artillery and tube artillery strikes made sure the Cavalrymen were not slowed down for long.

Commanders Praise Jeb Stuart Results

(The following letters written by the General of the Armed Forces, Republic of Vietnam, General Cao Van Vien, and Major General George I. Forsythe, CG, respectively; laud the achievements of each member of the first team during OPERATION JEB STUART. ED)

Dear General Abrams:

It gives me great pleasure to acknowledge the outstanding accomplishments of the 1st U.S. Air Cavalry Division during the period 17 June 1968 to 3 November 1968 in Operation Jeb Stuart III, conducted in Quang Tri and Thua Thien provinces.

In this remarkable series of actions, the valiant U.S. fighting men inflicted a continuous string of resounding defeats upon the North Vietnamese aggressor's force that have their best reflection in 2114 enemies KIA, 261 captured, 60 returnees, 1228 small arms and 133 crew-served weapons captured.

No victory, however, is without its price and, in the above operation the 1st U.S. Air Cavalry Division suffered killed, wounded and missing in action. To these heroes and their families, I would like to ask you to convey the gratitude of the Vietnamese Armed Forces and of myself for their incomparable contributions to the fight against Communism in Vietnam.

With my best personal regards and highest consideration, I should like to remain.

/s/ CAO VAN VIEN
General Cao Van Vien

TO: THE FIRST TEAM

It is with great pride that I pass on to all SKYTROOPERS this commendation for the 1st Air Cavalry Division from General Cao Van Vien, Chief, Joint General Staff, RVNAF. General Cao Van Vien's tribute highlights the outstanding accomplishments of THE FIRST TEAM during Operation JEB STUART III. This praise was amplified by General Creighton W. Abrams and Lieutenant General Frank T. Mildren.

THE FIRST TEAM has met, fought and defeated the enemy at every turn. You have put forth maximum effort regardless of the time of call, heedless of the danger involved, and mindful only of God, Country and mission. My sincere congratulations to each of you for your superb achievements. I have every confidence that you will continue to add to the illustrious record of the 1st Air Cavalry Division.

GEORGE I. FORSYTHE
Major General, USA
Commanding

A thin, taut wire was tripped, the grenade at the end of it exploded, and two 1st Air Cavalry Division troops lay wounded. Sergeant Donald Scott comforts one of his wounded squad members after the man had been treated by the field medic.

My 2nd Brigade change-of-command photo was on page one of the December 18, 1968 Cavalair newspaper.

24 A Surprise New Job at the Photo Lab

The street in front of the 1st Cav Information Office in the rubber trees at Phuoc Vinh.

Looking out the backdoor of the press/photo office in the rain, greenline bunker 35 was a short distance away.

Chapter Three I Will be a Photographer After All, But Where?

Dec. 20 - This morning, the major entered the press/photo office, walked over to me, smiled and said, "I was going to send you to 1st Brigade at Tay Ninh today, but changed my mind. Fred will assign you to a wider variety of jobs. Let's see what you can do here, but I may still send you to 1st Brigade."

"That sounds good to me, sir," I replied. *At least now there would be a chance for me to show what I can do.*

The guys told me Tay Ninh was a decent place about 70 km. west of here, near Cambodia. The large base was shared with a brigade of the 25th Infantry Division. We went north, they went south. Before, when I was in PV, there were four other photographers, now three, with two of them recently in from the brigades. Three others had gone home.

One of the short-timer writers, Bruce Burch (Chicago), heard the major talking to me. He said, "I stayed out with a brigade by choice. Most of the time was my own. I could go out a few days a week, take plenty of pictures, stay at the base camp the rest of the time, and write my stories. You would be better off at a brigade."

Christmas cards arrived in the mail from people who remembered me from my *Vista Press* work. A couple of weeks ago, I sent a 1st Cav Christmas card to Russ Dietrich, the editor, with my address. He quoted my whole text in his column. It was amazing. I received several more cards and letters from his readers.

2/20 Aerial Rocket Artillery Cobra Gunship at Phuoc Vinh

Dec. 21 - I had an early morning assignment at 2/20 Aerial Rocket Artillery, (ARA), the Division Artillery's gunship battalion, known as Blue Max. After the awards ceremony, they gave me a brief tour. *I must have really looked like a FNG.* It was my first close-up look at the shark-like gunships. They had narrow bodies with stubby "wings" holding large rocket pods. A turret mounted under the nose held a 3,000-round-a-minute minigun and a 40 mm grenade launcher they called a 'chunker.'

In the afternoon, we could hear heavy outgoing artillery fire and gunship miniguns in the distance. We heard rumors there was an NVA battalion in the area. Our scouts must have found a large enemy force.

Today, the officers and some other senior staffers went to Long Binh for the huge Bob Hope Show. *Sorry, no FNGs allowed.* If I had stayed at the photo lab two more days, I could have accompanied the lab guys. Captain Carrara said it was attended by 20,000 troops. When the entertainers arrived in a line of Hueys, General Abrams said to the crowd that it looked like a 1st Cav combat assault. That sparked a huge cheer! The Cav was well respected.

Our beer can Christmas tree brightened up the office.

Later in the evening, there was a nearby attack on the greenline, with heavy firing, numerous flares and explosions from M79 grenades. Everyone in our office was scared, and had their M16s ready. Being an FNG, I didn't know enough to be scared.

It had been so quiet at Bien Hoa.

Dec. 22 - Early morning, I was sent to take new Assistant Division Commander, Brigadier General William Shedd's portrait in front of his Huey. *This was certainly not a job for an FNG. The major was testing me.* We had a few minutes as we waited for the general's arrival. I had the pilot turn the Huey around so the light angle would be better. Later, everyone at the office was amazed I did that. Fred looked at me in disbelief and said, "You did what!"

"Just doing my job," I replied. "Backlighting would have been a problem." To the right is that photo, heavily cropped.

Sergeant Smart told me today that I would be sent to 2nd Brigade at Quan Loi when a camera for me returned from repair. It was a different day, different rumor, different source, different destination.

Greenline guard for me tonight with photographer Melvin Clarke. He had 13 days left, I had 326. We had a base-wide yellow alert, which meant two people awake at all times on each bunker. Before midnight, someone on another bunker fired an illumination flare too low. It started a huge fire that burned for over two hours with ten to fifteen-foot flames. Later, the lights that illuminated the wire area in front of our bunker went out. We couldn't see anything. That was frightening. It could have been the generator that powers the lights or the NVA could have infiltrated the wire. We loaded all our weapons, just in case and were ready to shoot illumination flares. An ambush, set up by our own guys, known as a 'trick or treat,' erupted several hundred yards beyond the wire. We had been told this could happen. There were many tracers and explosions. It ended abruptly. Poor Melvin was beside himself. He had severe short-timer paranoia. Having previously chain-smoked all his cigarettes, he was now visibly shaking, with just his lucky thirteen days to go.

Adjusting well, or just fortunate, I slept in the bunker from 3 to 6 a.m. while it was quiet.

*1st Cavalry Division
Headquarters, Phuoc Vinh*

Dec. 23 - At 7:30 a.m., I went to the Commanding General's (CG's) office for a routine medal presentation. After returning to PIO, I was having trouble with my old f2 normal lens, so the information office supply staff gave me a 50 mm, f1.4 normal lens, and a 35 mm wide angle lens. They had plenty of lenses but no cameras. They would have an Army issue Pentax camera for me soon, when it returned from repair.

In the early afternoon, I was called into Major McCarthy's office and introduced to Lieutenant Tim Millar, Officer In Charge (OIC) of our 3rd Brigade Information Office at Quan Loi. Immediately, I jumped to the conclusion that I was being sent to 3rd Brigade with the 7th Cavalry grunt battalions. This was Custer's famous regiment.

The major paused to look at some papers, then looked straight at me and said, "You will accompany Lt. Millar to Quan Loi now. Early tomorrow you will go to a Song Be area fire support base for a special job. I can't tell you what it is. You will be briefed by the battalion commander when you arrive at the LZ, and when the job is finished you will return to PV."

"Thank you, sir," I replied, surprised. *What! This must be an important job. Why me? I'm the FNG. At least I am not being assigned to 3rd Brigade.* Excited, I ran to get *all* of my camera gear.

The lieutenant and I bumped along in a jeep to the 15th Med chopper pad at Phuoc Vinh looking for a flight to Quan Loi. Soon a LOH (light observation helicopter, pronounced loach, photo at right) landed and Lt. Millar recognized the pilot. After a short, laugh-filled conversation, he gave us a ride to Quan Loi, 35 km north. This was my first flight in the smallest of the helicopters. We zoomed around, right on the tree tops, turning abruptly like an aerial sports car. The pilot was apparently showing off. I was sitting in the back with one leg dangling out into space, having a ball. We landed at the snoopy pad, with the famous beagle flying his doghouse painted on the PSP.

28   I Will Be a Photographer After All, But Where?

Aerial photo of the Quan Loi base camp

We walked a short distance to my accommodations with 3rd Brigade PIO in a building much like the press/photo office at PV. A short afternoon nap made up for missed sleep from greenline guard the night before. This had already happened to me a couple of times. Later, I didn't sleep well in this strange place with much louder outgoing artillery. My mind raced, anticipating my unknown job early in the morning. It could be anything.

Dec. 24 - Up early for my big mystery job, I caught a Huey at 6:30 a.m. to LZ Buttons, a Song Be area fire support base, 40 km east of Quan Loi. Two dog teams were in the Huey with me. One of the huge German Shepherds really liked me. He licked my face like he was a giant puppy.

We landed outside the perimeter wire of the fire support base (LZ). I could see all the deadly claymores and the two layers of jagged concertina wire with many trip flares in front of the defensive bunkers. It looked menacing. A four-foot-high earthen berm encircled the entire LZ with the bunkers built into of it. Carefully, I walked through the narrow gate into the LZ. I asked directions and was escorted to the command bunker. On LZs, all important operations were situated in underground bunkers.

My drawing of LZ Buttons near Song Be

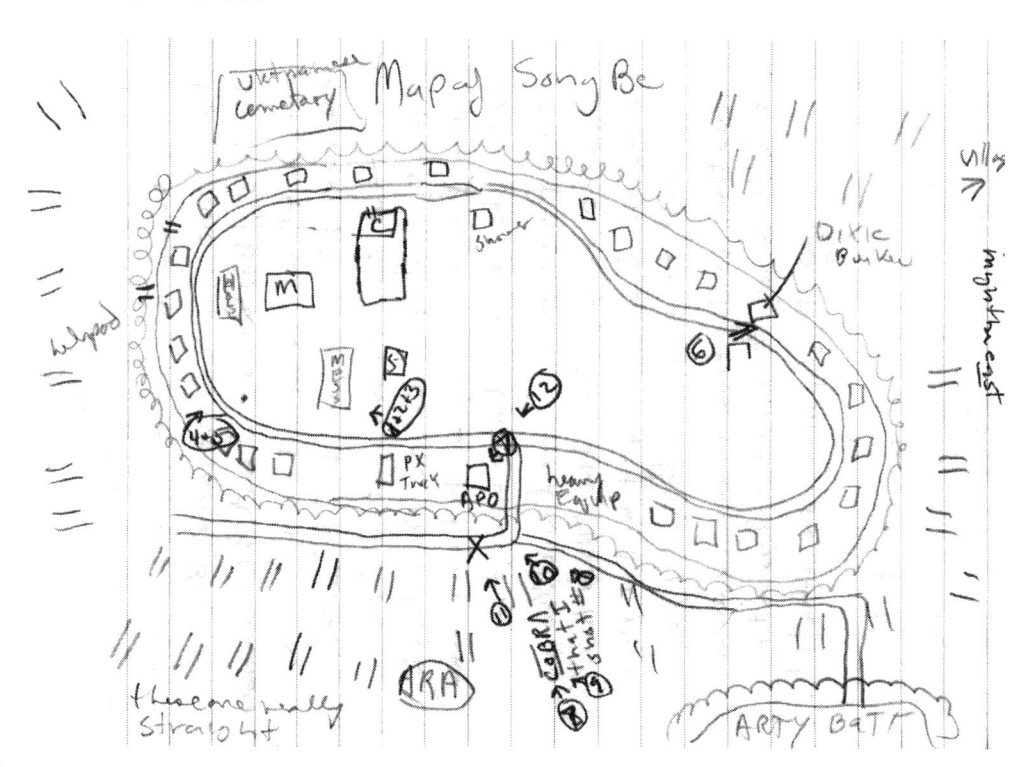

Lt. Col. John B. Blount, battalion commander of 2/12 briefed me quickly as we stepped outside the bunker, "You will be photographing the Christmas Eve goodwill tour of South Vietnamese President Nguyen Van Thieu." he said calmly.

My heart rate jumped. *What! I can't believe this.*

"He will arrive in an hour or so and quickly tour the LZ. Take as many pictures as you can of him with my skytroopers," he said.

"Yes sir, that's my job," I replied.

"You can have the run of the place. Get something to eat at the mess tent. How long have you been over here?"

"Five weeks, sir." I said.

"I thought so. Good luck son," he said smiling as he returned to the bunker. *FNG must be painted on my forehead.*

A quick stop at the mess tent for toast and coffee, and I was ready to go. This place was tiny, only about a half mile around the greenline. I quickly walked around the entire area. It had a very tight defensive perimeter, the bunkers were close together, and I could see another area outside the wire that looked like another LZ. They told me it was the artillery battery. Shortly, the sky was filled with descending Hueys and Cobras. The VIP entourage had arrived. The tour moved along quickly, 1st Cav Commanding General George Forsythe escorted the VIP. I had to keep running around to obtain good positions from which to photograph the diminutive President Thieu, casual in his white shirt and baseball cap. He talked to several skytroopers, having animated exchanges with each one. It was a festive scene. I had to move fast to get all the grunts' names. These photos would be great hometown news releases for them. I didn't see any CBS or NBC reporters. This tour was a well-kept secret. I had learned quickly that you couldn't trust the media here. Suddenly, it was over and the swarm of helicopters departed.

Returning to Phuoc Vinh was my responsibility. I convinced a pilot that I was important enough to overload his LOH for the flight to Quan Loi. For some reason, perhaps antiaircraft fire, he flew so high that it was bitter cold. I was stuffed in the middle of the back seat and mashed against the front seat so I couldn't see anything. At Quan Loi the "terminal" guys found a flight to PV for me as the only passenger in a Huey. I arrived about 4:30 p.m.

My M16 was a pain today, it kept getting in the way. I would try other ideas to secure it.

30   I Will Be a Photographer After All, But Where?

I learned that President Thieu toured only four places. Fred, our photo coordinator, covered him at Phuoc Vinh. The VIP also visited LZ Sue on the Song Be River north of Quan Loi and LZ Eleanor, 23 km north of Phuoc Vinh. LZ Buttons (Song Be) was my assignment. I had assumed that many more of our photographers were involved in this important job. It was satisfying to me that Major McCarthy gave me this opportunity, as I had been treated inconsistently since my arrival. *I will show him what I can do.*

For a late evening assignment, I walked in the light rain to take photos of Christmas dinner preparations at the 15th Admin Company mess hall. Upon entering, I sensed the holiday spirit. Everyone was smiling. Frivolity reigned as I took the pictures in the kitchen, and plenty of goodies covered one of the tables. I stashed my camera and helped make the rolls. The aroma was heavenly. We had a blast.   An instant camaraderie materialized.

A few hours later it was raining hard. I should have brought my waterproof poncho. I trudged out into the torrent. It was a no win situation. If you walked you were soaked, if you ran you slipped in the mud. I had to learn quickly how to better protect my cameras in the heavy rain.

Dec. 25 - The red dawn of Christmas morning found me heading to day guard on tower eight. The tower stood about forty feet high and had an expansive view. It was on the greenline by the rubber trees, about 200 yards east of our office. They told me nothing ever happened on day guard, and they were right. Shortly after noon, another guy, fresh from his Christmas feast, struggled up the many steps to relieve me. As he reached the top, he gasped, "You won't believe all the food."

I jogged to the mess hall for my much anticipated Christmas dinner. The menu looked like it was from a fancy restaurant. I ate so much a siesta was necessary. Now I understood why my replacement on the tower today struggled to reach the top. Work details were split up so everyone had at least a half day off to enjoy the festivities. Smiles appeared everywhere. I could sense the camaraderie among all the guys, no matter their job. We had been strangers, but after our Christmas dinner we were like old friends. From the commanding general, to the logistics people, to the mess hall cooks, they really tried to make holidays seem like holidays.

To top off the day, a big goodie package arrived in the mail from my girlfriend, Sally. *Perfect timing.* Inside were several wrapped gifts. They were carefully opened under our gleaming seven-foot beer can Christmas tree. She also sent a picture of the San Diego State Symphony Christmas Concert, where she played the double bass.

Three of my post office package sorting photos were in the Christmas edition of our *Cavalair* newspaper, (photo at right). That made me feel like I was a part of the PIO team.

My pleasant holiday came to a soggy end late in the evening, after I returned to the grubby tent. I had just settled into my cot, when my corner of the tent collapsed. Of course it was raining. I got soaked as I pulled the tent back up and pounded a couple of pegs in with a shovel. What a mess.

As I dried off and reclined on my cot ready to sleep, with my wet mosquito netting, mostly dry poncho liner, partially inflated air mattress and two precious dry towels, I thought about the camaraderie between the guys earlier. None of us wanted to be here, but we were making the best of it. What a great Christmas it turned out to be for an FNG in a war zone, more than eight thousand miles from home.

Merry Christmas to all, and to all a good night.

Christmas Day Dinner
1968

Shrimp Cocktail

Crackers

Roast Turkey　　　　　　　　　　　　Turkey Gravy

Cornbread Dressing　　　　　　　　　Cranberry Sauce

Mashed Potatoes

Glazed Sweet Potatoes

Buttered Mixed Vegetables or Buttered Peas

Assorted Crisp Relishes　　　　　　　Hot Rolls with Butter

Fruit Cake

Mincemeat Pie

Pumpkin Pie with Whipped Topping

Assorted Nuts　　　　　　　　　　　Assorted Candy

Assorted Fresh Fruits

Ice Tea with Lemon　　　　　　　　　Milk

32   I Will Be a Photographer After All, But Where?

Dec. 26 - I awakened feeling bad with a sore throat, there must have been some nasty microbes in the foul air inside the tent. I entered the office coughing. Sergeant Smart took one look at me and said, "Moon, you look like hell. Go see the medics." One of the guys suggested some orange juice at the mess hall, so I stopped on my way as I shuffled off to sick call for treatment of a cough and sore throat. I arrived feeling better, after the half-mile walk. The medics promptly gave me the FNG look, rolled their eyes and handed me cough syrup and drops. The Cav must have been a healthy place, because I was the only one there. By the time I returned to the office I felt better.

The copy film for the photo lab came in the mail last evening from my brother. He did a fine job of sending it quickly. Fred knew about this, so he sent me out on the 11 a.m. courier flight to the photo lab with the regular film packet. As had been prearranged with Lt. Sheridan, I received twenty rolls of High Speed Ektachrome color slide film in trade for the 100-foot roll of fine-grain copy film. *It was supply and demand, you know, basic economics.* I could shoot photos to send home with this film. I had the two cameras brought from home, and they hadn't given me an army camera yet.

It was great to see Lieutenant Sheridan and the lab guys again. I think they had more respect for me now. Some heavy-duty plastic bags from one of the lab's store rooms would help protect my cameras from the rain. My traumatized basic training friend, Glen was gone from next door. *I hope he is okay.* I grabbed the packet and barely caught the courier Huey back to PV, jumping on as it was about to take-off.

Dec. 27 - My assignment this day was a photo story on Military Police (MPs). Before we left, some Vietnamese women that entered the base to work, were questioned by a South Vietnamese Army MP, (photo at right). I rode with the MPs in a jeep all day. They checked around the outside of the greenline, and the nearby villages. Our incoming mortar attacks came from some of those areas.

Phuoc Vinh village, the largest, was primitive and filthy, a total contrast to the Saigon lifestyle I had seen earlier. It was the worst poverty I had ever seen, so many children. The 'roads' were extremely muddy with deep, water-filled potholes. Our jeep labored through a few tough spots. Most of the traffic consisted of motor bikes weaving around the potholes.

The 1st Cav MPs were cooperative and helpful, which made it easy for me take my pictures. They were courteous to the Vietnamese villagers, who were cooperative. The ARVN MP interpreter accompanied us. He was the first ARVN I had worked with. He smiled at me, pointed at my camera, and said, "You have a good job here." He asked me many questions about my job as a photographer.

As we drove along the outside of the base perimeter, we came across several water buffalo. "Water buffalo are very dangerous," said the ARVN MP. " I saw one knock over a jeep." The huge beasts gave us nasty looks, so we stayed a good distance from them.

Water Buffalo graze near Phuoc Vinh.

Scenes from a village just outside the wire at Phuoc Vinh.

As we swept through the more rural villages, the ARVN told me that some of the people in this area were Catholic refugees from North Vietnam where they had been persecuted by the Hanoi communist government. There was a large Catholic church nearby. *These people were fighting to keep their freedom just like we fought for our freedom more than two centuries ago.*

Tonight, I had compound guard duty by the division tactical operations center (DTOC) in a sandbag kiosk. It was less stressful and more boring than greenline guard. There were people coming and going. *I could have sold cokes and popcorn.*

Dec. 28 - Major McCarthy called me into his office, " You are doing well, so far, but I may send you to 1st Brigade in Tay Ninh in a few days."

"Fine, sir," I replied. "However, I was wondering why we don't have credit lines on photos and bylines for stories in the *Cavalair*? It is an incentive for photographers and writers to do a better job. All the places where I have worked have done this."

"Okay, we should do that. I will remind the editors," he answered.

We also talked about camera maintenance. Many cameras were out for repair, indicating that the guys should take better care of them. *I may be the only one here with my own cameras.*

Dec. 29 - In the middle of the night, although not near us, there was a large ground attack on the greenline. There were many explosions and heavy automatic weapons fire. We could hear the gunship's miniguns firing. There was no way you could sleep while this was happening. It was still scary even though it wasn't close.

I concentrated on administrative tasks today, logging in film from 2nd Brigade. In the middle of typing innumerable photo captions to be attached to prints for distribution to media, I snuck in another letter to Sally.

Dec. 30 - I hurried to a 7:30 a.m. award ceremony at Division Headquarters. A Silver Star was awarded to Lieutenant Keldson of the LRRP company for action in Hue during the February 1968 Tet Offensive. Then I walked to the chaplain's area and took photos of Bronze Star and Air Medal awards. Chaplains were helpful to the soldiers, and performed important support to division personnel. After I finished the job, the chaplain's assistants offered me coffee and we talked about cameras.

Dec. 31 - Day guard on the tower was my job today. With the big binoculars, I watched a long convoy of tankers and loaded flat bed trucks. Tanks and armored personnel carriers from the 11th Armored Cavalry Regiment (ACR) were escorts. They headed up from the South and trailed a huge cloud of dust.

Later, I spotted movement more than a kilometer away, outside the greenline, beyond the corner, but with the big binoculars the cows looked friendly.

In the evening AFVN radio finished playing the top 100 hits from 1968 as voted by the troops in Vietnam. We had a clean trash can full of ice with three cases of beer and a case of Pepsi. Somebody invited several cooks and, of course, they brought food. Everyone had a favorite song. We had fun, and it ended right before midnight. There was an instant camaraderie here that I seemed to find wherever I went.

The top song was "Love is Blue," a bit of a surprise to the guys, too mellow for them, but not for me. It was Sally's favorite song.

Jan 1, 1969 - At the stroke of midnight, all hell broke loose, with shooting all around us. We could hear bullets as they ripped through the rubber trees next to our building. Tracers were flying everywhere. Several different colored flares lit up the night. Countless explosions erupted near and far. We hid behind the sandbag wall of the office. Someone was shooting an M60 machine gun into the air as we looked out the back door. It was a massive celebration of the new year, as spectacular as it was scary.

Today I worked with Fred on some of the work orders, and helped prepare the courier packet for the photo lab.

Jan 2 - A big package of brownies from home arrived in the mail today, which I shared with the guys. Goodies were always appreciated. We played scrabble some evenings when time permitted. Of course, the PIO writers were extraordinary. They would come up with huge words that I had to look up in the dictionary.

It seemed like I was beginning to fit in, but I could be sent out to a brigade tomorrow. There was great cooperation from everyone I worked with, and the sense of teamwork was always evident. I was respected here and would be happy to stay in PV.

Jan 3 - Major McCarthy told us about a singer/songwriter, Bill Ellis, a grunt from A 1/5. Third Brigade Information Officer Lt. Tim Millar discovered him singing his songs New Year's Eve at Quan Loi. They would bring him here to audition for Commanding General (CG) Forsythe. Then he could be assigned to Special Services, and visit the Fire Support Bases of the 1st Cav to entertain the skytroopers. We heard him practicing his songs. His great voice and emotional lyrics impressed everyone.

1st Cav 545th MPs and ARVN NPFFs move into the village to begin the search.

Jan 4 - I left in the dark at 5:30 a.m. to go on a cordon and search of a nearby village with 1st Cav 545th Military Police (MPs) and the elite Vietnamese National Police Field Force (NPFFs). This was the first operation of its kind since the 1st Cav moved into the area. I accompanied MP Lieutenant Dennis Dillard and his radio operator (RTO) Spec. 4 Willie McGruder.

I saw plenty of children, chickens, dogs and rodents. We noticed the whole village smelled, emitting an obnoxious stench. This operation was more thorough than the sweeps of last week. Elements of the 2nd Battalion 5th Cavalry had surrounded and sealed off the village last night. No one could enter or leave the area.

We made three sweeps through the primitive hamlet, searching everywhere. The NPFFs would poke bamboo sticks into the ground looking for buried weapons. Some of our incoming mortar rounds came from here.

Disappointed in not finding more on the search, the NPFFs did take three people away for questioning. With my camera, I copied some Viet Cong propaganda leaflets found in the village for our MPs as the NPFFs took the originals.

An NPFF checks the papers of a man found in the village.

After my long busy day, I had greenline guard again tonight, tense as always, but quiet. Melvin Clarke joyfully left for home yesterday, chain-smoking all the way. Everyone was happy for him. We were now down to three photographers at Phuoc Vinh.

Jan 5 - Happy Birthday to me, I remain an FNG.
I'm in limbo you see, but I'm still here in PV.
I received a big package of cookies in the mail today, great timing by the family. The coffee can package was dented but the cookies were fine. It was such a special treat to receive a goodie package on my birthday.

Jan 6 - Today I shot a Polaroid job for the first time, with a Graflex XL camera, (photo at right). Twice as big a 35 mm camera, it had film backs that attach to it and use 120 or 220 film. I had used a big camera when I worked for the *Vista Press*, a twin lens Mamiya C-33.

Polaroid film was not user friendly. You had to take the shot, pull the sheet out of the camera by a small tab smoothly through two rollers, wait a minute, peel it apart slowly and coat it with the preservative. The photos required finesse, and I continued to improve with experience.

36   I Will Be a Photographer After All, But Where?

Two large packages arrived today, one from Sally, and one from my good friend, Bob Matush. Birthday gifts, recording tape, and C batteries were worth their weight in gold. Everyone was clamoring for more of Sally's fruitcake, *really*. I had to give out small pieces of my birthday cake.

Major McCarthy told me I would stay here at Phuoc Vinh a few more days. *I had heard that before.*

Jan 7 - We were all prepared for General Abrams to visit today, but he cancelled at the last minute, creating much wasted effort for several PIO staffers.

Everyone in our office kicked in a few bucks and we bought a TV set which had mysteriously appeared at the PX. Previously, we had to go to the service club, a half mile away, to watch TV. We would plan our week around *Rowan and Martin's Laugh-in*. *The fast-paced, zany humor was a welcome relief from the stress we faced every day.*

The mail brought sad news from home, my Grandmother Moon had a stroke, and was not doing well.

Jan 8 - I went out with a writer and shot photos of field medics working on patients. These guys were not seriously wounded and didn't need medical evacuation. The guy he was treating in the photo was just dehydrated. *I had learned about that earlier myself.* The writer did a story on medic Jerry Clark from Hurt, WV. He said the newspaper headline would read: "The World of Hurt."

Jan 9 - I awakened early, departed the grubby tent and signed out of the company for a two-day photo assignment. Staff Sgt. (E6) Matt Glasgow, a senior writer and scrabble hustler, accompanied me. We had an extended Huey ride with a stop at Tan Son Nhut en route to a large base called Bearcat, southeast of Long Binh. He was writing a story on helicopter maintenance with the 15th TC (Transportation Corps), a huge 1300-man Battalion.

An aerial photo of the expansive Bearcat base south of Long Binh.

At Bearcat, we went by jeep to Company A of 15th TC to observe Chinook maintenance in two huge hangers. Everyone was busy, the team spirit was evident. I shot photos of the different shops, including Prop & Rotor, Electrical, and Sheet Metal. The inspector showed us a Chinook being repaired in the big hanger. Several crews looked efficient and were proud of their excellent safety record. *In my year with the Cav, there was not a single Chinook accident.*

After lunch in their outstanding mess hall, we were driven to company C, a mile or two down the road at Long Thanh, where they repaired Hueys, Cobras, and LOHs. The chief inspector gave us a tour. I photographed numerous maintenance operations. It seemed like a very safe place. After a fine spaghetti and meatball dinner, we stayed the night in relative comfort with 15th TC. They had cold beers for us and we watched a movie, *The Deadly Affair*. Another photo job was scheduled early the next morning.

How Did You Get This Job?   37

A crew of mechanics from Company A, 15th TC work on a Chinook engine at Bearcat, on the left. Rotor maintenance at Long Thanh, on the right.

Huey engine replacement and LOH maintenance at Long Thanh

PFC Craig Thornburg (left) and SP4 Sidney Blythe, aircraft repair specialists with 15th TC Battalion, replace the rotor head on a LOH at Long Thanh.

Jan 10 - I awakened at 6:30 and hurried to shoot 25 promotions. It was still fairly dark at 7 a.m. when I began photographing the lengthy ceremony. This battalion was a haircut inspection, shined boots type of unit. They marched around in formation, strange for Vietnam, more like basic training. This place was a long way from the war. They had skilled jobs, relative comfort and almost no danger. After the ceremony, the 15th TC S-1 found a flight to Phuoc Vinh for us at 1 p.m. We arrived 45 minutes later.

Hooray! This afternoon, I finally moved out of the dilapidated old tent where I had slept since my arrival, into a real building with the other PIO guys. Next to press/photo office (photo at right), it had a cement floor, tin roof, screen around the top, sandbags around the bottom and electricity. Two big fans, one by each door, kept the air moving. It was more like the comfort of Bien Hoa. A 55-gallon drum stood on a rack nearby for a cool shower in the morning, or a warm one in the afternoon, if any water was left. Greenline bunker 35 was less than 100-feet from the back door. *I now felt a lot less like an FNG. However, I still needed to know where my permanent job would be.*

Tonight, I had compound guard by the Division Tactical Operations Center (DTOC), a walking post, 9 p.m.-12 a.m. & 3-6 a.m. This was a very different guard experience, walking around the huge, creepy DTOC bunker complex in the middle of the night, (photo at right).

Jan 11 - Late in the evening, a major ground attack erupted on the greenline, the largest one yet. We watched from the back door of the office. We could see their green tracers coming in and our red tracers going out. Muzzle flashes beyond the wire showed a huge NVA force. Illumination flares revealed NVA soldiers running beyond the wire. Rocket propelled grenades exploded on the chain-link in front of a bunker down the line from us.

Sergeant Smart burst in and yelled, "Everyone get two bandoliers of ammo and get out behind bunker 35."

Our M16s were in a rack by the back door along with the ammo. We grabbed our rifles and crept to the trench-line behind the bunker. The clerks, writers and photographers would be the second line of defense. We were not trained for this. I could see the wide-eyed, openmouthed faces of fear along the trench-line in the bright flashes of the explosions and in the flickering light of the flares. We could see muzzles flashes outside the wire with green tracers coming our way. The overall firing intensified again. An extra M60 fired from the top of bunker 35, about 25 feet in front of us. The one inside was also shooting. The explosions beyond the bunker in front of us disoriented me. *Were RPGs hitting the chain link in front of the bunker? Could it be the NVA were in the wire close to the bunker so that the guys inside were blowing the claymores around the front?* Flashes silhouetted the bunker, a grenadier was on top pumping out M79 rounds. The explosions could have been larger and further away, I couldn't tell in all the chaos. I had learned that explosions seemed closer than they really were.

This looks grim. Would my M16 work if I needed it? There are so many NVA. Heaven help us.

Two gunships appeared, one directly above us. The rockets from the cobras hit so close they made huge flashes and had the sharp sound of incoming. The roar of the cobra's minigun was deafening. They seemed to be shooting into the wire just beyond the next bunker down the greenline from us. A gunship weaved around about 100 feet directly over our heads when it fired. The scene was unbelievable. More brilliant flashes as rockets exploded nearby. The tracers from the Cobra's minigun resembled a glowing red firehose stream against the black velvet sky.

It ended soon after the gunships joined the battle. As the drone of the helicopters faded, silence. Only the ringing in my ears remained. All of our PIO guys and the grunts on the bunker were okay. Help from above had saved us.

How could I be so exhausted and so wired at the same time? Sleep was impossible. As I thought about the battle, I don't think we were in serious danger, but it didn't seem like it at the time. I was thankful I wasn't on guard duty in one of those bunkers down the line, where I had been a few times before.

Jan 12 - In the morning, they counted 247 dead North Vietnamese Army (NVA) soldiers in and outside the wire. There were also numerous blood trails where others had been dragged away. It was rumored that we were tipped off about the approach of the NVA battalion by a LRRP (long-range recon patrol) team. Our regular greenline bunker guards had been reinforced with extra men from the base defense force, a grunt battalion at PV just for this purpose. We were only on the edge of this maelstrom, but it seemed like we were right in the middle. Some of the guys walked down the greenline and said some of the wire was badly torn up and they could see numerous dead NVA soldiers. We heard nothing about American casualties and we should have since this was our sector.

After the sleepless night, I was surprised with my first KP duty. Last night's attack caused some confusion, so they sent me to the mess hall late. I was stuck with pots and pans cleanup, the worst KP job by far. It was a two-man operation, but the other guy never showed up. *What a drag.* The big pots had to be cleaned with huge long-handled scrub brushes in one of two steaming cauldrons. I drank plenty of water to stay hydrated because I sweated profusely all day. This was as difficult as any of my sandbag days on the greenline.

KP would become the scourge of an otherwise great job with PIO. I was not on the KP roster until I signed back into the company returning from Bearcat. *Win some, lose some.* Most KP days couldn't be this bad, but it was still a wasted day, because I couldn't do any photo assignments.

Jan 13 - I captioned the Bearcat maintenance photos today. They looked good, and it was important to me to see them. I tried to be creative. These maintenance guys were unsung heroes of the Cav, an important part of the team. They kept our helicopters flying. I was impressed with the quality of work I saw there.

Our resident intellectual, Assistant Press Officer Lt. Michael Harris, answered the question everyone was asking, why the NVA had green tracers. He calmly explained, "It is very simple, our tracers use a strontium compound to make them burn red, the Russian and Chinese manufacturers use a barium compound and it burns green."

A package of cookies and a fruitcake from Grandma Miller arrived in the mail, making it a pleasant day.

In the afternoon, I walked to the PX with a couple of the guys. We saw the engineers working on the airstrip, (photo at right). The PSP metal surface was extremely hot from the sun, making it was a tough day for the engineers. The Phuoc Vinh airstrip was closed to C130s while they repaired and lengthened it. This caused delays to our precious mail delivery as the C-130s unloaded in Quan Loi and smaller planes or Chinooks delivered it to PV.

Jan 15 - Day guard for me in the morning, and nothing happened as usual. I wrote several letters and worked on my tan. In the afternoon, we fixed areas on the greenline that had been damaged in the attack a few nights ago. The morning work detail had finished removing the large area of torn up wire, a difficult job. They would have easy day guard in the afternoon. It was only fair, everyone had a half day of work. It was cloudy, but hot and steamy.

40   I Will Be a Photographer After All, But Where?

I strung the wire while another guy unrolled the spindle to maintain tension, and others tightened and anchored it to the ground. I was careful, but still scratched my arms. This wire was close to the ground securing the concertina wire to prevent NVA sappers from crawling under or through it. Trip flares would be added next by experts.

Sappers were specially trained NVA soldiers who tried to sneak through our perimeter wire wearing only shorts and carrying a backpack-sized satchel charge to blow up everything from helicopters to bunkers. There were rumors they were high on drugs when they did this.

This week's *Cavalair* newspaper included Fred's photo of President Thieu at PV on page one, my Christmas dinner mess hall picture was on page six, and Captain Carrara's Bob Hope show photos as the center spread.

Major McCarthy told us he'd made some personnel changes. He also told me again that I may soon go to 1st Brigade at Tay Ninh. However, the longer I stayed, the better my chances were of staying here permanently.

Robert Mewes teaches first aid and Don Callahan demonstrates knot tying to the school children.

Jan 16 - This morning, I walked to G5 (civil affairs) where Major Sparks took me by jeep to the local elementary school. A few artillerymen from Headquarters Battery, Division Artillery, started a boy scout-like activity with the school children. Twenty-seven boys and fourteen girls ages six to twelve participated.

First aid, field sanitation, knot-tying and crafts were taught. They had a Vietnamese interpreter, but he wasn't often needed. One of the artillerymen, Don Callahan, had great rapport with the kids. The children had fun. Laughter was everywhere. The happy children addressed each of the Americans, including me, as "G. I." This type of activity happened frequently. This program was a weekly part of the school program. *I wish all Americans could see this, but they never would. It was ignored by the news media.*

Tonight was my first assignment at the commanding general's mess, an award ceremony with the Division General Staff, after their dinner. The CG's mess was more like a fancy restaurant than a mess hall. The awards reminded me of the Vista City Council awards I had covered for the *Vista Press* newspaper. It rained heavily as I walked a half mile to the headquarters area. My poncho did a fine job above my knees. Approaching the headquarters area there was an inch of water on the ground. I shot my photos and no one said anything about my wet pant legs. The staff treated me well. Photographers were respected here.

I wrote captions until after midnight. We had not received any more FNGs since my arrival seven weeks ago.

A typical Bunk in our Hooch with ammo box furniture.

Jan 17 - Early, I walked to the briefing bunker to photograph two medal presentations. The room was crowded and I had to push my way through. That went with the territory of this job.

I made a set of shelves from empty wooden ammo boxes for the foot of my bunk. Artist, and former grunt Larry Collins, showed me how to set up my cot with a partially inflated air mattress, and a poncho liner (a lightweight quilt-like blanket) on top. Of course, mosquito netting covered the whole setup. He placed a small fan, that someone had given me earlier, on the ammo box shelf at the foot, inside the net. It was quite comfortable and I slept well. My helmet and flak jacket were to the left on the floor, where I rolled instantly when we had incoming. *My reaction to incoming became so automatic that I would wake up already on the floor.*

Jan 18 - We had a multitude of captions to do today. One of my jobs that returned from the lab had some extra prints with it. Before I went to shoot the assignment, I tested my camera and flash by taking a picture of the guys in the office. Someone at the photo lab had made a couple of prints and sent them along with the job, (photo below).

The third photographer at PV left for rest and recuperation (R&R), leaving only two of us to handle all the photo work. The major kept telling me I would go to 1st Brigade as the other PV photographers continued to disappear.

The guys in the office, clockwise from left, Fred Fiallos, Larry Collins, Jerry Smith (back to camera), Dave Brady, Lt. Mike Harris, Eugene Christianson, and Frank Smart, sitting on the table.

Jan 19 - While we were briefed by the officer-in-charge of our sector for greenline guard duty, a speeding jeep hit a puddle and splashed us, totally soaking me. Then I took apart and thoroughly cleaned my M16. When you needed it, it had to work. The night was unusually quiet, only two outgoing artillery rounds were fired, usually there were several dozen.

Jan 20 - The Bearcat aircraft maintenance story, with my good photos, was killed by MACV (Military Assistance Command, Vietnam) censors because of Staff Sgt. Glasgow's story. This was a problem for the writers, they walked a fine line between writing a good story and saying something that might help the NVA. I was disappointed. I wanted to see my photos in print. This would have been a *Cavalair* center spread. Perhaps some of my photos could be released individually.

Most of the morning, I traveled by jeep throughout the base with a G3 (operations and training) major. He needed slides for his FNG officers training program. Most of the day was spent shooting photos of different helicopters. First, we drove to the Chinook area near the end of the airstrip on the far side of the base. I had to run around to find the best angles for photos of the large, dual-rotor helicopters. We went to the tower area of the airstrip next. Many helicopters were coming and going. It was easy to shoot the photos of Hueys, Cobras and LOHs. I moved quickly around the airstrip to take the photos he wanted. The steel plates (PSP) of the airstrip were so hot it even heated my boots. My feet were uncomfortable, but I kept moving. I drank my whole canteen of water. When I returned to the office, a short rest was welcome.

Later, I bought a small electronic flash unit at the PX. Now if a problem arose with my regular flash unit, I had a back-up. I tested it shooting our scrabble game with, from left, Assistant Press Officer Lieutenant Mike Harris, writer Dave Brady and clerk Larry Jones, my back was toward the camera. I won, with a huge triple word score, beating two writers! *As they would say on Laugh-in, look that up in your Funk and Wagnalls.*

Jan 21 - An FNG, Al Persons, arrived at the office today, the first since I arrived in November. He was a writer who had attended the University of Alabama.

In the morning, I received a phone call from Pete Sommers, my Fort Monmouth photo school friend. He worked in Long Binh with USARV and said Rick Keller was with the 101st Airborne up north in Hue. I told Pete that Jerry Born was with the 173rd Airborne in An Khe. We were now scattered throughout Vietnam.

Having heard about other state flags displayed in our area, I wrote to California Governor Ronald Reagan requesting a state flag.

Jan 22 - Thirty tons of NVA ammunition and rockets were found by 1st Cav grunts in a bunker complex near the Saigon River, southwest of Quan Loi. We would have ABC, NBC, CBS News teams and more journalists arriving tomorrow. This was a huge news story.

Jan 23 - What a bummer, I had day guard on the tower today, and missed most of the media commotion. We had several news teams come through the office. When I returned in the evening, one team was still there. Again, only one American, with a mostly Australian crew. I briefly talked with some of the Aussies. They were like no journalists I had ever met, mercenaries in the true sense of the word. If not in danger, they were bored. They wanted to make a name for themselves and did whatever it took to feed the antiwar sentiment in the USA.

In the evening, we watched the *Steve Allen Comedy Special*. It was entertaining, a welcome reminder of home.

Jan 24 - This morning, I was issued an Army Pentax Spotmatic Camera, with a Takumar 70-150 mm zoom lens. It recently returned from repair, and now I could shoot more pictures with my own cameras to send home.

Immediately, after receiving my Army camera, CID (Criminal Investigation Division) arrived needing a photographer. Of course, Fred sent me, I was still the FNG and he didn't want to go. I rode in their jeep to the 13th Signal Battalion area, a quarter mile away. The worst possible job awaited me, photographing the scene of a suicide. This was really ugly. They needed countless pictures, and I was there for an hour. The poor guy was lying on his bunk with his M16 pointed under his chin. CID performed a thorough investigation to be sure it was a suicide. I fumbled with my camera, which never happened. When they were finally finished, I couldn't get away from there fast enough. It was so distracting that I got lost walking back to the office.

Early this evening, I set up the group picture of the general staff, thirty-five officers. However, it was cancelled at the last minute, because one of them was missing. No problem, I returned to the office in time to watch the refreshing comedy relief of *Laugh-in*.

Jan 25 - Major McCarthy said he still wanted to send me to 1st Brigade at Tay Ninh, but our new NCOIC, Sgt. 1st Class Peter DeGard, and some of the staff, had been lobbying for me to stay. I had performed well on my assignments, and handled an increasing amount of the administrative work. I enjoyed seeing all the proof sheets of the photos shot by the photographers. It was important to me to see what my own photos looked like. The major would have to bring someone from a brigade to PV to replace me. Many of the photos in the recent *Cavalairs* were from 1st Brigade, perhaps there was an experienced photographer there who would become photo coordinator, and I would take his place in Tay Ninh. Fred would leave in about a week and in a few days, the other PV photographer would return from R&R.

Sgt. 1st Class Peter DeGard took a nap in the office during lunch break with a comfy case of Black Label Beer as a pillow.

Jan 26 - A couple of the guys that departed for home gave me some of their C-ration stashes. My holiday goodies were gone, so I would try these mysterious canned foods soon.

Some of the guys went to the EM club tonight where Special Services had a "Carnival" with games. I finished paper work for the next courier packet, having day detail the next day.

Jan 27 - Once again, I had day guard on the tower. *It was so much better than night guard, as the bad guys only came out at night.* Looking into the village with the high-powered binoculars, I didn't see anything suspicious. Having brought some of the C-ration cans, and not knowing what to expect, I tore open a "Hershey's Tropical Chocolate Bar" someone had given me. *How can they make a real chocolate bar that won't melt? Oh, I see, It's like chocolate-flavored chalk.* The date pudding and apricots were good. The tiny P-38 can opener worked quite well. It turned out to be a peaceful rest day.

After I returned to the office, Major McCarthy assembled the entire staff and announced, "Spec. 4 Terry Moon will take over as photo coordinator when Fred Fiallos leaves in about a week. He has a fine resume, has done well on his assignments and can handle the administrative work." He looked at me and smiled. "We ran him through the wringer a couple times and he responded well. Once, we yanked him out of bed after greenline guard, and sent him to Quan Loi for a big job. Tom Sheridan also tried to persuade me to let him stay at the photo lab. Spec. 4 Philip Blackmarr, a photographer from 3rd Brigade and another photo school honor student, will join him in this office in a few days."

There were smiles around the room, but mine was the biggest. Happy with the support I had received from everyone, they had my back. I finally knew what my job would be, the one I wanted all along. I remembered Don Lonsway's prophetic words to me, a new arrival, "Do your job well, and doors will open for you." Don was now in Tokyo editing and producing the *Cavalair* newspaper.

We learned later the photographer that was on R&R would go to 1st Brigade when he returned. Phuoc Vinh would only have two photographers now, where we had four in the past.

Later in the evening, I repaired an electronic flash unit for Captain Carrara, (a bent contact, an easy fix with my tiny screwdriver). As I casually flashed it around the room, he smiled and said, "Thanks, Flash."

Everybody laughed and someone yelled, "Way to go, Flash!"

Soon they would all call me "Flash," my nom de guerre, and now laughing with them, I was no longer an FNG.

44   I Will Be a Photographer After All, But Where?

Aerial view of Phuoc Vinh village, just outside the base. The huge Catholic Church is in the upper left corner.

The Huey of one of the assistant division commanders is serviced by the crew at Phuoc Vinh

Chapter Four From FNG to Photo Coordinator

Jan 28 - An early morning medal award ceremony for thirteen skytroopers was my assignment at Commanding General Forsythe's office. These were awards for heroism and valor, Silver Stars for the grunts and artillerymen, Distinguished Flying Crosses for the pilots. It went smoothly. The general was proud of these brave soldiers. He almost smiled.

The film from my Criminal Investigation Division (CID) suicide job was botched by someone at the photo lab who improperly loaded a film developing reel. Some photos were ruined, but I had taken so many that most were okay. For this, the lab culprit received article 15 punishment, probably a week of work details. *You did not want to upset CID.*

I received two goodie packages today that took over three weeks to arrive. However, they were packed so well, the treats were still in good shape.

Jan 29 - I prepared to take over the administrative duties of photo coordinator. We received multiple jobs from the photo lab, some with many prints to caption. A call to CID and Aircraft Accident Investigation Board (AAIB) notified them their prints were ready for pickup. Work orders arrived for several jobs. I had to shoot three assignments, some passport pictures and a couple of full-length photos of officers for their personnel files. We had a heavy load and we couldn't get behind.

Patience, grasshopper.

I enjoyed doing the administrative tasks, because that gave me a much better view of the overall picture of what the entire division did. I could also study my own assignment photos, to help improve my work in the future.

PIO writer Dave Brady tips his helmet on our way to a helicopter maintenance story at 227th.

After lunch, I walked to C Company, 227th Assault Helicopter Battalion (AHB) with jovial PIO writer Dave Brady (Philadelphia, PA). I took pictures to accompany his story on the Huey maintenance crews. It seemed hotter than normal, like a sauna. We could see the continuing work on our airstrip. A day like this was brutal for the poor engineers working on the hot metal decking (PSP) of the airstrip. When they finished lengthening the airstrip, the

C130s could return and our mail would arrive earlier. The large group of APO (Post Office) workers would then return from Quan Loi and be back on our duty rosters, making KP and guard duty less frequent for us. I had greenline guard again tonight, always stressful, but quiet.

Jan 31 - We finally took the group picture of the Division General Staff. I joined Photo Coordinator Fred Fiallos and Press Officer Captain Frank Carrara immediately after guard duty. We had to shoot this today because Brig. Gen. Irby would leave tomorrow. Commanding General Forsythe usually glared at the camera and I couldn't help noticing his shiny thirty-eight revolver. Major McCarthy was on the right end of the back row. I took about fifteen shots hoping we would have one where everyone looked good. Returning to the office, I had more administrative tasks before I could sleep off last night's guard duty.

Brig. Gen. Richard Irby, left, receives an award at his farewell dinner from CG George Forsythe.

In the evening, Fred and I went to the commanding general's mess with the Division General Staff. We photographed awards to departing Assistant Division Commander (ADC) Brig. Gen. Richard Irby. He had been interim CG before Maj. Gen. Forsythe's arrival last August 19 and was well-liked by everyone. I also shot Polaroids. It was fun now, since I had improved my technique. When Fred and I were finished, we returned to the kitchen where the cooks had large plates for us of delicious food, juicy steak, a steaming baked potato and complimentary side dishes. Fred smiled at me and whispered so the cooks wouldn't hear him, "This is a great job." We even made it back to the office in time to watch *Laugh-in*. It was a rerun, but that didn't matter, we loved it. We ignored the subtle antiwar messages.

Feb 1 - After an early job was delayed at C 227th AHB this morning, I walked to the VIP helicopter pad for Brig. Gen. Richard Irby's farewell ceremony and the arrival of new Assistant Division Commander Brig. Gen. Frank Meszar. The band, the colorful flags and an eleven-gun salute made it festive. Fred had day guard, so I was the lone ranger, so Captain Carrara helped me shoot the fast-paced ceremony.

Spec.5 Chris Miller awarded his 43rd Air Medal by C 227th CO Major Joe Miller, from the Cavalair. An award photo like this one was commonly called a "grip and grin."

Back at the office, I logged in fifteen work orders. Schedule changes and additions made it a hectic day. Later, I shot the award ceremony at C 227th AHB of a third term Huey crew chief with forty-three air medals on his shirt, (photo at right). That was a huge amount of flying time, you need 100 hours of combat flying time to qualify for an Air Medal. On the way back, I delivered prints to 11th Aviation group. I also had many work orders and rolls of film to log in. It was great to be busy. After dinner, back to the CG's office, but the job was postponed until the next day.

As I walked back to the office, the pace of the day caught up with me. I went right to bed and slept well.

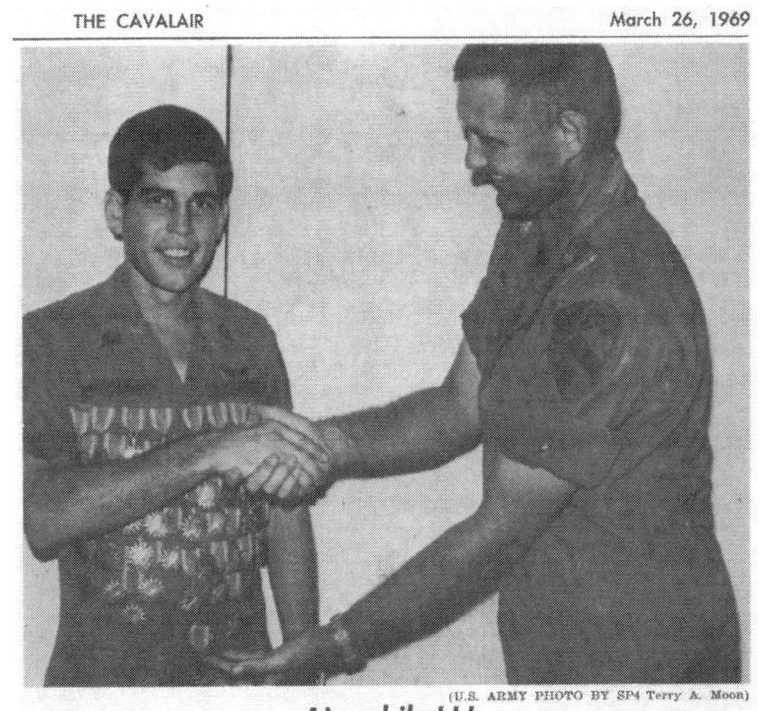

THE CAVALAIR   March 26, 1969

Airmobile!!!
(U.S. ARMY PHOTO BY SP4 Terry A. Moon)
SP5 Christopher A. Miller, 20, receives congratulations and another Air Medal from his commanding officer, MAJ Joe M. Miller, CO of Company C, 227th Assault Helicopter Battalion. The crew chief has flown enough hours to merit him 43 awards.

Feb 2 - Our 1st Brigade PIO guys were occupied with media the last few days covering major rice cache finds, northwest of Tay Ninh, totaling over 100,000 pounds. A huge bunker complex was discovered by 2/12 grunts not far away. It contained a hospital under construction with five plastic sheet lined operating rooms and six wards that could accommodate about 15 people apiece. They also found a bicycle repair shop with several bicycles and two mess halls that each seated 200 men. The NVA intended to defend this area from out helicopters, as several 12.7mm antiaircraft guns were found. The complex was so expansive, it had to be destroyed by B52 strikes. I spent most of January expecting to be sent to 1st Brigade.

I traded DTOC compound guard tomorrow with another guy in exchange for greenline guard tonight. Normally a bad trade, but clerks Larry Adams and Larry Jones from the information office (PIO) were with me on bunker 35, right behind the office. It was quiet, about as pleasant as guard duty could be. There had been a promotion party earlier in the evening and we drank leftover cans of Wink (grapefruit soda) and ate C-rations (I actually liked the date pudding and the fruitcake). At midnight, each of us took a two-hour shift until 6 a.m.

Feb 3 - I awakened at 10:30 a.m., and walked to a photo assignment in Brig. Gen. Shedd's office at division headquarters. After I took the photos, the general's aide, Lt. Hirsch, pulled me aside. He told me that the general really liked the portrait I had taken of him in front of the Huey, and it was rare for him to give out compliments. That made my day. It was great to be appreciated.

Spec. 4 Philip Blackmarr, the new PV photographer, arrived late in the morning from 3rd Brigade. Major McCarthy referred to him as a Fort Monmouth photo school honor student. He was a Princeton University graduate, an artist, and he played the violin. Tall and thin, he came to 1st Cav PIO in late September of 1968. He immediately went to 3rd Brigade and spent most of his time at Quan Loi and out in the field with grunts. The brigade commander also had him paint some artwork. It became a strange sight as he played Paganini Caprices on his violin with his music stand out by the greenline.

The two of us would be the only photographers at Phuoc Vinh. I worked with some of the base units to adjust photo assignment schedules so we could handle more work. Everyone had been very cooperative. We were earning their respect.

In a knock down, drag out scrabble game, I managed to hang on to beat three writers, a rare feat!

Feb 4 - Someone awakened me early and told me I had KP. What a terrible way to start the day. I had a kitchen job today. However, it didn't turn out that bad because it wasn't as hot as usual.

In the evening, Captain Carrara signed over to me the 45 pistol and the Graflex XL camera with the Polaroid backs. He went over the film logs, the work orders and the rest of the books. They passed inspection. The 45 would be a big help. No longer would it be necessary to take my M16 everywhere I went, since it was a nuisance while taking pictures. There was prestige in carrying a pistol. The holster attached to the belt along with my lens and film pouches that I always wore. I added another pouch to the belt to carry goodies, including two cans of C-rations, date pudding, and fruit cake. I could always find these items as they were unpopular, and I would always have something to eat with me.

I settled in as photo coordinator, PIO's head photographer. A week ago I was still an FNG. Fred left for R&R in Tokyo and he would soon leave permanently.

Phil was sharp and intuitive. We would handle the photo jobs here at Phuoc Vinh. *I felt confident about the future.*

Feb 5 - I had day guard on the tower, nothing interesting in view. I searched the village for suspicious activity but there was none. I wrote more letters and diligently worked on my tan.

This week's *Cavalair* had my MP cordon and search photos as the center spread (photo below) and the "World of Hurt," C 2/5 medic photo was on page eight.

Feb 6 - Today, I went on a VIP tour with the Army Chief of Chaplains, Major General Sampson, first to the brigade base camp at Quan Loi. Then we took the long flight to Tay Ninh. He also spoke to and presented Bibles to all the division chaplains at the Phuoc Vinh Chapel. (See photo at right.) Our chaplains were pleased with the way I handled the tour. However, they were *always* pleasant.

Previously, I had some discussions with CID and they now had their own camera, so hopefully we wouldn't receive too many of those grim assignments.

I had a mail call bonanza tonight, nine letters. Some of them were very old with wrong addresses. Two new ones were from Sally, a huge morale boost for me.

Feb 7 - I awakened at 9 a.m., Press officer Captain Carrara and NCOIC Sgt. 1st Class DeGard were gone. Phil shot the jobs and I prepared the courier packet. In the evening, I went to the CG's mess for awards. It was like a fancy restaurant. As a bonus, I always enjoyed a superb dinner. The kitchen staff knew me now, while I was shooting the job they would prepare an appetizing plate of food for me. It was a very pleasant relaxed atmosphere and I was usually asked photography questions by the General Staff and the cooks.

I received a California map from my family and I mounted it on the wall by my desk. I hoped to eventually have a state flag. We had several Californians here. The guys from other states said we were from the land of the fruits and nuts.

A low aerial photo of the south gate at Phuoc Vinh.

Feb 8 - I was assigned day guard at the main gate, which provided much more activity with frequent jeep and truck traffic than I ever saw on the tower. Many Vietnamese, mostly women, worked on the base. I watched them walk by in their white shirts, black pants and conical hats. MPs would check their papers.

In the evening, we had a Spec. 5 promotion party for our artist, Larry Collins (Oklahoma) with Larry Adams (Barstow, CA), Chuck Spicer (La Jolla, CA), Larry Jones (Reno, NV), Andy Anderson (San Jose, CA), our new writer, Al Persons (Alabama) and radio station announcer Dave Van Drew (Illinois). Larry was a fine artist, and he had several paintings in the last magazine. Phil missed the celebration, due to greenline guard.

I was already planning my R&R with my girlfriend Sally in Hawaii. I talked to guys that recently returned, and they provided good suggestions to help me plan.

1st Cav Chaplains Lt. Col. Michael Rosnock, left and Lt. Col. Raymond Foley hold Catholic and Protestant Church Services for 82nd Airborne artillerymen on desolate LZ Odessa..

Feb 9 - Early today, I flew to LZ Odessa, a desolate fire support base, 15 km northeast of Phuoc Vinh. My assignment, was to take photos of Sunday church services led by 1st Cav Chaplains for an 82nd Airborne unit. The Catholic chaplain, a priest, used ammo boxes for his altar. I took several photos of them with 105 mm howitzers, and a Huey helicopter in the background.

In the evening, I photographed a shooting victim at the PV medics for Criminal Investigations Division, a Vietnamese boy about ten or twelve years old. I took photos only of entry and exit wounds. They wouldn't give me any details. This wasn't as shocking as the suicide I photographed two weeks ago.

I immediately hurried to the briefing bunker for awards. I almost had to push the commanding general out of the way to get the shot. Division Command Sergeant Major Peters usually harassed me about my hair and mustache. *That was what sergeant majors did.* My curly hair looked messy, even when it was short, so a haircut today would save me some grief.

Feb 10 - Early in the morning, I began photographing a VIP tour with four-star General Ralph Haines, US Army Pacific Commander. It would last all day. The Division Tactical Operations Center, (DTOC) was the first stop for an intelligence and operations (G2-G3) briefing. The tour with Gen. Haines and Commanding General Forsythe then took a lengthy Huey flight to LZ Cindy, a desert-like fire support base next to the Dong Nai River, northeast of Bien Hoa. A and E Companies, 1st Battalion, 12th Cavalry had fought off a major NVA attack during the night. They had many incoming mortar rounds, and several skytroopers were wounded.

The generals gave out medals to grunts and artillerymen. They toured the LZ and talked with many of the skytroopers. I shot pictures, obtained the grunts' names and the photos eventually could be sent to their hometown newspaper (see photo below). This was an important part of my job. I noticed a California flag standing by ammo boxes in one of the 105 mm howitzer pits, (photo at right). *Soon, I hope to have my own state flag from Governor Reagan.*

As I was doing this, one of the dirty, tired grunts approached, smiled and asked me. "Hey man, how did you get this job?"

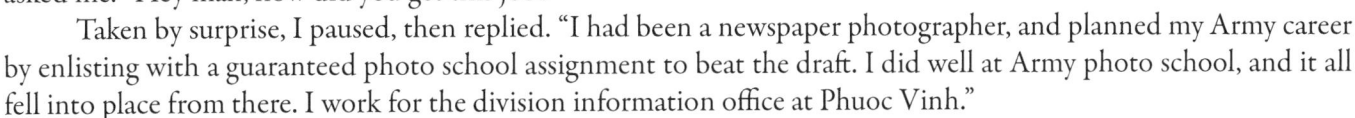

Taken by surprise, I paused, then replied. "I had been a newspaper photographer, and planned my Army career by enlisting with a guaranteed photo school assignment to beat the draft. I did well at Army photo school, and it all fell into place from there. I work for the division information office at Phuoc Vinh."

He shook my hand, smiled again, and said, "Good thinkin' man, I was fuckin' drafted. I am an alpha company, first of the twelfth, grunt." *I would hear this question about my job frequently during the rest of my time with the 1st Cav.*

General R. E. Haines, CG, US Army Pacific, talks with E 1/12 mortarman Spec. 4 Samuel Faulk of San Diego at LZ Cindy. Guiding Gen. Haines on the tour are Maj. Gen. George Forsythe (second from left, actually smiling) 1st Cav CG, and Col. Karl Morton, 1st Cav 3rd Brigade Commander.

This is a classic home town news release photo.

We flew to Quan Loi where I photographed a huge display of captured Chinese-made weapons, (photos above and below). Dozens of 122 mm rockets were stacked in the front. The NVA shot these monsters at us frequently, and up close they looked enormous. Also, rows of antiaircraft guns still encased in grease. *With my frequent flying, I didn't even want to think about antiaircraft guns.*

Numerous mortars of different sizes stood by large piles of ammo. I looked closely at one of the 82 mm rounds (setting on the box, lower right in the photo). Heavy and much larger than a grenade, it was unnerving just holding it. A while back, one of these nasty bastards almost got me on a greenline bunker. There was also a huge pile of AK-47s, some with bayonets. It made me uncomfortable being close to the weapons that wounded or killed our guys.

MG George I. Forsythe, 1st Cav Commanding General (left) shows a captured AK-47 to Gen. R.E. Haines. Commanding General, US Army Pacific. The weapon was part of a huge cache captured by 3rd Brigade skytroopers.

Next, we flew west to LZ Jake, near Cambodia, a strange fire support base with an airstrip, and a separate special forces camp at the other end of the runway. It was shaped like a giant dumbbell, with a circular base on each end of the airstrip. More Chinese rockets, ammo, and mines uncovered by 5/7 grunts within the last few days, were shown to General Haines. Another long Huey ride, and we arrived back at PV about 6 p.m.

I did captioning later of all thirty-five of the names on the general staff photo, along with other paperwork. I prepared the film that was shot earlier, to send to the photo lab tomorrow.

This was a long, busy day with new, interesting elements. *The 1/12 grunt I spoke with today was right, this is a great job.*

Feb 11 - It was a very odd, slow day in the office. We sometimes shot passport photos, but usually not that many. Strangely, today, I shot fifteen of them. Some R&R destinations required passports.

I received a large goodie package in the mail from the family. The brownies were always a welcome lift. We watched *Star Trek* and *The Dean Martin Show* on TV in the evening.

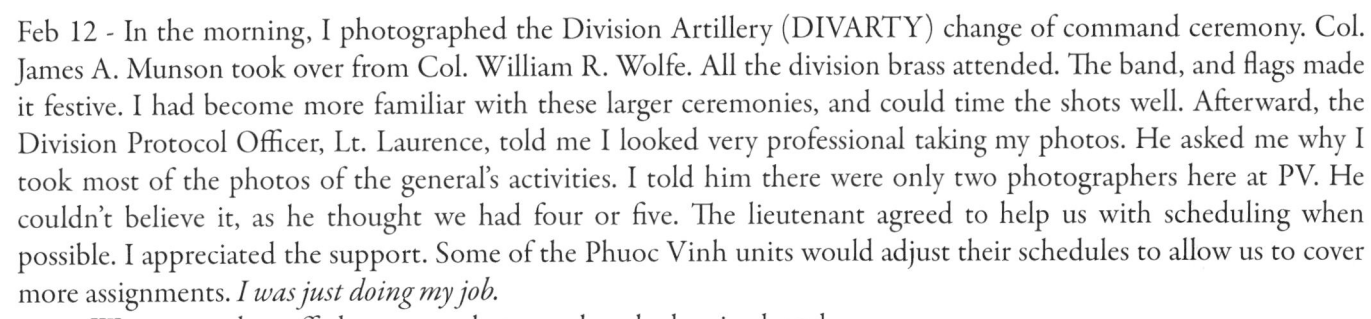

Feb 12 - In the morning, I photographed the Division Artillery (DIVARTY) change of command ceremony. Col. James A. Munson took over from Col. William R. Wolfe. All the division brass attended. The band, and flags made it festive. I had become more familiar with these larger ceremonies, and could time the shots well. Afterward, the Division Protocol Officer, Lt. Laurence, told me I looked very professional taking my photos. He asked me why I took most of the photos of the general's activities. I told him there were only two photographers here at PV. He couldn't believe it, as he thought we had four or five. The lieutenant agreed to help us with scheduling when possible. I appreciated the support. Some of the Phuoc Vinh units would adjust their schedules to allow us to cover more assignments. *I was just doing my job.*

We were understaffed, no new photographers had arrived, and six had departed. The brigades were also thin. However, Phil and I had been able to handle the jobs at PV with few problems. We adjusted well on the fly to last-minute changes. Phil was good with a camera, and remarkably calm. He seemed to enjoy this as much as I did, and had learned the paperwork quickly. In the photo to the right, he took a shot of me with the Polaroid back on the Graflex XL camera. He learned to use that swiftly, as well.

After lunch, I walked to the MP area where I photographed several awards. They had their ceremonies outside in the yard in front of a formation of the company. The poor MPs had to stand out in the heat during the lengthy ceremony.

I received another care package from my old friend Bob Matush. He had been in Vietnam before on Navy river boats, so he knew what I would need, cotton socks, batteries, lens cleaner, a collapsible drinking glass, and other useful items. It was thoughtful and much appreciated.

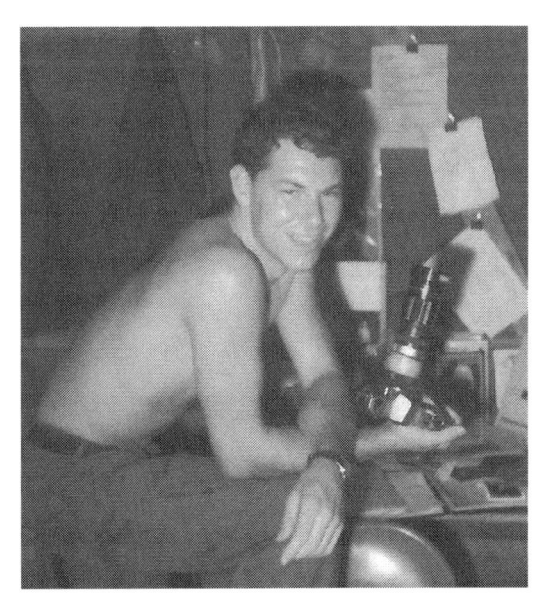

Feb 13 - I rode with our chaplains to visit the local Buddhist Monk with Tet (Vietnamese New Year) holiday gifts. He gave us tea and watermelon.

We also went to the local Catholic church, (see photo above). It was huge, made out of plywood and partially painted white. It looked totally out of place. There were a large number of Vietnamese Catholics in this area, due to the French influence. Several had also escaped the severe communist persecution in North Vietnam, to settle in this area. However, the priest wasn't at the church because he had an accident on his motorcycle, and was recovering in the hospital. He was 85.

Feb 14 - With a little help from my alarm clock, I awakened at 5:30 a.m., and hurried over to the mess hall for the best job on KP, dining room orderly. It beat working in the hot kitchen, or God forbid, in the pot and pan shack. The first KP guy to arrive, would choose which job he wanted. I learned quickly how to play the game, grabbing several snacks during the easy day.

The January issue of the *1st Cavalry Division Magazine* arrived. Most of the pictures in it, were shot by photographers who had already gone home (DEROSed). Fred had a great article on the LRRPs, called the "dirty half-dozen." Unfortunately, the magazine had major production delays. It was supposed to be out in December.

Feb 15 - Early in the morning, I walked to the VIP pad to take the portrait of new Assistant Division Commander Brig. Gen. Frank Meszar in front of his Huey. He looked similar to Telly Savalas, with a big, ugly cigar.

While we waited for the general, I noticed the crew's uniforms were a lighter color. I asked the crew chief, "What are these different uniforms you're wearing?"

He replied, "This fabric is called Nomex, it's fireproof. You have a much better chance to escape from a fire when wearing these uniforms."

"Really, that's cool, where can I get one of those?" I asked.

"You can't, they're for aviation crews only."

"What a bummer. OK, will one of you sharp-dressed skytroopers take my picture?" I asked. I handed one of my cameras to the shaky door gunner to photograph me in the general's chair in front of his Huey (photo on previous page). He was so nervous, like Don Knotts, I had to tell him to hold the camera still a few times. Meanwhile, the crew chief was laughing. He was still snickering when the general arrived a few minutes later.

"What's so funny?" the general asked.

The crew chief could only point at the door gunner. The general shook his head, smiled briefly and sat in his chair for the portrait (photo at right). I took several shots quickly, the general then took his place in the copilot's seat. As set by tradition in an airmobile division, all 1st Cav generals were aviators. The pilot cranked up the Huey, and as they ascended, I received a wave and a thumbs-up from the crew chief. *I would fly with these guys countless times in the future.*

In the evening, we finally viewed the Super Bowl on TV. We could see how slick Joe Namath carved up the Colts defense.

Feb 16 - We heard an interesting story from our 2nd Brigade PIO guys. They were working with the South Vietnamese Marines 3rd Battalion who discovered a huge cache of weapons near the Saigon River. Included were modified 122 mm Rockets with warheads nearly twice as large. They were called "Flying Trashcans." It was bad news that some of our future incoming rockets may be even more destructive.

Ed Koehnlein, our 2nd Brigade photographer, went to the site, and took photos. They also found 105,000 rounds of AK-47 ammo, 216 B-40 rocket propelled grenades, over 500 mortar rounds and other enemy supplies. It took several days to remove the weapons from the massive bunker complex.

Feb 17 - Today was Tet, the Vietnamese New Year, and everyone was wary. We knew what happened last year, the huge countrywide wave of attacks. We were expecting the same this year.

High aerial photo showing the convoy crossing the Song Be Bridge

Throughout the day, writer Al Persons and I flew in a LOH helicopter, shadowing a large convoy traveling from Bien Hoa to Quan Loi. We had been briefed earlier by an MP lieutenant, who would be flying the cover mission. As we approached from PV, a huge cloud of dust appeared. When we moved in closer, many tanker and flatbed trucks suddenly materialized with 11th Armored Cavalry tanks and armored personnel carriers (APCs) riding "shotgun" for them.

In the morning, we were in the air over two hours following the convoy from Bien Hoa up the dusty road to Phuoc Vinh. They crossed the strategic bridge over the Song Be River, (photo on previous page), just south of PV. Two places along the way, were groups of APCs with huge tracked tow vehicles, (photo to the right), in case of breakdowns or attacks. Fortunately, they weren't needed today.

After lunch, we flew from Phuoc Vinh to Quan Loi. Part of the area was thick jungle, so it had been cleared 200 yards on each side of the road to avoid ambushes, (photo at left, the dark areas are shadows of the clouds). The engineers cleared the areas with special tree-cutting bulldozers called rome plows. Convoys still frequently received enemy fire.

For better photos, I had the pilot fly low beside the convoy. To tell him what I wanted, I had to lean forward between the seats, shout at him, and he would nod. Al was in the left seat writing notes for his story. With the extensive dust, sometimes I could see only the first few vehicles. I was in the back of the LOH attached to a harness, so I was free to move around to either side for whatever picture opportunities arose. I could lean out far, to take a shot like the one on the facing page, and not fall out. Enjoying this immensely, it was an adrenaline rush, another E-ticket ride for me. The harness usually secured M60 gunners on scout flights.

As we approached Quan Loi, green tracers streaked by our LOH. Our pilot reacted quickly with evasive action, darting one way, then the other, to avoid the NVA fire. I bounced around in back, grateful to be secured with the harness. We were a big target, and there was no place to hide. The seats in the front of the LOH were armored on the back, sides, and bottom, but I had nothing in the back. The lead tank was also fired upon, and the convoy stopped briefly while air strikes hit the area where the enemy fire had originated.

How Did You Get This Job? 57

I am leaning out to shoot the convoy as we fly by very low; that is our tail rotor on the left.

The lead tank of the convoy as it approaches Quan Loi.

After arriving at the Quan Loi base camp, we rode around in a jeep with the MPs. The heat was oppressive, and the fine red clay dust was everywhere. My wraparound shades kept it out of my eyes. I appreciated the "natural air conditioning" of flying in the helicopters. Later, I took photos of a few convoy trucks being unloaded by 15th S&S (logistics) guys. They gave us some apples. We rode back to the MP office, situated in one of the old French brick buildings. While munching our juicy fresh fruit, we watched Jackie Gleason on their TV until our LOH returned.

We flew over the huge rubber processing plant, (photo at right), outside the Quan Loi base as we returned to PV, arriving at 5 p.m. My clothes were filthy from the red clay dust, it also stuck to your sweaty body, and created a fine layer of mud. I had been told the red clay would stain your skin if you left it on too long. That late in the day, there was no water left in our shower, so I scrounged up some canteens, filled them at the drinking water trailer, and took a slow, cool, satisfying shower, one canteen at a time.

I received a letter from the *Palomar College Telescope* newspaper editor, Steve Krueger. They had run a story about me. He sent me a list of questions to answer, similar to an interview. As a member of the *Telescope* staff in 1966, I wrote a page one lead story on the draft as one of my assignments. I knew the photography instructor at Palomar, Mr. Justus Ahrend, was behind this story. He sent me a copy of the newspaper that arrived at the same time. Earlier, I sent him one of the 1st Cav Christmas cards, and we exchanged a few letters in January. He was pleased that I had applied some of the lessons he had taught me. *He definitely helped change me from a guy with a camera, into a photographer.*

The Tet Truce ended at 6 p.m. We had nearby B-52 strikes at 6:05, and many during the night. My cot was shaking enough to awaken me. It was surprising how much I had adapted to the heavy rumbling sounds of the B52 strikes.

Some of the guys in the office, clockwise from front, Chuck Spicer, Larry Adams, Al Persons (FNG), Fred Fiallos (extreme short-timer), and Andy Anderson. Al and Andy were excellent guitar players. Al was working hard to play "Classical Gas."

Feb 18 - Fred Fiallos, and writer Jerry Smith returned from R&R in Tokyo. Apparently, they spent a few extra days with the REMFs in Bien Hoa. Fred had bought a motor-drive Pentax Spotmatic camera. It was really slick. *I want one.* He would leave for home tomorrow, so we partied. I would have large shoes to fill, as he was well respected by everyone. Later, I had to catch up on office work.

Feb 19 - I shot one award job today, and wrote countless captions. I was fortunate it was a slow day because Phil had KP, and I was alone to handle the work.

After a "drought," the PX finally had some soda available, but only root beer. Sometimes we had to resort to Kool-Aid. The only flavor anyone liked was black cherry.

My picture of Brig. Gen. Irby's departure ceremony was on page one of the *Cavalair* this week.

A shower setup similar to our old one.

Feb 20 - Several of us worked on our new shower most of the hot day. This work was entirely voluntary, and everybody helped. This was important to us. When you needed a shower, and the water was gone, it turned ugly. I had never been as dirty as I was here, total misery. This one would be larger, two 55-gallon drums, instead of one.

Feb 21 - I wrote captions most of the day, and prepared the courier packet. Phil took the few jobs that were scheduled. I played horseshoes in the afternoon, and had an amazing comeback win from a 20-8 deficit over clerk, Larry Jones. He couldn't believe it. We had light rain later in the afternoon, unusual because we normally had heavy rain, and the temperature remained over 100.

Feb 22 - In the morning, I shot Polaroids at 8th Engineers of CO Lt. Col. Walter and his staff for their headquarters chart. After lunch, there was an awards ceremony for me to photograph with several medals awarded at Civic Affairs (G5). It rained like hell only minutes after I arrived back at the office. *It's all timing.*

Feb 23 - In the middle of the night, about 3:30 a.m., we had heavy incoming, much of it extremely close. One of the guys in our building panicked, ran screaming down the center aisle, right past me, toward the back door. He ran into the tall, heavy, pedestal fan, crashed into the door frame, and crumpled to the floor. This was another intensely disturbing incident. A flashlight beam showed blood. More lights showed his arm was badly cut. Groggy, he may have hit his head. We wrapped his bloody arm in a towel and drove him to the medics. After our return, more incoming struck at 6:15 a.m. An intense level of fear existed during incoming, prompting these fear-driven incidents to happen occasionally. Everyone reacted differently. We rallied behind him, and he knew he had our support.

The spectre of incoming was always there. The next one could get you.

The mortar rounds were more concentrated in small areas. The rockets were much larger and more random. It seemed like they were aiming the mortars at the greenline bunkers near us. That usually meant a ground attack would follow, but not this time.

Our injured clerk's arm took several stitches, but he would be okay. They thought he might have a concussion, but he passed the tests. The fan, on the other hand, took a while to fix, the cage was smashed, and we had to straighten the blades. We kept tweaking it, but it still wobbled slightly. *We needed it whether it wobbled or not.*

Mysteriously, we acquired a large, 65 cubic foot refrigerator today. *Fantastic!* We would now have the luxury of cold drinks. *I had no idea where it came from, no one was talking, and no questions were asked.*

Feb 24 - Today all our jobs were cancelled. We had an unusual base-wide red alert. There were several rocket and mortar attacks during the previous night over the entire area. Long Binh, Bearcat, and Bien Hoa, normally safe bases, had also been attacked. My scheduled all day work detail, never happened. *Again, it's all timing.*

We were building a large bunker with a heavy wood frame, (photo at right) PSP roof reinforcement, and hundreds of sandbags outside the back door of our bunk building. There we could safely watch TV, and quickly hide from incoming.

Greenline guard duty for me this evening with the PIO clerk who had run into the fan the night before. He recovered quickly, and embarrassed by the incident, kept his shirt sleeve down to cover the bandage.

Red alert status on the greenline meant everyone stayed up all night. Several base defense force grunts were with us on the bunkers, and guys crouched in the defensive trench behind us. This by itself was scary. A major ground attack was expected, and the stress level was off the chart. We watched closely, and sweated profusely throughout the night, but nothing happened, except the relentless attacks of the hungry mosquitos.

Two LRRPS in the "jungle."

Six man LRRP team look like they are out on a mission (above) and pose as a group (below).

Feb 25 - I awakened, just in time for lunch, after I slept off the extremely stressful night of greenline guard. Writer Al Persons and I walked to the Long Range Reconnaissance Patrol (LRRP) compound. We then traveled by truck with a six-man LRRP team, to a remote area in the rubber trees, behind tower eight. I shot photos of the team, so it would look like they were on a mission in the jungle. With their "camo black" applied, their faces would disappear in the shadows. It looked good for a "photo op." No photographer could go with them on an actual mission, because it would be easily compromised by an untrained man.

We rode back to their area, where they posed for a team photo (see previous page). One LRRP showed me an interesting Chinese folding-stock AK-47, (photo at right). Soon after, we were interrupted by a 1st Squadron, 9th Cavalry Huey, and the team jumped on, and left on a mission.

On our way back to the office, we saw a 1st of the 9th scout team far beyond the greenline. A LOH searched low, and the Cobra waited up high, which made a deadly hunter-killer team. *What a great concept.* Al and I discussed setting up a job in the near future to fly with them. It would be tough, as they had a crazy, rowdy reputation, and didn't like writers or photographers. Al would use his southern, "good ole boy" diplomatic skills, to set this up with them.

Feb 26 - I shot photos of a 1/7 FNG officer initiation. It was strange, as they acted like little kids. One of the events, they tied two guys wrists together, blindfolded them, and they swatted each other with big, rolled up papers. Everyone was laughing.

In the middle of the night, a mortar attack struck near us. Again, the NVA appeared to be aiming at the nearby greenline bunkers. Some debris from the blasts banged and clattered on our tin roof. Fear overwhelmed one of our guys, he ran screaming down the middle aisle, through the back door, and out into the night. We hugged the floor with our own fear. The screaming just made it worse.

Quickly, our gunships arrived, and fired a spectacular display of red tracers from their miniguns, beyond the village outside the greenline.

After that, the incoming abruptly ceased, and the screamer was nowhere to be found. However, he returned about an hour later, unhurt, just extremely embarrassed. He knew we were there to support him, because the same powerful fear was in all of us.

The gunships had fired from more than 4 km outside the greenline, where the mortar fire originated, but it seemed much closer. We needed to finish building our bunker as soon as possible.

Feb 27 - KP today, and I went in early again to secure the best job. Being an easy day, I snuck out in the afternoon and did some caption work. I had learned the times when I wasn't needed in the mess hall, and they wouldn't miss me. Sometimes, it was fun to play the game, and see what I could get away with.

Two of my photos of the artillerymen teaching the local elementary school kids, were in the current *Cavalair*.

I received a big goodie package from my girlfriend, Sally, and enjoyed some of the varied cookie assortment, along with a quart of chocolate milk I smuggled out of the mess hall. This milk was different. It said on the carton it was "filled" milk, reconstituted with palm oil. If it had a funny taste, the chocolate covered it up, but I wondered if this was safe for me to drink. The goodie packages and mail were so important to me. What great support I received from Sally, and my family.

Feb 28 - We heard Major McCarthy would leave tomorrow, but no one knew for sure. Lately, we hadn't seen much of him. He had done a fine job of fading away. Captain Tom Kallunki, would be interim information officer, until our new leader arrived.

Our other PV photographer, Phil Blackmarr, had performed well, and was always calm. He could shift into meditation mode at will. Both of us adjusted quickly to schedule changes on the fly, earning the respect of the units we worked with. We could easily take over the administrative tasks from each other. The office continued to run smoothly, with an increased workload. I would shoot jobs during the day, and tend to the administrative tasks in the evening. I enjoyed that, when busy, the time passed faster.

Mar 2 - I caught an early flight to the Bien Hoa photo lab by way of Long Binh. Several of the proof sheets from my jobs were critiqued by Press Officer Captain Carrara. We went over more than a dozen of them. He liked several of my jobs, and gave me an excellent review.

"You have done well, Flash. Work with the writers and think up some interesting jobs, or come up with photo ideas yourself," he said. "If it looks good, we will run it in the *Cavalair*. Also, think about color photo stories for the next magazine. The clerks can also help you with your paperwork."

"Great," I said. "Al Persons and I have already discussed some ideas."

This critique never happened to me again. They were clearly happy with my work, so I would look for more interesting subjects to photograph on my own, and train others to do some of the paperwork.

It was too late for a ride back to PV, so we ate spaghetti and meatballs at the marvelous mess hall, watched a movie, and drank beers with the photo lab guys.

Mar 3 - This morning, I went to one of the small Vietnamese speciality shops by the huge Bien Hoa PX and had them make a black name badge that said, TERRY MOON 1st Cav Photo (two lines). Now people wouldn't ask me who I was as often. After walking around wide-eyed at all the stuff in the PX, I bought a quart pitcher for my iced tea. Captain Carrara and I flew back to PV on a Huey, a quick half hour flight, arriving at 5:30 p.m.

"Flash" in base camp mode, with his shiny new name tag, ever-present shades, and of course, his flash.

Mar 4 - When the packet arrived from the photo lab, several jobs were ruined, or of very poor quality, they must have had film developing problems. My LRRP color slides looked like bad high-contrast copies. *They had real potential, but not the way they looked now.* I felt so disappointed, but it only started a bad day for me.

In the afternoon, I had a greenline sandbag and bunker repair detail. Bad memories of this flooded my mind. It was extra hot, and I remembered past days of sandbag hell. Now I was prepared with two canteens and a towel. The dust in my nose and mouth was unbelievable. Sweat and dust made a layer of mud all over you. *Yes, everywhere.*

"Mama said there would be days like this."

When I returned, our new larger shower still had water. It was he best thing that happened to me all day.

Mar 5 - Just when I thought things couldn't get any worse, this morning, I had first sergeant's work detail. I had skillfully avoided it for a long time, but I was finally stuck with the notorious shit-burning detail. It was usually handed out as punishment, so non-offenders were spared this curse, most of the time. I wore extra-large gloves to drag two of the cutoff 55-gallon drums from the back of the outhouse to burn. A generous amount of fuel was added. I tossed a match into each one, then quickly backed away, and watched the thick black smoke rise above the rubber trees. They burned, until nothing was left. The same routine for the other two. I only had one more four-holer to do, so I finished before lunch. Later, one of the guys told me that I was lucky, shit-burning was usually an all day job. *Fortunately, this never happened to me again.*

We had another late night rocket attack, not near us, but an entire pallet of beer behind the PX took a direct hit, and was destroyed. The guys couldn't believe it, one of our most precious commodities. There were pieces of beer cans scattered throughout the area. Indubitably, this was a tragedy. At lunch time the next day, everything stopped briefly as someone from the band played "Taps," and we all had a mournful moment of silence.

Mar 6 - An anonymous writer or editor arranged for me to fly a night mission on a "heavy gunship" (50 Cal) with "sniffer radar." *Whatever that was.* I would be shooting infrared film, with red flashbulbs, inside a helicopter. I didn't have a lens wide enough to do this. I had no idea what they wanted, however, it was cancelled. I never found out who had this strange, but creative idea. I thought maybe it was total BS, but the photo lab told me they received the infrared film, and flashbulbs. Weird things like this would mysteriously show up on the schedule.

An aerial photo of LZ Grant.

Mar 8 - Last night, a major attack occurred on LZ Grant, 72 km northwest of PV. American casualties were ten killed, including the 2/12 Battalion Commander Lt. Col. Peter Gorvad. The LZ's tactical operations bunker took a freak, direct hit from a rocket. Thirty grunts and artillerymen were wounded during the battle.

A C 1/77, 105 mm howitzer crew member tosses away the shell casing as they prepare to fire another round on a busy day at LZ Grant.

There were heroics by the two artillery batteries, A 1/30 (155s) and C 1/77 (105s). Like giant shotguns, the artillerymen fired their cannons with beehive rounds, directly at the attacking NVA troops. Filled with thousands of tiny dart-like flechettes, beehive rounds were nasty, creating a strange buzzing sound when fired. Also high explosive rounds were fired directly at the NVA with extremely short, timed fuses. They exploded just above the ground, and beyond the berm, just seven-tenths of a second after they were fired. One of the 155 mm howitzers was destroyed in the attack. Outside the wire, 154 NVA lay dead, also many more blood trails left the area, as the enemy later dragged away some of their casualties.

A 105 mm howitzer on LZ Grant takes a well deserved break.

A 1st Cav MedEvac Huey hoists a grunt on a litter from a wooded area where they could not land.

Mar 9 - While Phil went on a tour with the commanding general, I shot a Medevac jungle penetrator demonstration, with a CBS News team. A seat, or litter would be dropped by cable into the jungle where the Huey couldn't land. Then a wounded grunt sat on the seat, or was placed in a litter, hoisted aboard, and evacuated for treatment.

The Medevac jungle penetrator view from below.

With activity near LZ Grant, we followed a Medevac Huey, and I took several shots of the wounded grunt being hoisted aboard (see photo above). Later, we set up photos of the operation from the ground as a guy was hoisted into a Medevac Huey (photo at right). Then a wild ride back to PV in another chopper, very low and very fast. These pilots were tremendously skilled. They loved to scare passengers, and on occasion they would hit a tree with the skid. *Hang on to your fillings!*

Word of our refrigerator had spread rapidly. Strangers would enter our office, and want to buy cold beers or cokes. We discouraged it with high prices. The beer shortage worsened, and demand increased. While I was out shooting my assignment, they caught a guy from another unit stealing a case of beer, a rare occurrence. Our NCOIC, took care of it with the company commander, and the first sergeant. He said, if it were up to him, the punishment would be a deterrent, a whole week of all-day shit-burning.

CHAPTER FIVE A DIFFERENT JOB EVERY DAY

Mar 10 - At 8 a.m., I walked to the VIP pad to accompany Commanding General Forsythe on tour. Being the only passenger, besides the general's aide, the crew gave me a headset. Because I was only a photographer, that was surprising, but now they knew me. It was interesting listening to all the conversations. Our first stop, that lasted about an hour, was at Quan Loi, for a 2nd Brigade operations briefing. Next, we made the long flight to USARV (U.S. Army, Vietnam) Headquarters at Long Binh to pick up Brig. Gen. E.B. Roberts. I gave him the headset. He would become 1st Cav Commanding General, and receive his second star when CG Forsythe left in about six weeks. We visited company C, 15th TC, a Huey repair unit, at nearby Long Thanh. Then, we took a 20 minute flight to company D at Phu Loi for continued helicopter maintenance inspections.

USARV HQ Buildings at Long Binh, The Dong Nai River flows by in the background.

Aerial photo of LZ Cindy, northeast of Bien Hoa. The smoke marker tells our pilot where to land.

68   A Different Job Every Day

After lunch, we flew to LZ Cindy, 22 km northeast of Bien Hoa, (photos previous page and to the right) a desert-like, fire support base next to the Dong Nai River. Running ahead of the CG, I took photos of him talking with grunts and artillerymen, for hometown news releases. Most of the day, I sat quietly, then I ran around like hell for a half-hour.

The next stop was Tay Ninh, after another long Huey ride, for a 1st Brigade operations briefing. I met Colonel Lieu, the 1st Cav's ARVN Liaison Officer. He was pleasant and enjoyable to talk to. Command Sergeant Major Peters yelled at me about my mustache (that was what sergeant majors did). Then we flew to Bearcat, where I enjoyed a nap in the Huey.

We returned to PV in time for my greenline guard duty on bunker 32, the most distant one in our sector. Thankfully, it was uneventful, except for the relentless mosquitos. I had adjusted well. Sleeping in the bunker was easier now, and I could be alert instantly when necessary.

March 11 - Captain Carrera awakened me at 11:30 a.m., so I could finish work orders for the day's courier flight to the photo lab. Office talk centered on the large attack at LZ Grant last night. Heavy incoming mortars struck first, followed by a ground attack from two NVA battalions. This time, it was over quickly, with few American casualties, as gunships ravaged the enemy. The NVA left 62 dead behind at the LZ, and later, 1/9 scout teams located groups retreating to their Cambodian sanctuaries, and killed 51 more. *I would see LZ Grant for myself tomorrow.*

Mar 12 - I flew to Nui Ba Den Mountain, north of Tay Ninh with the engineers. They had installed a huge searchlight on the mountain top. Nui Ba Den was a massive mountain standing strangely alone on the flat plain. It dominated the entire area, (see photo to the right).

An aerial photo of Nui Ba Den, the legendary "Black Virgin Mountain." Of course it's raining.

Our first stop was LZ Dolly, (photo at right) on a hilltop at the end of a long, steep ridge, called the Razorbacks, about 25 km east of Nui Ba Den, and 52 km west of PV. It overlooked the famous Michelin Rubber Plantation to the East. I took photos of 105 mm howitzer crews. I also talked with some of the grunts from the heavy weapons (mortars) company, and one guy told me the wax on 81 mm mortar round containers was great for mustaches. I scraped wax from one to curl my mustache, put it in a film can, and would try it later.

Next, we flew to LZ Grant, 72 km northwest of PV. Grunts from 2/12 were rebuilding several bunkers damaged in the previous night's NVA mortar attack. They added another layer of steel decking (PSP) and sandbags on top of the Tactical Operations Center and Fire Direction Control (artillery) bunker (see photo at right). The TOC had taken a direct hit on March 8.

The accompanying ground attack last night was stopped cold by C Battery, 1st of the 77th 105 howitzers firing "beehive" rounds directly at the enemy. Also, the heavy fire power of the quad 50 was effective. It was comprised of four 50-caliber machine guns mounted together on a truck so it could be moved quickly to where it was needed. (See photo at right.) They also had a huge helping hand from the gunships. I felt strange and uneasy visiting the site of so much carnage. The LZ was about 200 yards long and 100 wide, in the middle of an NVA supply route from Cambodia to Saigon. In the past three days, ten Americans and over 200 NVA died there. However, the LZ guys went about their jobs like it was just another day.

The quad 50 at LZ Grant, known as "Zorba."

An Air Force F-100 fighter-bomber buzzed the LZ. A large communications tower in the center of LZ Grant was 60 or 70 feet high (photo at right). The F-100 didn't miss it by much. These pilots were exceptionally skilled, and like to show off.

Explosive Ordinance Disposal (EOD) was detonating captured munitions, so we were startled a few times by random, large explosions.

Finally, we flew back to Nui Ba Den, only 11 km southwest, where I photographed the searchlight on its platform. It dominated the entire area. A quick flight to Tay Ninh followed, where we ate lunch at 1st Brigade Headquarters. I enjoyed working with the engineers, because they did interesting projects, clearing the jungle, building roads, and they could, with help from grunts, put together a defensible fire support base in one day. After a pleasant lunch, we flew back to PV.

Today, Phil Blackmarr flew on a four-engine C-130 cargo plane to An Khe to do a story about our urgent care medical clinic that served the local Vietnamese community. This was a terrific humanitarian story. You wouldn't hear anything about compassionate, merciful programs like this from the news media.

I received a letter from my photo school buddy, Jerry Born. He was in An Khe, near where Phil was doing his story. Jerry shot additional photo assignments now for the 173rd Airborne Brigade, along with his daily lab work.

Mar 13 - I had KP, a wasted day. I had learned when the slow times of the day would occur, and could usually leave for a while and catch up on office work. More people were on the KP roster now, so for me, it came up less often.

Sad news in the mail, my Grandma Moon passed away, she never recovered from the stroke.

Mar 16 - During the last week or so, our artist Larry Collins broke his right index finger playing volleyball. He was unable to continue drawing, so he became the 15th Admin Company courier. We had a new artist, Ron Doss, a friendly Texan. He painted one of his favorite subjects in the photo to the right.

Mar 17 - Early in the morning, I was the only one available to photograph a helicopter crash for the Aircraft Accident Investigation Board (AAIB). The communication facility helipad on top of Nui Ba Den was the site, 80 km to the West. An upside-down Huey wasn't badly damaged, and no one was hurt. Numerous pictures were needed for their investigation.

On our flight back, we briefly stopped at Lai Khe, then on to PV. We flew past a busy air strike by A-4 and F-100 fighter-bombers, referred to as "Fast Movers." After the quick trip with AAIB, I arrived in PV in time for lunch.

Mar 18 - I traded night greenline guard duty, for one hour of stringing barbed wire. *Only an hour, what a great trade!* I finished it quickly, without a scratch.

I received a letter today from Rick Keller, my photo school classmate. He was with the 501st Signal Battalion, a photo support unit of the 101st Airborne Division in Hue, not the information office as I was. They hadn't issued him a camera yet, however, he had other photo related duties.

Phil had the page one lead story, and photo in the *Cavalair*. He was "humping in the boonies" with A and C companies of 2/7, about 12 km north of Quan Loi. They discovered a huge bunker complex that included a hospital with a large cache of medical supplies, and a plastic sheet lined operating room inside a 12 by 15 foot underground bunker. Phil shot this during his 3rd Brigade time, before he arrived at Phuoc Vinh.

Cavmen Uncover NVA Hospital

Operating Room With Huge Medical Cache

By SP4 Phil Blackmarr

QUAN LOI, Vietnam—"It didn't look like anything special at first," related Staff Sergeant Jimmy M. McCurry, acting platoon leader of the first platoon, Company A, 2nd Battalion, 7th Cavalry: "A punji pit and some bunkers. Then we investigated and began to see how big it really was."

Companies A and C of the 2nd Bn., 7th Cav were conducting reconnaissance in force mission recently when each found a trail. Both trails converged on a thickly jungled area one mile south of the battalion base camp, Landing Zone Jill, and about 10 miles east of Quan Loi.

Almost simultaneously, the two companies — Company A working from the southeast and Company C from the northeast — came upon enemy emplacements. Inside one bunker complex, Company A discovered caches amounting to three tons of rice and 100 pounds of rock salt. Meanwhile, Company C found a cemetery with 11 graves.

In addition, Company B, which had been patrolling just west of the other two units, began to uncover its share of bunkers and equipment.

Although there were indications of recent occupation throughout the area, no resistance was encountered. Staff Sergeant Warren L. Brown, platoon sergeant of Company C's first platoon, commented. "When we started spotting bunkers and hootches, everyone flattened out on the ground. But nothing happened."

In the early afternoon, Company A observed three armed individuals approaching and killed one in a brief skirmish. A little later aerial rocket artillery was called in when movement was detected again, but there was no further contact.

A further search disclosed large caches of clothing, food, and equipment. It soon became evident, as the three companies worked in close proximity to each other, that their separate finds were all parts of a single base, larger than a quarter mile square. Hootches and bunkers were well hidden under tall forest growth and thick clumps of bamboo which blocked out the sky.

The main portion of the area consisted of a hospital and related medical facilities. The operating room was a 12 by 15 foot bunker, dug down six feet with a thatched roof three feet above the ground. Plastic sheets lined the inside to guard against moisture, and there were three plastic-covered tables, tin water troughs, and several sterilizing canisters. Lighting was provided by portable battery-powered units. Most of the surgical instruments had been removed but large quantities of medical supplies remained there and in adjoining storerooms.

Specialist Five Jerry S. Coleman, senior medic with Company A, estimated that 800 to 900 pounds of drugs and medicines were found and shipped out to the 3rd Brigade at Quan Loi: "There were bottles of Russian, and Chinese manufactured drugs. They had plasma and blood supplements, good equipment, and undoubtedly skilled personnel."

Surrounding the hospital were classrooms, living quarters, mess and supply structures, a bicycle repair shop, enough clothing to outfit at least a company, a shrine with propaganda material, and hundreds of records and documents. Two days were spent cleaning out the site while soldiers from Company C, 8th Engineer Battalion set about destroying 200 bunkers. Finally, by midday of the 24th, the companies pulled out, detonating charges behind them to demolish the remaining structures.

Major James W. Napier III, 3rd Brigade Executive Officer, stated: "The presence of ether and suture materials indicated that almost any kind of surgery could be done there." He estimated that the complex could have supported a division or more.

Constructed perhaps a year ago and possibly used during last year's major offensives, the base is now destroyed, severing a vital enemy link between Cambodia and the Saigon region.

NVA Hospital
Cavalrymen from Company C, 2nd Battalion, 7th Cavalry search one of the 'hooches' that is part of a large NVA hospital complex recently found by the company.
(U.S. ARMY PHOTO BY SP4 Phil Blackmarr)

Cavalair

Vol. 3, No. 12 — 1st Air Cavalry Division — March 19, 1969

Four Skytroopers Awarded AM With 'V' for Action

QUAN LOI — The night of Jan. 21 was quiet and dark at Quan Loi, the base camp of the 1st Air Cavalry Division's 2nd Brigade. But at 10:30 a six-hour drama began which ended with four Air Medals with "V" device for three pilots and one sergeant attached to the 1st Battalion, 77th Artillery.

First Lieutenant Stephen Kollstedt (whose wife lives at 1627 S. Argyle Place, Cincinnati, Ohio), First Lieutenant David R. Owen, Warrant Officer Norman L. Helmke, and Sergeant Wallace E. Gordon Jr. were enjoying a cool soda and admiring a deluxe tape recorder one of their buddies had just received that day. Abruptly, a call came through stating that Loc Ninh and areas around it were under an intense barrage of mortar fire.

Within minutes, WO1 Helmke, 1LT Owen, and SGT Gordon had their light observation helicopter (LOH) in the air headed for the troubled area, accompanied by two Cobra gunships for which they were going to locate enemy positions.

No sooner did they reach the area of Loc Ninh than the enemy opened up on the LOH with .50 caliber machine gun fire. SGT Gordon and 1LT Owen immediately started plotting targets for aerial rocket artillery (ARA).

When asked why ground artillery wasn't used, 1LT Owen stated: "The enemy mortar tubes were located too close to the Special Forces Units in the area."

SGT Gordon summed up the situation like this: "You could clearly see light flashes in about twenty different enemy positions, and I could hear considerable small arms fire in various locations. We directed ARA and the Air Force 'Spooky' team to enemy positions from the air by marking targets with tracers from an M-16 rifle. We know that we destroyed three enemy mortar tubes and one .50 caliber machine gun."

After enemy mortar fire was successfully subdued, the LOH returned to Quan Loi to refuel and to change pilots. 1LT Kollstedt then took control of the ship and along with 1LT Owens and SGT Gordon returned to the embattled area to find that a village five miles south of Loc Ninh was under attack on the ground. Approximately 50 per cent of the village had been overrun.

1LT Kollstedt quickly established communications with the Special Forces Camp at Loc Ninh. Thus, members of the Special Forces were able to direct the artillery observers who in turn could pinpoint quickly and accurately the enemy positions for ARA. Thanks to the cavalrymen's quick reactions, the attack was beaten off.

Major Earns Silver Star For Action

TAY NINH — The Long Range Patrol had been inserted into the thickly vegetated area. Only minutes after the team touched the ground, a hidden enemy released a heavy barrage of fire.

"I knew that I had to give them all the support I could," said Major Bradley Johnson, commander of Company C, 229th Assault Helicopter Battalion. "We had just inserted the team and were still in the area when the contact was made."

MAJ Johnson decided to land in the area once again — this time to rescue the team from the murderous enemy fire. Swooping downward to a small clearing, he and the pilots of the other helicopters made a successful extraction of the team.

For his bravery, MAJ Johnson was awarded the Silver Star on Feb. 4, 1969, during ceremonies in which he turned over command of the company to Major Franklin Haar.

Thanking all of his men for their efforts, MAJ Johnson said, "The courage of this company is well known. I think one thing that makes this an outstanding company is its fantastic safety record. We are the only company in the Cav that has not had an accident in the last seven months."

"MAJ Johnson said he was proud to have been a member of this company," said MAJ Haar. "I might add that I am proud to became a member of Company C, 229th Assault Helicopter Battalion."

Rat Patrol Outguns Enemy, Uses John Wayne Tactics

QUAN LOI — "It was just like a scene from a John Wayne movie when he stood up and peppered the enemy positions so that I could get to cover," said Staff Sergeant Richard E. Olson, as he described the actions of a fellow member of the 1st Squadron, 9th Cavalry during a recent contact five miles southeast of here.

The 1st Air Cavalry Division's "Rat Patrol" was maintaining security along the roads surrounding the 3rd Brigade's base camp near here when it ran into a platoon-sized enemy force.

The cavalrymen jumped out of their vehicles and set up positions to counter the crossfire coming from a forest on one side of the road and a clearing on the other. Moving into the clearing to provide cover for his vehicle, SSG Olson soon found himself under heavy AK-47 fire.

From the center of the column, Specialist Four Louis Marciano, made his way to the lead vehicle to lend a hand. "My platoon leader didn't need me any more where I was, so I wanted to get to the front to see what was going on," he explained.

Telling the pinned-down sergeant that he was going to lay
(Continued on Back Page)

A Different Job Every Day

Mar 19 - In the morning, I photographed operations at 15th Medical Battalion. Several Medevac Hueys transported wounded to the 15th med helicopter pad at PV. A milestone day for the medics as they brought in their 40,000th patient. What a grim, disturbing job. *I didn't want to think about it.*

In the afternoon, I took photos of a G-5 civic affairs project. Artillerymen from 1/30th built a swing set for the local elementary school. This was a happy job. A large crowd of Vietnamese villagers, including several children, watched. A few gathered into my photo (at right). The man in white, on the left of the photo, was the Mayor of Phuoc Vinh.

The engineers had also built numerous humanitarian projects for the local villagers, drainage, roads, and other infrastructure.

Today, I received another letter from my photo school friend, Jerry Born with 173rd Airborne Brigade. He spent time with the REMFs in Qui Nhon and Cam Ranh Bay, similar to the time I spent with the REMFs in Bien Hoa.

Mar 20 - I photographed an all-day VIP tour for the pretty, blonde AFVN-TV weather girl, Bobbie Keith, "The bubbling bundle of barometric brilliance." She visited the CG, and he made her an honorary skytrooper. That was followed by a stop at the medical wards, where she talked to, and perked up some of the patients. Then we visited the base defense force, 5/7 grunts, called the "Palace Guard." Wolf whistles filled the air. Subsequently, we took the 52 km flight west, to the Air Force weather station on hilltop LZ Dolly. Of course, she talked with the Air Force guys about weather. The grunts had a different agenda. The Tay Ninh 1st Brigade VIP center was the next stop, more upscale than the others. She played cards with A Company, 2/8 grunts in from the field, many with wide eyes and open mouths. Lai Khe followed, where we visited 2nd Brigade Headquarters, and the D 227th gunships with their clever names and fancy artwork. Today, I heard it several times again, "You lucky SOB, how did you get this job?" The last stop was the Bien Hoa 3rd Brigade VIP center, where she visited B 5/7 grunts, and was met with stares and hoots. She had been here 21 months, and would return to the USA in June. Finally, we let her off at Tan Son Nhut airport.

We stopped at the huge Long Binh PX, where I bought goodies I rarely saw, like orange juice, small cans of real chili and greeting cards to send Sally.

On AFVN-TV, Bobbie said she really enjoyed the attention she received from everyone touring the 1st Cav bases. It was 100 degrees in Phuoc Vinh today. She didn't usually mention us since we were close to Saigon, and our weather was similar.

Mar 21 - In the morning, I took photos of a visiting general at the 8th Engineer Battalion Headquarters. The entire group stood in formation, and he congratulated them for their excellent work. They had developed a fast system for building fire support bases. They had many motivated, skilled soldiers.

When I returned, Phil shocked me with distressing news. PIO had suffered its first casualty since well before I arrived. It was bizarre, the lab chief had been killed in a jeep accident at Bien Hoa. I had often worked with him when I made the courier run. His job, at the photo lab, was equivalent to mine as photo coordinator in Phuoc Vinh. How ironic, he was in the Cav's safest place. He and his expertise would be greatly missed. *No one was safe here.*

Pink Team heads out on their mission.

In the afternoon, Al Persons and I flew with 1st Squadron, 9th Cavalry LOH scouts, the division's reconnaissance unit. They had an attitude, and did not like writers or photographers. Al, a sharp "good ol' boy," from Alabama, did a fine job persuading 1/9 to let us fly with them. We flew in a second LOH, along with a recon "pink team," comprised of a scout LOH (white) and a Cobra gunship (red). The LOH was low, looking into the jungle, and the Cobra waited high above, ready to pounce.

They showed me armor plating for protection under, and behind my seat. Also, they gave us thick armored chest plates, called "chicken plates," to wear. This was alarming by itself. What the hell were we getting into? Flying about sixty feet above the ground, we were an easy target. Since Al had the front seat on the convoy job, it was my turn to sit in the more secure spot. Al felt better after they gave him another "chicken plate" to sit on. Smoke grenades were attached along the edge of the door, behind the pilot's seat. The gunners used them to mark the spot if they saw something suspicious or from where enemy fire originated. Then the Cobra would swoop in, and blast the area. We hoped the NVA would think twice before shooting at us.

It was clear that our presence was not wanted, as no information was provided about the mission, only dirty looks. We were REMFs to this hardcore unit. Skimming along the jungle canopy with assorted zig-zags, we searched for signs of the NVA. The pilot pointed out trails and a few bunker shapes in the jungle. Some of the area was open terrain, it was not all thick jungle (see photo at right). This was scary, I really felt like a target, and only 60 feet up, *a big target.*

They couldn't have two LOHs flying close together, and they couldn't fly too slowly. The pilots flew erratically to avoid being easy targets, and reacted immediately if they received enemy fire. I expected to see green tracers appear throughout the afternoon, but there were none. I asked if we could go higher a couple of times, but was ignored. How could I take good pictures if we stayed low all the time? I wanted to be higher to photograph the other LOH against the jungle below. I asked again for better photo angles, but the pilot turned to me and shouted into my face, "Shut the fuck up, or I'll throw your ass out."

We saw some of our grunts below. I assumed the "pink team" was scouting for this grunt unit, however, they didn't tell us what was going on.

It was easier for me to support my camera from the left front seat, than it was from the back. I needed a longer lens and better angles for this job, so no great photos today. It was almost dark when we returned to PV.

In their own world, this hard core unit was the exception to overall spirit of cooperation that I saw elsewhere. Many of the skytroopers of 1/9 had volunteered for the prestige and danger of this elite unit. They were extremely good at finding the elusive NVA.

We had a great evening in the office, highlighted by our guitar players. Al was working on "Classical Gas," and of course, *Laugh-In* from beautiful downtown Burbank, was "verrry interesting."

Mar 23 - I awakened late, 10.30 a.m. It was Sunday, and I was tired from yesterdays tense job. It was stressful, feeling like a target, and not knowing what was going on. I suppose those guys were used to it, the scouts and grunts did this almost every day.

I went to greenline guard early at 4:30 p.m., more stress, but a blissfully quiet night.

Mar 24 - Late this morning, I photographed wrecked jeeps and trucks at 27th Maintenance Battalion. They repaired anything that didn't fly. After the tragic loss of one of our own, we would run a safety story in the *Cavalair* to alert others to be more careful.

After lunch, Al Persons and I flew in a 1/9 Huey on a LRRP team extraction. Al was on a roll, as he lined up another interesting, but dangerous job. The six-man team had been out on a four-day recon mission west of Phuoc Vinh, and had seen a forty-man NVA force. With a predetermined pickup point, the Huey would drop in quickly, the team would come out of hiding, immediately jump on, and be withdrawn from danger.

In the middle of nowhere, we dropped down to an open area. Everyone was alert, expecting enemy fire at any time. As the Huey approached the ground, the LRRPs materialized out of the bushes (see photo above). I shot a couple of photos, but the whole operation took only seconds. All six of them jumped in, and swiftly pinned me in the middle of the Huey. We rapidly ascended. I was mashed by the heavy "G force." *Hi-Ho Silver, Away!*

Although I could hardly move, I was able to take a shot inside the Huey of a weary and relieved LRRP lighting up, framed by an out-of-focus M16 barrel and a smoke grenade (photo at right).

Mar 25 - Our bosses were gone this morning, so we did our own thing, making it an easy day. I received a letter from my brother, Dennis. He now had my old job as photographer for the *Vista Press*. Editor Russ Dietrich had also printed some of my letters in his column.

Everyone was counting their time left here. I had 227 days to go until I would leave for home.

We had a late night, distant mortar attack. If it wasn't close, we didn't really notice. *Have we become complacent?*

Mar 26 - Hilltop LZ Dolly was attacked last night by sappers. These were specialized NVA soldiers, wearing only shorts, skilled at penetrating barbed wire defenses with their explosives. They climbed the steep east face where there were less perimeter defenses. No one on the LZ thought that would ever happen. No further details were available. A rare occurrence, LZ Dolly was relatively safe, and my favorite fire support base.

Mar 27 - Most of the morning, I shot several slides of buildings and areas around the base for a G1 (Personnel) briefing. I had a photo in the *Cavalair* of the C 227th Huey crew chief with 43 air medals on his shirt. An air medal was awarded for 100 hours of combat flying time, or 25 combat assaults.

Mar 28 - I flew to LZ Lois, 16 km north of Bien Hoa, and LZ Terri, 20 km south of Tay Ninh on a VIP tour. This moved quickly, and only a few incidental photos were taken. *I don't know why I went.*

Mar 30 - I had planned to go to Bien Hoa, but Aircraft Accident Investigation Board (AAIB) called and needed a photographer immediately. I was the only one available, and they arrived before I could load my camera. We rushed to the 2/20 ARA pad and caught a former gunship, an older, shorter Huey C model. They gave me an armored "chicken plate," always worrisome. We flew to the crash site about 5 km south of the base, directly out from our section of the greenline, near the Song Be River.

A Cobra had lost pitch control of the rotor, and hit the ground hard. The skids were smashed and a rocket pod was damaged. The pilot and gunner were unhurt. It was in the middle of an open area a couple hundred yards from the Song Be River. We saw the 1/9 rapid response infantry platoon, called "Blues," arrive in their Huey, and form a defensive perimeter around it.

A Chinook came in quickly and picked up the Cobra as the "Blues" hooked up a sling-out. The damaged chopper was lifted, its broken skids dangling, and they flew back to PV. I shot the entire operation from the air in less than half an hour. It was very efficient.

The rest of the day I did captions, office stuff, and worked on our bunker.

Mar 31 - Several of us continued to work on the bunker, adding considerably more sandbags. The spectre of every incoming attack gave us more incentive to finish it.

A new photographer arrived, Eric White (New Hampshire). He extended to come to PIO, and then would receive an early out from the Army. He had already been in Vietnam for a year with the chemical unit, so naturally we called him "Agent Orange." He immediately left for 1st Brigade at Tay Ninh.

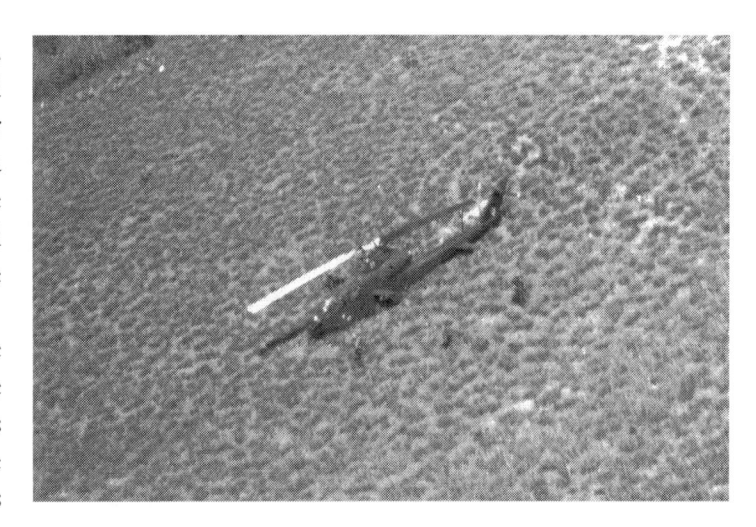

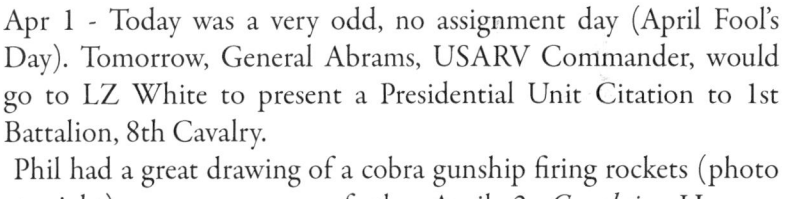

Bringing Smoke
(COMBAT ART BY SP4 Philip Blackmarr)
An ARA Gunship from 2/20th Artillery bears down on enemy ground troops with its deadly rockets.

Apr 1 - Today was a very odd, no assignment day (April Fool's Day). Tomorrow, General Abrams, USARV Commander, would go to LZ White to present a Presidential Unit Citation to 1st Battalion, 8th Cavalry.

Phil had a great drawing of a cobra gunship firing rockets (photo at right) on page one of the April 2 *Cavalair*. He was multitalented.

Apr 2 - Phil shot the 1/8 Presidential Unit Citation award with General Abrams, while I flew to An Khe for a ceremony at the An Tuc Dispensary on April 3. Phil told me, I really needed to see this magnificent place. He had written a story about the facility for the next *1st Cavalry Division Magazine*.

I signed out early, and beat the duty roster for the fourth straight time. It was a bunker building detail on the greenline. I paid attention to everything, and knew how to play the game.

I spent the morning at 15th Med. Thankfully, there weren't many patients today. It had the look of a giant emergency room. I told them about my dehydration episode in November, when I was rushed here unconscious by the guys from the mess hall. They said I wasn't the only one, many FNGs had this problem.

After lunch, I flew to An Khe on a C-130 with Lt. Col. Guthrie L. Turner Jr., Commanding Officer of the 15th Medical Battalion. I would have a chance to visit my photo school friend, Jerry Born, at the 173rd Airborne Brigade Photo Lab in An Khe.

The An Tuc Dispensary was an impressive urgent care facility. They provided extensive medical care to the local residents. It was started from scratch, three years ago, by Staff Sgt. John D. Rozzell. He had scrounged up much of the equipment and supplies. It was a great cause, and everyone wanted to help. In the last year, they had served over 2000 of the local Vietnamese, providing all types of medical care. They also delivered 350 babies.

Some of the staff were Vietnamese volunteers. Several orphan children were cared for, (photos at right) and they did small chores to help out. It was a warm, welcoming place. Sleeping on a real innerspring mattress and taking a hot shower were welcomed luxuries to me.

Apr 3 - I shot several photos of the impressive ceremony, celebrating the opening of two new buildings that increased their bed capacity to 86. When they reached 100 beds, they would meet the criteria to be an accredited hospital. Many Vietnamese helped setup the ceremony. Several local dignitaries spoke, with deep appreciation, for the facility. Lt. Col. Turner cut a ribbon to signify the opening of the new wing. A huge crowd of spectators cheered. An Tuc was so popular with the local residents, that earlier, when VC rockets hit close to the dispensary, the VC promptly apologized. Lt. Col. Turner had given me his camera to take some shots and an An Tuc staff member, Spec. 4 Lilley (Garden Grove, CA) had me shoot his Instamatic. So, I photographed the ceremony with four cameras.

About 2:00 p.m., I rode into An Khe with Staff Sgt. Rozzell and visited my photo school friend, Jerry Born, at his photo lab. He gave me a tour and we spent an enjoyable two hours swapping stories. One of his photos made it into the *MACV Observer*, a countrywide newspaper, which was a big deal. Riding through An Khe was nostalgic, I had spent ten days here last November for orientation. *That seemed like a long time ago.*

Lt. Col. Turner and Spec. 4 Lilley picked me up in a jeep at 4 p.m. on their way to the airport. We boarded a waiting C-130 and left for Phuoc Vinh, arriving at 5:30 p.m. I had an enjoyable dinner with Lt. Col. Turner and the medics. Later, I caught a ride to the information office with the chaplain's assistants, known as the "God Squad." This was one of my best days in Vietnam. Everything about this trip was positive. *Phil was right, a great story here. Happy to witness this myself, I wished every American could see how much good was provided by the An Tuc Dispensary.*

Apr 4 - I covered the office while Phil flew to Bien Hoa. We were planning more magazine jobs. I would set up one with Division Artillery (DIVARTY) on the 155 mm artillery. We would also do a magazine photo shoot on Huey door gunners with E/82.

We continued to work on the bunker. The entrance remained the last part to be finished. This had taken countless hours of work from all our guys.

Apr 5 - I walked to the VIP pad early, and took pictures of Commanding General Forsythe and his helicopter crew. He actually smiled today, and would leave on April 21st.

Later, we had a big party with food and drinks. I shot polaroids and gave them out to the guys. I heard "Thanks Flash," many times.

The power went out this evening as quickly as Arte Johnson's tricycle crashed, so we missed *Laugh-In,* one of the highlights of our week. No ringy-dingys tonight.

80 A Different Job Every Day

Apr 6 - Today was Easter Sunday, and we had no power for the entire day. The temperature was over 100 with steaming humidity. No fans, and the refrigerator was off. Everyone had a towel to soak up the sweat. *Oh well, war is hell. We could be in a worse place than this. Couldn't we?*

Apr 7 - Phil, Larry Adams, and I had day bunker detail. We had to be sure a grass fire didn't get too close to the Foo Gas (Napalm) emplacements on the greenline. We had shovels, and we were certainly motivated. If we were close to this and it ignited, we would be incinerated, and they wouldn't find a trace of us. We did an exceptional job, and finished before noon. Executive lunch was noon to 2 p.m, then more fire tending till 4 p.m. There were a couple of photo jobs, but we rescheduled them for the next day. We received excellent cooperation from everyone involved.

Our bunker was finally finished (see photo at right). You could see the huge tank on top of our new shower behind the bunker. Power was off again this evening.

Apr 8 - My assignment today was a VIP tour for Senator John Tower of Texas. He was extremely pale, and looked odd in a fatigue uniform. The tour went quickly. He was obviously nervous, I don't think he really wanted to be there. He "inspected" LZ Dolly, easily our safest fire support base, for maybe ten minutes. Then we toured Phuoc Vinh where it was really safe. It was over by 11 a.m. The tour moved so quickly the backlit photo at the right was the only one I could get with my own camera.

During lunchtime, I went to the PX, bought a footlocker and a case of Dr. Pepper. I carried them all the way back to the office, and no one came by to offer me a ride. How strange. I put the footlocker under my bunk. The area looked better after I stored my stuff in it, including my growing stash of C-rations. Pound cake was very popular, and hard to find. It went well with the peaches and apricots. I liked the spaghetti with meatballs, and the frankfurters and beans, commonly called 'beanie weenie.'

Lt. Col. Raymond Foley a 1st Cav Chaplain holds church services for an 82nd Airborne unit at LZ Odessa.

This weeks *Cavalair* had my convoy pictures as center spread with the biggest credit line I had ever seen. One of my chaplain photos, from February, with the log bird in the background, was on page eight (see photo above).

Back at the office, power problems continued, so we used a special "borrowed" generator for our TV tonight. We were watching *Laugh-In* about 10:30 p.m. when two rockets hit nearby. That was it. Nobody moved, as we kept watching the "flying fickle finger of fate."

Apr 9 - I walked over to 1st Battalion, 30th Artillery to organize a photo story about them for the magazine. Later, I would go to the fire support bases for the pictures. The artillery moved frequently from one LZ to another.

AFVN news said the 1st Cav base camp was hit with a big rocket attack last night, an exaggeration to say the least, or maybe they were messing with NVA intelligence.

I heard the new San Diego Padres baseball team won their first-ever Major League game.

My girlfriend Sally visited Hawaii on spring break with friends, a reconnaissance mission to help plan our R&R in July.

Apr 10 - It rained heavily on us as we returned by jeep from a job at DIVARTY, located on the far side of the base. It would have been worse if I had walked to the job, and I did walk to many. It continued raining hard for most of the afternoon. By now, I had fine-tuned my plastic bag system for protecting the cameras and lenses. It worked well.

82   A Different Job Every Day

Apr 11 - Today, the 11th Armored Cavalry Regiment (ACR) was attached to the 1st Cav. We would see more of their tanks and armored personnel carriers since they would now be working closely with us. Most of last year, until January of this year, 11th ACR was commanded by Colonel George S. Patton IV.

A few days ago, I took a relatively haze-free aerial photo of part of Phuoc Vinh. The east end of the airstrip is visible on the right. The information office is located in the rubber trees to the left, near the small plume of smoke.

This 227th Huey had the most appropriate name.

Chapter Six A New Information Officer

Apr 12 - We left before dawn for a cordon and search operation with 1st Cav Military Police and ARVN National Police Field Force (NPFFs). A village, near Phuoc Vinh, was sealed off the night before by an infantry company, prohibiting entry or exit by anyone. We knew some of the enemy mortar attacks came from this area. Today's photo assignment was for the next *1st Cavalry Division Magazine* with senior writer Steve Haldemann.

1st Cav Huey with loudspeakers tells residents of the village to go to the school while the ARVN units and 1st Cav MPs (entering from the left) search the area cordoned off during the night by infantry units (some of them were visible under the tree on the right). They were searching for mortars after tips from villagers.

All the villagers congregated at the school, with one of the fully loaded grunts.

The NPFFs thoroughly searched the village.

MPs moved around in two jeeps with M60 machine guns mounted in back. The NPFFs swept through the village searching everywhere. They poked the ground with sticks looking for buried weapons. The homes were thoroughly inspected, even the clay-covered charcoal pits. A huge booby trap was found, a wired 175 mm round buried in a four-foot high ant hill. If exploded, it would have thrown shrapnel over a wide area. It was setup to be command detonated by the NVA at the far end of the wire. We were lucky, that we couldn't set it off ourselves. Since the village was sealed off, no one could sneak in and trigger it while we were there. When the lengthy search was finished, they didn't find any evidence of mortars.

The NPFFs begin to dig up the buried 175 round.

A small boy tells how the NVA snuck into his village at night. NPFF in his jeep with the 175 artillery round booby trap they dug up during the search.

The villagers were cooperative. A small boy in a floppy hat (photo above) told the NPFFs how the NVA would sneak into the village at night, shoot some mortars, and exit quickly, leaving no trace. Mortar attacks were always relatively short, since we had radar that could pinpoint their position. This job lasted well into the afternoon. It was cool today, only 93 degrees.

When I returned to the office, Captain Carrara said he was going to Tokyo and offered to buy camera equipment for me. Great! I wanted a Pentax motor drive camera kit and two more lenses.

My 400 mm lens with its mount that was shipped by my brother, arrived in the mail. He had packed it well. The support was like a gunstock with a shoulder plate, a solid rail that the camera attached to, and a forward pistol grip with a trigger cable release. It allowed me a much better chance to hold the camera steady while using the long lens, increasing my photo capabilities.

I returned late from a headquarters award job, grabbed my guard gear, and headed directly for greenline guard at 7 p.m. We usually reported at 4:30, but they knew I would be late. It was another stressful, but quiet night. Guard duty happened every five days now. We would receive clusters of attacks and then a lull, sometimes for weeks. *We never knew when an attack would occur.*

A New Information Officer

Our new Information Officer, Major J.D. Coleman, a Montana native, arrived today. Previously, he had served with the 1st Cav as a captain in 1965, when they were the first combat division deployed to Vietnam. He was assistant information officer for the first half of his tour. The second half, he was the grunt company commander of Company B, 2nd Battalion, 8th Cavalry. On an early combat assault operation in the central highlands near An Khe, his company was ambushed and surrounded by a much larger Viet Cong force. His expert leadership and specific radio directions to gunships, saved his troops from being overrun. He was awarded a Silver Star for valor and his unit was awarded the first Valorous Unit Citation of the war.

Major McCarthy left several weeks ago, and few decisions were made in the office. I had complained earlier about the poor quality of prints from the photo lab, and was told if I kept complaining, they would send me out to a brigade. The rumor now was, Major Coleman would listen.

Apr 13 - In the morning, Major Coleman called me into his office and asked several questions about the photo operations. He inquired about my background and what I thought about some of the current situations. My college journalism classes and newspaper experience impressed him. Apparently, he heard positive reports about me, because he didn't change anything. Phil and I would continue as before. Our biggest problems, I told him, were poor quality prints from the photo lab and we were understaffed.

Someone checked the temperature today. We usually didn't bother to look. It was a steamy 103 degrees, and last night it went down to a cool 78.

The next day was my girlfriend Sally's birthday. Earlier, people from home had sent me blank greeting cards, so I mailed them to arrive on her birthday. One of our clerks, Chuck Spicer, made an excellent pencil drawing of Sally from one of the photos on the wall above my desk, (photo to the left). I packed it well and shipped it from the APO. *She loved it.*

Apr 14 - KP was not bad today. *Was it possible that I had become used to it?* Of course, I had the easy dining room job because now I knew how to play the game to minimize the misery, but it was still a wasted day.

I had a full page of photos of the AFVN weather girl visit in the current *Cavalair*. Another chaplain photo from February at desolate LZ Odessa was on page three. I also had a nicely composed shot of an ARVN officer talking to a Vietnamese woman from the December village sweeps on page eight.

Today, I did poorly on the hearing test that was given to everyone in PIO. No surprise there. My hearing hadn't been right since the close incoming on the greenline bunker in November. *Now I always wear my ear plugs when flying or near artillery.*

Giant Skycrane helicopter lifts the 155 howitzer from LZ Grant creating a huge dust cloud.

Apr 15 - On an all-day job at LZ Grant, I photographed the giant Skycrane helicopters relocating three 155 mm howitzers to LZ Jess, about 30 km to the West. The heavy-lift helicopter would hover while the artillery crew hooked up a sling-out rig to the howitzer. Then the Skycrane hauled it away, dangling below. At the new location, the crew would immediately begin setting up the gun for a fire mission.

A few times today, while I was taking pictures of them, artillery crew members asked me the all too familiar question, "How did you get this job?"

One artilleryman approached me and said, "You are a Spec. 4, just like me, how come you carry a 45? I thought you were an officer."

"It goes with my job, I'm PIO's photo coordinator. We produce the *Cavalair*," I replied.

He smiled, "Oh yeah, we read it every week," he quipped as he sauntered back to his crew.

Later, I was sandblasted in stereo by two Chinooks that came in on each side of me filled with troops. I took several shots of a 155 on a fire mission, trying to capture a different part of the firing sequence each time they fired a round. This was for the magazine story on 1/30 artillery.

A 228th AHB Chinook lifts off from LZ Grant with a California State Flag in the foreground.

Artillery crew member from 1/30 rammed another 90 pound round into the 155 howitzer at LZ Grant, as they continued a lengthy fire mission.

F-100 fighter-bombers were pounding an area about a mile away, but too far, and too hazy for photos. I also saw an A-1 Skyraider, an old WWII style propeller plane, flown by the South Vietnamese Air Force. They were called "spads," and very effective.

One time, I walked too far around in front of a 155 when it fired, and the muzzle blast rung up my ears. My earplugs were overmatched. Then, six Hueys took grunts on a combat assault, but I couldn't get there in time for photos. I didn't run that often, it just made me sweat more. My pistol belt with its canteen, 45 pistol and pouches filled with film, camera lenses and C-rations weighed over 20 pounds. As always, dust and sweat made mud.

I waited until 6 p.m. for a ride back to PV. I had run around LZ Grant several times, but was slightly late each time for a chance at another good picture. However, there would certainly be numerous future opportunities. Back at the office, they told me it had been 105 degrees today.

A 155 howitzer crew at LZ Grant, the 90 pound round is lifted on a cradle by two guys, then it was pushed in snugly. The white powder bag was put in behind the round and the breech was closed. Everybody held their ears, (low tech ear protection), a yank of the lanyard and BOOM!

Apr 16 - At the ceremony that dedicated our repaired and enlarged airstrip, sarcastically referred to as "Phuoc Vinh International," both the 1st Cav Commanding General, and the 31st Engineers Commanding Officer, pounded in the last spike. Solid brass, it was symbolic of the old railroad golden spike. These engineers specialized in the construction of airstrips. Now, C130s could land and our precious mail would arrive earlier.

The photos from the cordon and search job arrived today in the packet from the photo lab. We had numerous shots of the different activities, and writer Steve Haldemann was pleased. He had taken a photo of me during the operation as I tried not to look kerfuffled walking away from the booby trap wire discovery. This was the first picture of me actually doing my job, with the 45, wrap around shades, two cameras and the pouches on the pistol belt. He also caught the NPFFs in the background. *Steve, a fine writer, would soon become the editor of the Cavalair.*

90   A New Information Officer

Apr 17 - On a rare, slow day, I took photos of the promotion of Brig. Gen. Shedd's Huey crew chief. We joked around as I took the shot in front of the helicopter. They knew I was from California, and proclaimed it the land of fruits and nuts.

Vista Press editor Russ Dietrich ran another of my letters in his column. My brother, Dennis, now had my former job at the *Vista Press*, using my heavy, twin-lens C-33 camera. I received the paper weekly in the mail. It was great to see Dennis' credit lines on his photos. He also showed Russ a *Cavalair* newspaper.

It was the normal, steamy, 103 degrees today. We hardly noticed anymore. It also rained hard from 3 to 4 p.m. At 9 p.m., it was still a humid 90 degrees. Later, it dropped down into the cool 70s. Phil Blackmarr and I were both assigned greenline guard duty on Bunker 32. We were rarely assigned guard duty on the same night. That meant no photographers would be available the next morning. A quiet night on the greenline was still stressful, as all hell could break loose at anytime.

```
RONALD REAGAN              State of California
  GOVERNOR                   GOVERNOR'S OFFICE
                             SACRAMENTO 95814


              March 25, 1969


        SP/4 Terry A. Moon
        RA 18863138
        15th Admin. Co. FWD IO/Photo
        1st Cav. Div.
        APO San Francisco, California 96490

        Dear Mr. Moon:

        I am more than pleased to be able to meet your request
        for a California State Flag for use in Vietnam, and I
        am sorry for whatever delay there may have been in
        getting this flag to you.  I know you will fly it
        proudly.

        We here at home, in turn, are proud not only of the
        job California men are doing in this difficult situ-
        ation, but also we know that your service over there
        will bring honor to both our state and our nation.

                                Sincerely,

                                Ronald Reagan
                                RONALD REAGAN
                                Governor


        P.S. Since there is no provision in the state
             budget for the purchase of flags, I am
             pleased to inform you that this flag was
             made possible through the generosity of
             a grateful citizen of the state of
             California.
```

Apr 18 - Following guard duty all night, I slept from 7a.m. to noon. The California flag I had requested from Governor Reagan arrived in the mail along with the letter to the left. The flag had previously flown over the Capitol, but now hung on the wall by my desk in the front corner of the press/photo office. In the photo above I wrote a letter at my desk in the presence of the new flag.

I loved my nickname, "Flash." Now, they called me "The California Flash." I saw California flags flying on LZs. A Maryland flag hung in the office a few months ago. Many Californians livened up our office: Phil, Larry Adams, Chuck Spicer, Andy Anderson and Bill Ellis.

How Did You Get This Job?   91

Apr 20 - It was the largest ceremony I could remember, with all the troops in formation and more media than I ever had seen before. The 1st Cavalry Division received the Vietnamese Presidential Unit Citation, only the second unit that received this prestigious award. A streamer was attached to the 1st Cav Colors by the ARVN III Corps Commander Lt. Gen. Do Cao Tri at the VIP pad. This award was for the 1st Cavalry Division's successes inflicting heavy casualties on the NVA invaders. Also, the Cav was cited for cutting off major enemy supply lines from the Cambodian sanctuaries with their wide-ranging, helicopter-borne forces. The fast paced ceremony only gave me time for a few photos.

As his aide explained things to Lt. Gen. Tri, it seemed like CG Forsythe, on the left, was glaring at me while I was taking the picture.

Apr 21 - Today, I photographed seven jobs. First, at Division Artillery (DIVARTY), I flew in an E/82 LOH to shoot aerial door gunner photos. E Battery, 82nd Artillery was the air support unit for Division Artillery, flying LOHs and Hueys, the artwork on the gunner's pouch showed the company's nickname "woodpecker." We flew close to the E/82 Huey and the door gunner faked shooting. I took several shots.

Then, back to DIVARTY at Phuoc Vinh, where they wanted a photo of their spotter plane called a "Bird Dog," with artillery shells exploding in the background. Flying in the same LOH, I now wore Captain Carrara's headset to talk with everyone involved, coordinating the position of spotter plane and the artillery fire. I used the radio call sign "California Flash." They had a target area set. I told the Bird Dog pilot to fly really slow in a circle between our LOH and the target. We tried to keep the Bird Dog in line with the target as we flew a larger circle. When the artillery fired the first shots at the target area with normal High Explosive rounds, the black smoke was difficult to see against the dark green trees. The artillery crew chief on the radio, call sign "Yankee 3," suggested "willie peter" (white phosphorus). A great idea, the big white puffs showed up well, (see photo at right). We were flying so fast that the LOH was shaking. Superb skills by both pilots and cooperation from everyone involved, made this picture possible. I took a couple of good shots.

Later, after several routine awards ceremonies I had earlier scheduled sequentially, I photographed an accident for AAIB, near the PV airstrip. Two cobras flew too close together and their rotors hit. What a mess. They were close to the ground, so no injuries, but the rotors were shattered and looked vaguely like spaghetti.

Apr 23 - A light schedule today, so Phil handled the jobs. I went on the courier flight to the Bien Hoa photo lab in the afternoon. We rotated this job between us depending on the work load. Late in the day, there wasn't a ride available back to PV, so I stayed at the photo lab and watched a strange movie with the guys, *Bye Bye Braverman*. Lt. Sheridan had departed, but several members of the crew remembered me from my time at the lab last December. One of them took over the job of lab chief and did well.

94 A New Information Officer

Apr 24 - In Bien Hoa, I looked for an early ride back to PV. One Huey pilot said he was flying passengers into Saigon, back to Bien Hoa, then on to Phuoc Vinh, and I could tag along. That sounded interesting. I would see most of Saigon from the air, an excellent photo opportunity.

We flew over part of downtown Saigon

The Saigon dock area, with many ships, was a very busy place.

I shot aerial photos of the city and ships at the busy docks on the river. We landed at a pad in the city, where I stayed in the Huey, so I would be there when they were ready to leave. When the passengers returned, we flew back to Bien Hoa, where everyone, but me, disembarked. After another half hour flight, we arrived in Phuoc Vinh in the early afternoon.

Tan Son Nhut Airport, was on the north side of Saigon.

Apr 26 - An excited Major Coleman burst into the press/photo office with a newspaper in his hand. Cheerfully, he congratulated me on a full page of my photos in the April 25 *MACV Observer*. I took them on the January 4 cordon and search operation with the MPs. It was rare and prestigious for our photos to appear in the larger, 100,000 circulation, countrywide newspapers.

One of my photos from March 20 was selected as it showed the 40,000th MedEvac patient. United Press International in Saigon called and wanted more details. This would be widely distributed by UPI and I would receive a photo credit line, but I didn't want one for this kind of photo. Unfortunately, this was a war, and the media focused on what was news.

Apr 27 - Sunday, everyone had a half day off, unless you were assigned KP. I awakened at 5:30 a.m. to secure the easy dining room job, but it was still a wasted day as I was stuck in the mess hall.

Apr 28 - After an early awards ceremony at division headquarters, one of the guys in the room was talking about his MARS call, from here in Phuoc Vinh. The station was nearby so I stopped in and set up a MARS call to Sally. They would call me at PIO and patch the call through when it was ready.

Back at the office, a Civic Affairs (G-5) officer needed a photographer, so I left the office immediately with him. We flew in a LOH to photograph a cache of weapons near LZ Jamie, 72 km northwest of Phuoc Vinh. On the way, we saw 11th Armored Cavalry tanks and armored personnel carriers in thick underbrush, blasting an NVA bunker complex. Our pilot tried to fly closer to the action, but the gunships overhead forced us to stay out of the way. I took some aerial photos, but it was distant, and the heavy dust and smoke obscured the operation. (See photo above.)

When we arrived at the cache, weapons were stacked neatly for me to photograph. There were several rockets, thankfully, a few less the NVA could shoot at us. These guys were proud of all the weapons they captured, and rightfully so. I took several photos of the displays, and rode back on the same LOH, since I wanted to quickly return to PV. After a short flight to Tay Ninh, we had lunch with the 1st Brigade staff. I fell asleep in the back of the LOH at 1:30 p.m. and woke up just before we arrived in Phuoc Vinh at 3 p.m. We must have stopped somewhere else, but I slept through it. Sadly, my MARS call never came through.

I received a letter today from Greg Michaud, the fifth and final guy to contact me from our photo school group. He was with the 9th Infantry Division in the Mekong Delta, no doubt he sloshed through shallow water or was an easy target riding in boats. I was grateful to be here on solid ground with all the helicopters. The rest of our group, Jerry Born was with the 173rd Airborne in An Khe, Rick Keller was with the 101st Airborne in Hue, and I heard Pete Sommers was now with the 25th Infantry in Cu Chi. Our group that cruised New Jersey together, and competed fiercely for the top spot in class, were now scattered throughout Vietnam.

Apr 29 - About 7:30 a.m., writer Al Persons and I met a Civic Affairs (G-5) Major at the VIP Pad. We flew south to the 1st Logistics pad by the Dong Nai River, near Saigon. We waited over an hour to pick up two former NVA soldiers from the Chieu Hoi (defector) program. South Vietnamese Army (ARVN) intelligence officers directed the operation.

The Chieu Hoi (open arms) Program encouraged defection by Viet Cong and North Vietnamese Army soldiers by the use of propaganda leaflets and radio broadcasts. Offers were made to those who were tired of B-52 strikes and gunships, who would cooperate with the South Vietnamese Government. Those who surrendered were known as "Hoi Chanh" and often joined allied units as Kit Carson Scouts, assisting Americans and ARVNs in the same areas from which they had defected. Several made great contributions to the effectiveness of U.S. units, and distinguished themselves in combat.

Downtown Tay Ninh street scene.

The Tay Ninh West Base, 100 km northwest of Saigon, was our next stop, then we rode jeeps into Tay Ninh City. I shot photos of one of the NVA defectors on a downtown street.

We ate lunch in a nearby restaurant, with traditional Vietnamese cuisine, including local beer. The G5 major said, "Just eat it, don't worry about what it is." I faked it with the chopsticks and did okay. The food tasted strange, something shrimp-like with rice. Poor Al was eating so slowly, that they gave him a fork. This was a popular place, filled with local Vietnamese. The din of their high-pitched voices was distracting. However, it turned out to be a memorable, unique experience with an inside look at authentic Vietnamese culture.

High aerial photo of Tay Ninh City, 22 km east of Cambodia, with the Vam Co Dong River flowing in the background

Returning to our Huey at the 1st Brigade helicopter pad, we took off north for An Loc, another large city, just west of Quan Loi. I photographed the other NVA defector in the center of town. Then, on to the An Loc Chieu Hoi Center where I took photos of a third NVA defector. These pictures would be made into propaganda leaflets and dropped the next day, where the NVA defectors' units were presumed to be. I gave my film to the ARVN intelligence officer after we finished. They did the rest.

The Chu Hoi program was frequently an intelligence bonanza. The media rarely, if ever, mentioned this great program.

98   A New Information Officer

The huge Catholic Church in Tay Ninh served the innumerable Vietnamese of that faith in this area.

We returned to PV about an hour before my greenline guard duty on bunker 32 at 4:30 p.m. Because of my scheduled job at 7:30 a.m. the next morning, I was assigned an early shift by the sergeant of the guard, who was one of our office guys. *I get by with a little help from my friends.*

Al took a picture of me photographing the NVA defector in An Loc. Behind me was the ARVN Intelligence Officer.

Apr 30 - In the morning, I went to Division Headquarters for an awards ceremony. Brig. Gen. Meszar was acting commanding general now that Maj. Gen. Forsythe had quietly departed.

Radio operator (RTO) checks in while members of his platoon wait.

May 1 - Leaving early, I flew to LZ Grant for another small weapons cache, consisting of mostly mortars. I searched in vain for a flight to PV riding a Huey around the rest of the morning, and spending time at LZs Jamie and White. Finally, I caught a ride to a grunt company in the field and spent the afternoon with them. The terrain wasn't jungle at all, mostly waist-deep grass (see photo above). I rode out to the field company on a Huey with grunts returning to this unit, and departed on the evening log bird. I stayed with the command platoon most of the time, keeping close to the radio operator (RTO) so I knew what was going on. They answered my questions about their procedures. Only a few good shots for me, but not as many as there could have been. The stress level was high. I had to pay attention to what was going on around me and couldn't think primarily about composing photos, as all hell could break loose at any moment.

Earlier, one of the grunts saw my name tag, smiled, and said, "Do you take pictures for the *Cavalair*? Your name is familiar."

"Yes, I work for PIO, and I try to show what you guys are doing out here in the bush."

That made my day.

I was very careful not to "get in the way" of the field unit. A couple of weeks ago at the office, I had received an irate call from a grunt company commander complaining that one of our photographers out with his unit, had been careless, made noise after being warned to be quiet and nearly caused a disaster. This angered Major Coleman when I told him. He knew how serious it was as he had been a grunt company commander. It was common sense to me to stay out of the way, but some guys couldn't figure that out.

The field grunts were happy to get their C rations and water. Clutched tightly in his hand was the red bag of precious mail. I shot this photo as I left on the evening log bird.

May 3 - The PX was low on soda, so we resorted to Kool-Aid. I also had my pitcher of instant iced tea. We were certainly thankful for our refrigerator. How could we complain? Others had far worse conditions than we did.

I always carried two C-ration items in one of my belt pouches, and they were often eaten on my busy days. My supply needed replenishing frequently and friendly grunts would give me a can or two. I found the jewel of C-rations, pound cake. It went well with the peaches, apricots and fruit cocktail. I added that to my regular rotation of date pudding and fruitcake. The tiny P-38 can opener was an amazing tool, a brilliant design.

The meat units needed to be heated to make the grease palatable. An empty short can could be vented on the side, top and bottom, so air would flow through creating a small stove for the burning of a heat tab or a small chunk of C-4 explosive to warm the food. The meat can was opened leaving the lid attached and folded as a handle. The grease could then be melted as the meat unit was heated, and stirred to avoid burning. Some of them even tasted good. *It was all relative, because out with the grunts it was all we had.*

May 4 - Today, I received the only mail for the entire section, two letters and a package. I had such great support from my family and friends. The mail was extremely important to all of us. It also raised the spirits of everyone when we shared our goodies from home.

Only a few more days and my long year in Vietnam would be half over.

Chapter Seven A New Commanding General

May 5 - Today was the Division Change of Command Ceremony for Major General E.B. Roberts. A large contingent of media attended, because the 1st Cav was the elite division in Vietnam. I bumped elbows with an NBC cameraman jockeying for position. Major Coleman pulled Phil off KP duty to help shoot the important ceremony.

MACV Deputy Commander General William B. Rosson passed the 1st Cavalry Division colors to our new commanding general, symbolizing leadership of the division. The various flags and the band made it a memorable, colorful ceremony.

New 1st Cav Commanding General E. B. Roberts.

I had met the new CG previously when he toured with the former division commander. He was pleasant, and struck me as being too nice to be a general.

New II Field Force Commander Lt. Gen. Julian Ewell attended. After the ceremony, I heard him insulting the Cav and almost threatening CG Roberts. He said we wasted the use of all the helicopters. Later, when I told Major Coleman about this, he said that Lt. Gen. Ewell had no understanding of helicopter cavalry interdiction operations. Formerly, he had been the 9th Infantry Division Commanding General. A "body count" guy, he gave almost no value to our cavalry sweep operations where many tons of weapons and rice were captured.

General Roberts' military career included parachuting into Normandy with the 101st Airborne Division on D-Day, and as a Colonel, he led the Cav's 1st Brigade when the division arrived in Vietnam in 1965.

May 6 - Early in the morning, I photographed the 8th Engineer Battalion change of command ceremony. New Commanding Officer Lt. Col. Andre Broumas was charismatic and enthusiastic. He spoke to me after the ceremony, which was unusual, and told me he hoped I would take many photos of his "skybeavers". *No problem, I always enjoyed photographing the engineer's operations.*

It rained every day now, the dust had turned to mud, but there were beautiful clouds. Our TV was finally in the bunker, and I saw *Laugh-In* this evening for the first time in three weeks. *Sock-it-to-me.*

102   A New Commanding General

An aerial photo of LZ Carolyn, with its airstrip.

May 7 - Last night, LZ Carolyn (86 km northwest of PV, near Cambodia) was attacked on opposite sides by two NVA battalions, a bad scene. The wire was breached on both sides. The NVA came close to cutting the fire support base in half, but there were many heroic acts by the 2/8 grunts, A Battery, 2/19 and B Battery, 1/30 artillerymen. Hand to hand combat broke out in several places as the LZ was partially overrun. One of the artillery pits changed hands more than once during the battle. 1st Cav Cobras, Air Force "Spooky" (AC-47) and "Shadow" (AC-119) gunships finally drove off the enemy. The NVA left 172 dead. Our grunts captured thirty more, including a high-ranking officer, an intelligence bonanza. American casualties were ten killed and eighty wounded. At first light, 1/9 LOH-Cobra teams killed sixty retreating NVA as they headed back to their sanctuaries across the Cambodian border.

Grunts test their M16s outside LZ Carolyn.

This morning, we had several journalists come to the office clamoring for rides to LZ Carolyn. I called my friends at 227th and E/82 and secured rides for several of them. Our press officer took care of the others.

Since there were several attacks throughout the area last night, my greenline guard shift, midnight to 3 a.m. was extra tense, as we expected further attacks. Fortunately, it was quiet, except for a few close B-52 strikes that produced dramatic chains of brilliant flashes in the blackness. They called them "arc lights" for good reason.

My photo of the Vietnamese Presidential Unit Citation Award was on page one of the current *Cavalair*.

We continued to be understaffed. Major Coleman ran ads in the *Cavalair* for photographers, looking for a grunt, who was also a talented photographer. He also had the staff at the orientation center looking for experienced journalists among the arriving FNGs.

It still rained everyday, and the weather continued to get hotter.

An aerial photo of a B-52 strike, from a long way off.

May 8 - Today, more B-52 strikes hit nearby, and the eastern horizon was full of smoke. I hurried to finish the office work, due to a big job tomorrow.

I received a goodie package in the mail with a new variety of treats, as always, a welcome psychological lift. I liked the Nabisco Raisin Biscuit Cookies, and the dried apricots. My C-ration stash was growing as I was on the lookout for pound cake and fruit.

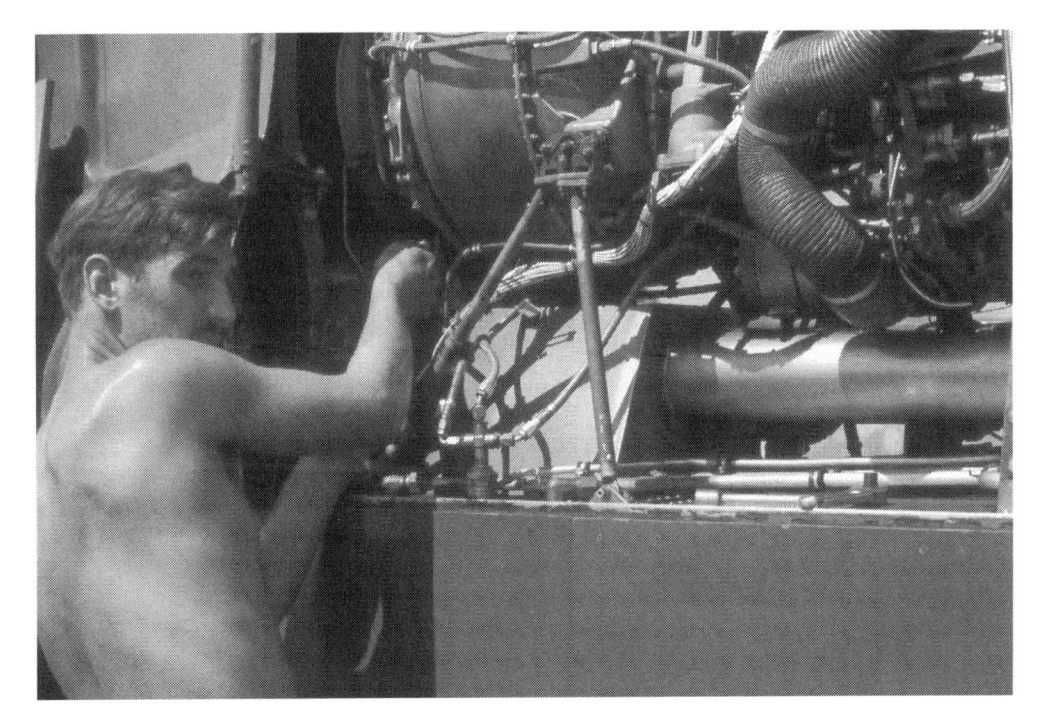

A 15th TC maintenance team member works on a Cobra engine.

May 9 - I had an extensive aircraft maintenance assignment today, an important part of the division's operations. At 7:30 a.m., I went to the 227th AHB pad and caught a Huey to Long Thanh (near Long Binh). On the way, we stopped at Lai Khe to pick up parts from another 227th company to be repaired by 15th TC (Transportation Corps). Next, we flew to Dau Tieng, 32 km west of Lai Khe for more parts from 229th AHB, including a tail rotor.

Two hours after we left PV, we finally landed at Long Thanh. I shot photos of Company C, 15th TC Battalion, as they repaired Hueys, Cobras, and LOHs. I walked around with one of the supervisors, and took photos of various aspects of maintenance including rotor heads and engines.

I hitched a ride on a truck over to 15th TC Battalion Headquarters at nearby Bearcat, and talked with the guys. They were proud of their excellent safety record. We enjoyed lunch in the outstanding mess hall.

An aerial photo of one of the Chinook repair hangers at Bearcat.

After lunch, I visited company A, situated in two huge hangers, where they worked on Chinooks. With the two large rotors and the long driveshaft, the Chinook was far more complicated, and required more maintenance than the other helicopters. I toured the shops and took pictures of their operations. It appeared organized and efficient.

The 15th TC S-1 found a flight for me to Bien Hoa. It had started to rain at Bearcat, but not in Bien Hoa, as I strolled up the hill to the photo lab. Later, I walked over to the 101st Airborne PX. There I ran into my friend from the FNG orientation camp at An Khe. Mark Orthman was now with 15th S&S (logistics) Battalion at LZ Jake, an unusual LZ with an airstrip, west of Quan Loi. He was in Bien Hoa on light duty after a fall. We talked at length, since we had great times together at An Khe, about six months ago.

I couldn't find a ride to Phuoc Vinh, so I stayed the night at the photo lab. In the evening, we watched *The Rogues*, and *The Tonight Show Starring Johnny Carson*.

May 10 - I caught an early Huey ride back to PV with the Lab's courier pack. My brother Dennis had worked hard sending me camera accessories, so I bought a "Bush hat" for him from an Aussie I met at Bien Hoa.

In the evening, the office had a party, and we enjoyed the music provided by our guitar players. I shot Polaroids of groups of buddies and gave them out. I heard "Thanks, Flash" many times.

May 11 - KP was more difficult today. We had a tough inspector general inspection, so everything had to be exceptionally clean. We passed easily, as everyone pitched in and worked hard. I drank a lot of water, because I sweated all day.

Sgt. 1st Class DeGard had nominated me for promotion to Spec. 5. He was happy with the way the photo operations were managed. I hadn't been in the Army long enough to be eligible for promotion, so he was trying to obtain a special waiver for me. I had filled an E5 slot since February 2, and felt fortunate to have such excellent staff support.

May 12 - Our base was attacked just after midnight at four different places by NVA sappers, with one extremely close to us. We saw some of the base camp defense force 1/8 grunts arrive to reinforce the bunkers on the greenline. Heavy firing and explosions continued throughout the night, and we saw the green tracers coming in. We heard gunships, and saw the red stream of tracers from the Cobra's miniguns. The greenline bunker behind the office was firing heavily as dawn approached. They had several extra guys on the bunker and there was much more outgoing fire than usual. We were in the office building with our M16s ready. Sometimes the gunships hovered directly above us. The stress level was high throughout night. Then it just stopped, resulting in an eerie silence. In the morning, there were many dead NVA in and beyond the wire. I didn't get a number, but we could see bodies from the office. None of us had any sleep.

An aerial photo of LZ Jamie, north of Tay Ninh.

Major attacks also occurred at Quan Loi and LZs Grant, Ike, and Phyllis, but the worst was at LZ Jamie (2/7 and B 2/19 Artillery). Seven Americans were killed. The artillery crews had to resort to "Beehive" rounds, similar to huge shotguns, fired directly at the attacking enemy. There were over seventy dead NVA.

After a night without sleep, I had a busy day scheduled, photographing 7 a.m. awards at Division Headquarters, and the command portrait of our new CG at his desk. Then on to the VIP pad for a ceremony celebrating the 25,000th aircraft repaired by 15th TC Battalion. They did a great job keeping our helicopters flying. There had not been one Chinook accident in the last six months.

Back at the office, Captain Carrara had the camera equipment that he bought for me in Tokyo. It included a Pentax Spotmatic Motor Drive Camera Set, a Pentax SL Camera body, and Super Takumar 24 mm wide angle, and 200 mm telephoto lenses. I barely had time to look at them.

I grabbed a quick lunch, and hurried to catch the Huey for a VIP tour with General Haines (US Army Pacific Commander) to picturesque, hilltop LZ Dolly for a brief tour. I shot photos of him talking with 1/5 grunts. (Photo at right from the *Cavalair*.) Then to LZ Carolyn, scene of a recent major attack. Most of the LZ looked intact. The 105 mm artillery pits had been rebuilt. They were still repairing a few damaged areas from the massive attack of May 7. I shot generic pictures of LZ Carolyn for my sister, who's name was Carolyn.

(U.S. Army Photo By SP4 Terry Moon)

General's Visit

General Ralph E. Haines, USARPAC commander, chats with SP4 Lawrence Thompson, a rifleman with Company C, 1st Battalion, 5th Cavalry at LZ Dolly.

A muddy day at recently repaired LZ Carolyn.

From there, we went to Lai Khe. With only one Huey on this tour, I was bumped off the flight by a Colonel. My USARV press card only allowed me to bump Majors and below off flights. I had to find another ride back to Phuoc Vinh. I met two guys from Criminal Investigations Division who were also looking for a ride to PV. A thunderstorm rolled in and blasted us. We were soaked running around the airstrip looking for a flight, but late in the evening we finally found a Huey flying back to PV. The pilots told us they could fly around the storm. Usually it was a fifteen or twenty minute flight. *What happened next was a perfect setting for a horror movie.*

The thunderstorm was wider than they thought, so we had an insane, wild ride through it. The Huey bounced around violently in all directions. On the floor, we wrapped ourselves around the slippery, wet bench posts and hung on. One of the CID guys wedged himself under the copilot's seat hanging on to the frame. The rain blew in, one way, then the other. Sliding around on the wet floor, we struggled to hang on and could easily have been thrown out of the wide open doors, and over dense jungle, lost forever. It was completely dark except for the red glow of the instruments. (See photo at right.) The lightning flashes froze our bewildered faces in time. I was thankful for my helmet as my head kept banging into the post. We were too busy holding on to be scared. Then, we were out of it. *What a relief!* The last few miles into Phuoc Vinh were extremely calm.

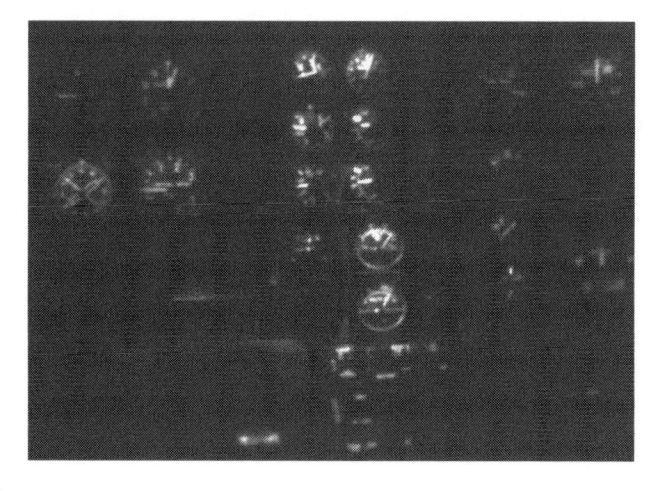

My cameras were dry in their plastic bags, passing the toughest test yet. This was a long, nasty night and day. I was soaked and absolutely beat as I trudged back to the office. When I entered, everyone looked up and someone said, "What the hell happened to you?"

If there was incoming during the night, I slept through it.

May 13 - I slept late in the morning, and no one said a word. They had seen how I looked when I returned last evening, and none of us had any sleep the night before. One of the clerks helped me catch up on the paperwork.

I received a goodie package today from Grandma Miller that contained chocolate chip cookies. The chocolate was almost liquid, so I kept them in our refrigerator. They were delicious.

That night, I had greenline guard duty. We were on red alert status, so everyone on the bunker stayed up all night. It was really tough to stay awake around 5 a.m. *Unless you thought you saw movement outside the wire.*

May 14 - My bunk looked great at 7 a.m., and I slept soundly until 1 p.m., paying off a huge sleep debt, as I only had slept one night in the last three.

I had a photo in this weeks *Cavalair*, on page six from the weather girl tour. An FNG motion picture photographer arrived at the office today. Today a letter arrived from Sally's mother, a wonderful lady.

May 15 - I tested some of my new cameras and lenses, but it rained most of the day, so I didn't accomplish much. The 24 mm lens was extremely wide.

Poor Phil had guard duty tonight. It was even more miserable when it rained, but not as bad as red alert status.

May 16 - In our bunker, from 3 to 6 a.m., we hid during another close rocket attack. The massive amount of work we did building the bunker was well worth it. The North Vietnamese Army was apparently "celebrating" Ho Chi Minh's birthday three days early by attacking us. I was scheduled to fly to LZ Grant this morning, but most of today's jobs were cancelled. Later, at 4 p.m. I photographed 11th Aviation Group medal presentations by Commanding General Roberts.

After the general's ceremony, I walked over to E-82 to photograph a gunship mission. Sgt. 1st Class DeGard set it up with DIVARTY, so I flew in an E/82 LOH with 2/20 ARA "Blue Max" gunships to a nearby target area. I would take photos of the Cobras firing with my new Motor Drive Pentax Camera. It was late in the day, almost 6 p.m., and light was waning. I didn't know how the photos would turn out. *One came out great, (see photo at right), with the rockets frozen right in front of the cobra. The motor-drive could take 3 frames per second, that helped with timing the shots.*

The famous "Top Hat" flagpole at LZ Jamie.

May 17 - I wrote captions most of the day. Later, greenline guard for me on Bunker 34 with first shift. It was a stressful, but quiet night. I had adjusted, and slept well in the bunker after my intense three hours of watching for the NVA in the rain.

May 18 - Major Coleman, Phil and I shot more photos of CG Roberts in front of his Huey. I used the new camera. *I loved it, so smooth, so easy.*

May 19 - I flew to LZ Jamie with a visiting general. We saw numerous craters from the early morning mortar attacks. I shot several photos of his fast-paced visit with the grunts and artillerymen. AFVN-TV evening news had Don Webster's CBS News report from LZ Jamie early this morning while incoming mortar rounds exploded. Some of the guys I photographed today were the same ones interviewed by CBS. LZ Jamie looked different now, the 11th Armored Cavalry APCs and self-propelled howitzers were gone, and so was most of the bamboo.

LZ Jamie grunts repairing damage from a mortar attack.

Newly rebuilt culvert, ammo box, and sandbag hooches at LZ Jamie, with M16 and 105 ammo on the right in the foreground.

Back at the office, I noticed darkening around the edges of each frame on one of my proof sheets. The culprit was my zoom lens, one inside glass element had mold growing around the edge, and it was beyond repair. *This was a tough environment for photo equipment.*

May 20 - Today was a rare slow day, no jobs on the schedule, so I reorganized and cleaned up my desk area, while Phil took the courier pack to the photo lab.

To make up for the loss of the zoom, I would carry the 200 mm in one of my belt pouches, changing to the other lens instead of just zooming.

Now I had 56 days to go until R&R, and 174 left before departure for home.

May 21 - My D/227 Cobra gunship photo from Lai Khe was in this weeks *Cavalair*.

Greenline guard for me this evening, it seemed to come up again too quickly. The rain was heavy, except for the what was normally the worst shift, my quiet one from midnight to 3 a.m. So far I had been lucky not to have been on greenline guard during a ground attack.

A New Commanding General

May 22 - I found the perfect subject for my new 24 mm super-wide lens, the long-barreled 175 mm self-propelled howitzer. The 6/27 Artillery Battery in the center of the base, where these big guns were located, was a short walk from our office. The super wide lens made it look absolutely unreal, extremely long. I shot several different angles. *Major Coleman and the editors would love these photos.*

When the big guns fired, we heard the shell screaming through the air on its way to the target, with an eerie, unearthly sound.

May 23 - I had the dreaded KP today, but we had some unexpected excitement. An immersion heater started a fire in the pot and pan shack. Our fire extinguishers were overmatched. We called the Phuoc Vinh fire department to put it out. The shack had a new scorched look, but was still functional.

One of the cooks, a pleasant, heavy guy that everyone called "Cheeks," (photo below right,) received word his wife had a baby girl. We all celebrated with him. He was kind to the guys on KP. Later, one of the outside stove burners exploded, spewing gas all over one wall. It ignited, and we had to put the fire out with CO2 extinguishers. Then, of course, it rained the rest of the day. At dinner, when everyone came through the mess hall, popular "Cheeks" received more accolades.

A letter arrived from my photo school friend, Jerry Born. His unit, the 173rd Airborne Brigade, was moving to Qui Nhon, where he would be even more of a REMF.

May 24 - They cancelled my scheduled D Troop, 1st Squadron, 9th Cavalry combat assault job. D Troop was the ground recon unit using jeeps and light trucks. I had no idea what this really was. It was probably a different operation or another unit. Odd things like this showed up on the schedule occasionally with no clue as to where they originated. Everyone denied responsibility.

May 25 - In the morning, we received word that photos were needed of a large cache of rockets and other weapons found near LZ Jamie. Phil was out shooting a series of jobs. I had a ton of office work to do, but I searched around and hitched a ride on an A Troop, 1/9 Huey to LZ Jamie. He dropped me off on his way to another LZ. I flew out to the site with supplies on the logbird. They had several dozen AK-47s, a large assortment of ammo, and dozens of rockets, in two sizes, already neatly displayed. I quickly photographed the entire layout, returning to the LZ on the same logbird.

A logbird was a supply or logistics helicopter. Each fire support base was staffed by a grunt battalion with one grunt company, and the heavy weapons (mortars) company at the LZ. The other two or three grunt companies were out in the field. The logbird delivered ammo, water, C-rations (sometimes hot food), and precious mail, in a red nylon bag, to them. Grunts, including FNGs, also caught rides going to the field units.

I just missed this Carabou flight to Phuoc Vinh. It left Quan Loi just as I arrived.

I checked with the two choppers on the ground. One was the logbird and would be flying supplies to field units all day, the other one was cranking up, so I jumped on. It was headed to LZ Phyllis, 10 km northeast, where they dropped off a couple of guys, then on to the large 3rd Brigade base at Quan Loi. The guys in the airstrip "terminal", who were always helpful, told me there wouldn't be any flights soon to Phuoc Vinh. I had just missed the regular Carabou flight, so I ran back, jumped on the same Huey and flew back to LZ Jamie.

Patience, Grasshopper.

LZ White (about 12 or 15 km south) was the next stop, and I stayed onboard. We continued on to a field unit and picked up several officers. There wasn't room for me, so they left me stranded. I took pictures of the grunts setting up for the night as they made shelters from their ponchos (see photos at right and next page). It occurred to me that I might be spending the night with them.

This is the grunt's field shelter for the night, made with a poncho and hidden with grass.

About a half hour later the Huey returned, (see photo above), picked me up, and went back to LZ White. After a brief wait, we flew to LZ Jamie. It was almost dark when I returned to PV on the original logbird that had been there throughout the day. Entering the office at 7:30 p.m., they told me I had greenline guard. I grabbed my guard gear and hurried out to bunker 34 and ate C-rations for dinner. *Bon Appetit*. I was lucky, as it was quiet all night. I only had to pull one short shift, midnight to 2 a.m. I would need to catch up on a load of office work tomorrow, and one of the clerks had overheard Major Coleman say that I would soon be sent on an unusual job.

CHAPTER EIGHT ONE JOB THAT CHANGED EVERYTHING

May 26 - I had the morning off to make up for greenline guard duty the previous night, and slept well. Phil and the clerks had completed most of the paper work. Waiting for me was the previously rumored, strange assignment. I would photograph the creation of a "Daisy Cutter" instant landing zone (LZ). A C-130 would drop an old World War II, 10,000-pound bomb into the deep jungle, detonating it above the ground. The blast would clear an area in the dense vegetation, allowing the Hueys to deliver troops. The operation of bringing troops into an LZ by helicopter was called a combat assault (CA).

I caught a flight in the afternoon to Blackhorse, the 11th Armored Cavalry Regiment base camp southeast of Bien Hoa, where some of the 1st Cav's 3rd Brigade were temporarily based (see photo above). The rumor was an NVA division was approaching from the East to attack the Bien Hoa and Long Binh bases. The editors, who decided what photos and stories appeared in the *Cavalair*, wanted me to use my long 400 mm lens and motor drive camera, to photograph the operation. We couldn't fly close to the blast in a helicopter. However, they thought I could shoot this with my specialized equipment. It seemed like an impossible situation for good photos. My lens and film were too slow to shoot sharp photos of the operation from a helicopter. But I was curious, and wanted to see the bomb blast for myself, so I didn't tell them what a bad idea I thought it was. I spent the night with the 3rd Brigade Information Office team at Blackhorse.

May 27 - Late in the morning, on the way to catch my flight, I took some photos of a base defense team testing a tripod-mounted minigun for perimeter defense, (see photo at right). The firing rate of three thousand rounds a minute was impressive. I had never, in the past, been so close to one firing, because they were usually in gunships. It was loud, and the spent shell casings were flying out around me as they shredded a 55-gallon drum over a hundred feet away. They offered to set it up so I could sit there and fire it, but I had to catch my LOH ride to photograph the bomb drop. I had to be there when they were ready to go, and I didn't know exactly when that would be.

At 1:30 p.m., after some delays, PIO writer Dave Wolfe and I finally took off in a LOH. We followed the bomb-laden C-130, and moved into position for me to take the photos. Dave was in the front seat with a headset, listening to the Air Force crew. I wore a harness, in case I leaned out too far. Wedged in the back of the helicopter, I was trying to figure out the best way to steady my 400 mm lens. All helicopters vibrated, and that made it difficult to shoot sharp photos. The haze was another problem, as

we followed the C-130. Dave echoed the countdown, three, two, one. We saw the bomb on a pallet as it came off the lowered ramp in the back of the plane. Under a parachute, it dropped slowly, and exploded just above the ground, creating a huge orange and yellow fireball. From our distant viewpoint, massive concentric ripples, caused by the gigantic shock wave, rolled through the jungle like the surface of a quiet pond hit by a rock.

An immense mushroom cloud billowed skyward. The Air Force said we had to be at least a mile away because of the nasty shock wave. We were probably much further. I took fifteen shots with the motor drive, however, the big mushroom cloud would probably be the best. (See photo at the right.) I doubted that any of the pictures would be sharp, and even with the long lens, the image was minute. It was difficult to capture something so dynamic with a still photo.

By the time we returned to Blackhorse, it was too late for me to fly back to Phuoc Vinh, so I decided to visit the supermarket sized PX to check it out. It was enjoyable looking at the abundance of merchandise, but it made me realize how many items we used to take for granted, that we didn't have here. It would be necessary to carry any purchases around with me until I returned to PV, but I did buy some orange marmalade and a small pair of scissors that easily fit in my pistol belt pouches. I spent another night with 3rd Brigade PIO.

May 28 - Before dawn, the FNG PIO lieutenant, writer Dave Wolfe and I flew out to LZ Rock, a fire support base 25 km north of Blackhorse. It was still dark when we arrived. Dave and I were going to fly on a combat assault into the jungle LZ created by the bomb blast that we observed the previous day. I could have flown back to Phuoc Vinh this morning, but I was curious about the Daisy Cutter LZ. There should be dramatic photo opportunities on the combat assault, but we might be the target of enemy fire, as an entire NVA division approached.

Six Company B, 227th AHB Hueys picked up the Company C 1st Battalion, 8th Cavalry grunts. Dave and I caught the lead chopper of the second of three waves. They wouldn't let us fly on the first wave, thinking we would be in the way if enemy fire was encountered.

The 227th Huey drops into the tiny LZ, as a machine gunner rides on the skid

Six fully loaded grunts were packed into the chopper, so I had to stand on the front of the skid and hold on, like the machine gunner in the photo above. I glanced back at the grunts inside the Huey as they waited, grim-faced and fidgety. When I first saw the LZ created by the bomb, it was much smaller than expected. A large tree trunk, and a few small ones, still stood in the center. Only one Huey could drop in at a time. It was dark, with a heavy overcast, almost drizzling. Possibly, it was too dark for photos, but with absolutely no shadows, and with my fast black and white film, I would have a chance.

When we were close to the ground, I jumped off the skid, and immediately began taking pictures as the others exited the Huey. *What great action, with grunts jumping off the skids of the Hueys.*

I caught an RTO (radio operator) as he stepped off the skid (photo at left).

116 One Job That Changed Everything

A machine gunner jumped out of a Huey from about ten feet up, and I captured his image in midair, (see photo above). He hit the ground hard, and with his eighty-pound load, crumpled into a heap. His helmet rolled away, but he jumped up, grabbed it, and ran to the perimeter.

All around, it was an unearthly scene of devastation from the big blast. I stood in the center where the few tree trunks had survived. They were still smoldering and the helicopter's arrival made them smoke even more. Shredded stumps that looked like oversized shaving brushes swayed from the rotor wash. Boulders were setting around loose where they had been casually tossed by the powerful blast. Further out from the center, debris was plastered against the still-standing trees. The Hueys came in close to the tree trunks. The door gunners had to watch and direct the pilots around the hazards. I was standing by the tree in the center, and the Hueys squeezed in between me and the edge of the small landing zone.

A medic stepped off the skid, and came rushing toward me to help an injured lieutenant who had jumped out too soon, landed hard on a stump and injured his ankle. A couple of grunts quickly dragged him out of the path of the next onrushing Huey.

When the second wave of six Hueys had left, it was deathly silent. Everyone was straining to hear any sounds in the jungle. We knew there were NVA out there. Many grunts, in defensive positions, were around the perimeter ready for a possible attack. I crouched between trunks and stumps as I scanned the full circle of destruction.

This was a challenging situation for photos. I needed a fast shutter speed for the action, therefore the aperture was nearly wide open in the gloom, making accurate focus critical.

The third wave arrived, led by a shotgun-wielding grunt riding on the skid of the first Huey. (See photo to the right.) I took more shots of the grunts arriving, and a grenadier, (a grunt with an M-79 grenade launcher), who was the last guy out of the last Huey, (see photo next page). Now the entire company of about a hundred grunts was on the ground. Dave and I helped carry the injured lieutenant, and lifted him into the last Huey. We also jumped in, and headed back to LZ Rock.

As we lifted off and gained altitude, I looked back at the hole in the jungle, and realized what an easy target I had been, standing in the center. There was a good chance we could have been shot at by the NVA on the combat assault. *I learned later that the other nearby CA (B 1/8) today met fierce enemy resistance. My good luck continued.*

A grenadier from Company C, 1st Battalion, 8th Cavalry is the last one out of the 227th lift ship. One of his buddies waits, and a machine gunner struggles with his heavy load. They will quickly join their comrades on the perimeter of the LZ as shown below.

The trip back to LZ Rock seemed much quicker than the earlier flight to the jungle combat assault. Dave and I went to the mess tent for coffee, but we didn't need it, as we were still wired. He said I was constantly running around during the combat assault, and thought I would have some exceptional photos.

Soon, fatigue hit both of us, so we rested against some convenient sandbags. I kept checking for flights to Blackhorse as helicopters came and went.

Patience, grasshopper. This time I would wait, and not go on another wild-goose chase, like last week.

During one of my walks to check on a flight, I shot a picture of other 1/8 grunts as they received their mail, a dramatic study of faces, (see photo at right). It was the final picture on my last roll. Now for the first time in Vietnam, I was totally out of film.

I was supposed to have been out on a one day job, but this was my third day away from PV. I finally found a flight back to Blackhorse at 5:45 p.m. I picked up my camera case, with the lens and camera from the bomb job, but by then, it was too late to fly back to Phuoc Vinh. The Blackhorse flight operations staff tried to help, but no rides were available.

The FNG lieutenant was pissed that Dave and I weren't shot at. We looked at each other in disbelief. He was just assigned to PIO, so we didn't know where he would end up. We heard the other combat assault, that also left from LZ Rock, with Company B, 1/8, met enemy resistance. That CA was not far from ours.

May 29 - I caught the scheduled 11:30 a.m. flight to Bien Hoa, where I soon found a Huey headed to PV. My odyssey had lasted four days. There was a sign on my desk, "Welcome back Flash." Phil had flawlessly covered the photo assignments. Sgt. 1st Class DeGard, our office NCOIC, shot a few jobs to help. A Dave Wolfe phone call had informed the office of my combat assault photos, and there were questions from writers and editors. They were eager to see the pictures.

Heavy incoming had struck the area near the office two nights earlier. Our new bunker had been crowded. Phil had a close call on greenline guard duty that night. As he sat on the folding chair on top of the bunker, watching the wire, he saw a sparkling trail in the sky heading his direction. He yelled "Incoming!" as he ducked behind the front sandbag wall on top of the bunker. Immediately, a huge explosion scattered shrapnel above him, and into the sandbags in front of him. He was lucky to have seen the rocket in the air, and to have reacted quickly. He scrambled down into the bunker, injuring his knee, but he would be okay. This was the only time I knew of, where someone yelled "incoming" before the first rocket or mortar round hit.

Two of my photos appeared in the May 28 *Cavalair*, the bird dog spotter plane over the artillery bursts, also the LOH maintenance photo with the dramatic cloudy sky background. Phil also had a shot in the paper of the division change of command ceremony, with the face of the monument statue as foreground (see photo at right). A creative shot of what was a routine ceremony. *Looking closer, you could see me with my camera beside the flags in front of the Huey.*

Earlier, the 3rd Brigade Information Officer told me by phone, they were sending a photographer back to PV. He had been there since September, and was productive until recently, but they didn't want him anymore, as his attitude was a major problem. He refused to do any work. Major Coleman told me not to assign him important jobs, because he couldn't be trusted. We would have to watch him now. This would make my job much more difficult.

Jun 1 - I had some catching up to do on office work, but it went quickly. In the evening, I took some artistic photos of Phil Blackmarr with candlelight and a full moon, as he played his violin, testing the Graflex XL and color Polaroid film. He had an idea of what he wanted, so we adjusted until it looked right. They came out well. Phil had decided to stay with PIO instead of joining Special Services. *I was extremely pleased about that.*

Jun 2 - The fighting continued in the area where I went on the C 1/8 combat assault on May 28, near Xuan Loc, by the Dong Nai River. The other CA that day with B 1/8, was a hot LZ (they met enemy resistance). Several tons of supplies and ammunition were found by both companies soon after the CAs. We learned an NVA Division was planning a major attack on Long Binh and Bien Hoa. The 1/8 skytroopers and many others prevented this from occurring. Companies A and B of 1/8 killed 54 NVA by the Dong Nai River today to bring the operation total to 132. The 1st Cav's ability to quickly place two companies of troops into the middle of a wide area of dense jungle, made the difference.

Most of the day, I did office work, logged in brigade film, wrote captions, the normal fare. (See photo at left.) We had a close late evening mortar attack of 12-15 rounds. It was comforting to have the protection of our bunker.

Jun 3 - I had greenline guard again, first shift, the best one from 9 p.m. to midnight. It soon became a weird evening. Small talk flowed between our sector bunkers on the phone, mostly BS. Tonight, a female impersonator, who sounded like a real girl, talked on the greenline phone. She called herself Cindy, and denied being a male. The other men on the line grilled her with probing questions trying to expose her as a guy. She handled them well in a coy, feminine way, complete with giggles. Perhaps, she was a real girl. Cindy disappeared about 11p.m. The phone was quiet after that with only the periodic checks of each bunker, until my shift ended at midnight.

FNG PIO writer Joe Kamalick listened in another bunker and was impressed. He investigated and wrote a story that appeared in the *Cavalair* a few weeks later. Cindy was never heard from again. Could a guy really have pulled this off? The mystery was never solved.

I had two photos in a Chinook center spread, and a photo of Gen. Haines with a C 1/5 grunt at LZ Dolly in the current *Cavalair*.

June 4 - Today, I flew to LZ Grant and photographed 105 mm artillery crews on fire missions. One crew stood out above the others. They were like a well oiled machine pumping out the rounds. They posed for me in the photo to the right, with the enthusiastic crew chief on the left. When I started looking for a ride back to PV a Huey arrived immediately. *It was all timing.*

Jun 6 - I received a letter from my photo school friend, Rick Keller. He suffered through two horrible days with his 101st Airborne comrades on "Hamburger Hill." A dire situation, he had several extremely close calls, but survived intact.

Jun 7 - A large package of fudge and cookies arrived in the mail, always a big lift. Sally also sent me interesting poetry, she was, after all, an English Major.

I had greenline guard on bunker 34. It rained during the night, that added to the misery so the long shifts seemed even longer. I stayed on top of the bunker in the rain, so I could see the entire wire area. I wore my poncho, but was soaked anyway. After my shift, inside the bunker, I tried, in vain, to sleep in my wet clothes. It was strange, I felt cold.

Jun 8 - After wringing out my guard clothes, I dried them with a fan, (it took all day). It felt good to be dry again, thanks to my precious towels. I slept until 11a.m.

My C 1/8 combat assault proof sheet came in the courier packet from the photo lab. Word had spread about this earlier. I had previously been asked about the mission. The guys crowded around for a look at the contact sheet. The photos lived up to the hype. Someone ran and told Major Coleman. When he saw them, he was excited and enthusiastic. "This is what the Cav is all about," he exclaimed.

It happened so quickly, and I was intensely focused while I shot the pictures, now it was surreal looking at the sequence of still shots on the proof sheet. I had one shot where writer Dave Wolfe looked just like a grunt with a camera among the heavy debris out on the edge of the LZ. (photo at right). Dave also shot film of the CA, but I didn't see any contacts of them. He may have had slower film than I did. The jungle LZ had been very dark.

Major Coleman took my proof sheet with him to the General Staff evening briefing. Most of the 20 shots were even better than I expected. The bomb photos from my original assignment, were lost in the shuffle, and forgotten.

Jun 9 - Shortly after dawn, I photographed the 13th Signal Battalion change of command ceremony, as Lt. Col. James Cook took over from Lt. Col. Billy Thrasher. Some units conducted their ceremonies first thing in the morning.

Immediately after finishing, I returned to the office, grabbed the heavy Graflex XL camera, loaded up the cargo pockets of my pants with Polaroid film packs, and hurried to the VIP pad. I flew with Assistant Division Commander Brig. Gen. Frank Meszar (he looked like Telly Savalas, cigar and all) as he visited wounded troops in a hospital in Long Binh. For over an hour, I shot Polaroid photos of the general as he spoke with the soldiers and presented medals. Each 1st Cav soldier's bed was marked with a Cav placard. The 1st Cav pride was quite clear. The Cav stationed liaison NCOs in each field hospital to help with any problems the patients had, and to make sure they quickly received their mail.

I expected a grim scene, but it wasn't. A few of the wounded were in bad shape, but they would be quickly airlifted 2700 miles to fully equipped hospitals in Japan. If the wounded soldier wouldn't be able return to his unit in thirty days or less, he was sent to Japan. Most of the skytroopers had shrapnel wounds, however they were in good spirits, thankful to be alive. The general knew about the incidents where these guys were wounded from battlefield reports. He talked with each one about how things were going with his squad. Some of the grunts stories were amazing. These guys just wanted to return to their units. *I could appreciate the courage, and sense the powerful bond between these "brothers."*

THE CAVALAIR   July 30, 1969

10,000 Pounds Creates Instant Assault Position

BLACKHORSE — "Squire 899, you are left of track," said the voice over the plane's radio. "Come right two degrees to a new heading of 108 degrees."

After the words came into the ears of the crew, the gigantic Air Force C-130 made the change and continued on its way to the target area, a heavily wooded strip about 30 miles north of here.

The plane made several additional corrections in its course, and then the voice on the radio blurted out, "4...3...2...1...now!" At that moment a parachute opened at the rear of the giant aircraft, and an enormous bomb slid out the tail of the C-130, drifting toward its target below.

A few feet above the triple-canopied jungle floor, the 10,000 pounds of destruction exploded, sending a huge red and yellow fireball approximately 200 feet into the air.

The blast cleared an area big enough for two helicopters to land safely. Another instant landing zone (LZ) had been constructed through the teamwork of the Army and Air Force, this one for the members of the 3rd Brigade.

The dense trees which had covered the area five minutes earlier were strewn about symmetrically in a large circle with their trunks pointing toward the center of the blast.

When all was in readiness, the first UH-1H Huey of the 227th Aviation Battalion dropped into the small landing zone, evading remnants of the previous day's bomb drop.

Gnarled trees, burning stumps fanned by the wind blast of the helicopter, crumpled rocks and tropical vegetation bent out of shape created an awesome sight for the soldiers as they entered. Approximately 75 meters in diameter, the area was nearly circular.

Skimming the trees surrounding the perimeter, the helicopters dropped sharply into the ready made pad. Only one spot was clear enough to accept the assaulting soldiers. Each ship nearly touched down as the experienced Skytroopers of the 1st Bn, 8th Cav rode the skids, or awaited quick exit near the ship's doors.

Immediately jumping to the ground while the ship hovered, each soldier assumed a combat ready position around the perimeter. Any enemy soldiers in the area would have their work cut out for them if they chose to attack, as a tight defense was asserted once the first ship was on the ground. Buffered further with each landing troop, the new landing zone was quickly secured.

Radios, heavy packs and equipment such as chain saws clammered off the ships on the backs, or across the hips of the assaulting troops. A 90mm recoilless rifle was shouldered by a young soldier, who faltered slightly as he jumped from the ship. He recovered and moved to his position on the perimeter.

A tall, charred tree remained standing near the center of the blast, somehow having withstood the impact of the bomb. Nearby were trees lying on the ground, their roots yanked from the ground by the ferocious explosion. A slight indentation in the ground, surrounded by shattered rocks, marked the center of the explosion site.

The last Skytrooper was on the ground, and it was time to move toward their objective. A long trek through the heavy jungle awaited them, but now that they were on the ground in what had become their natural habitat in Vietnam, the soldiers grimaced and smiled at the same time.

Dave Wolfe's story on the C 1/8 Combat Assault (finally) ran in the July 30 Cavalair.

We ate lunch at nearby Bearcat in the exceptional mess hall of 15th TC Battalion. After a delicious meal, we headed to a hospital in the beach resort city of Vung Tau, 55 km south of Bearcat (photo at right). It was a welcome sight to see the ocean again. A Navy ship was firing its guns off the coast to the North.

There were fewer skytroopers here, and they were also in good spirits. Again, I sensed a huge amount of courage. I took more Polaroids and each shot turned out well, so the general was pleased. He gave a print to each of the wounded soldiers. Polaroids were not user-friendly, and the general knew it. He complimented me a couple of times. I was focused, as it was the least I could do to take a quality picture for each of these heroic warriors.

Author's Note: This journal was drawn from the letters I sent home. I didn't tell my family everything, and cause them needless worry. I had visited hospitals with the generals for several months, but never mentioned them in a letter until now. This was my first visit to Vung Tau, and I took several aerial photos to send home.

Next, we flew north to LZ Joy, about 70 km northeast of Bien Hoa. It started to rain so I stayed in the chopper. The general received a briefing from the battalion commander, no photos required. We stopped at Long Binh next, where it was raining heavily, (photo at right) to pick up a General Staff member.

We returned to PV about 5:30 p.m. I had just arrived at the office when eight or ten incoming mortar rounds struck nearby. It surprised everyone, since we rarely had incoming in the daytime. That was it. The NVA knew the radar would pinpoint their location quickly and our artillery would blast their position. It was a reminder to us that they were still out there.

I received a letter from my friend Allan, stationed in Korea. We were trying to coordinate our leaves to Tokyo in September. We planned to buy camera and stereo equipment.

Jun 10 - KP for me today, I arrived early and had the easy job, Dining Room Orderly. Not bad. What could I say? It was still a wasted, but tasty snack-filled day.

NVA Onslaught Fails At LZ

Cavalair

Vol. 3, No. 24   1st Air Cavalry Division   June 11, 1969

Six Hour Battle Rages At Jamie, 2/7 Holds

By CPT Peter Zastrow

LAI KHE—A desperate attempt by North Vietnamese regulars to storm a Cav firebase was repelled by Skytroopers May 11th.

The target was Landing Zone (LZ) Jamie, base camp of the 2nd Battalion, 7th Cavalry. When the sun rose after a furious night, 75 NVA bodies were counted on and around the LZ.

When a trip flare went off near the LZ at 12:45 a.m., no one was surprised. At 1:10 a.m. another trip flare sprang into the night; an observation post reported five individuals lying on the ground. Cavalrymen responded immediately by spraying the area with artillery and organic weapons fire.

At 2:40, the men at LZ Jamie knew the attack was for real. Between then and approximately 3 a.m., some 200 rounds of 107mm rockets and 60 and 82mm mortars slammed into the firebase.

In the midst of this deafening mortar and rocket barrage, the crackling of small arms fire was barely audible. From three sides the North Vietnamese poured toward the perimeter. "Just as the mortars were hitting, sappers blew the wire," said Sergeant Vaughn G. Hood, a squad leader with Company D, 2nd Bn, 7th Cav. "We opened up with M-60's, M-16's and claymores, and the 2nd Bn, 19th Arty fired at Charlie point-blank."

The concentrated enemy fire and the holes in the wire, blown by bangalore torpedoes, allowed the NVA to penetrate the wire and charge three of the perimeter bunkers. "They occupied three bunkers — our men moved in toward the TOC when they saw they would be overrun. There were at least 12 NVA in each bunker," said Sergeant First Class Durwood L. Potts.

Some of the bunkers had been built with cyclone fence surrounding them. "That fence saved our lives," said PFC Larry M. Huff. "The NVA got up to the fence, tried to blow it, but couldn't. We were able to direct mortar fire on the gap in the perimeter wire, and kept on firing all night long."

Atop another bunker was Specialist Four Larry Smet, armed with his M-60 machine gun. Only the machine gun and his hands could be seen over the top of the sandbags as he pumped round after exploding round into the charging enemy soldiers. Inside the bunker, the Skytroopers manning the firing ports shouted directions through the din.

Meanwhile, with the violent sounds of battle all around, three bunkers were filled with NVA. One bunker was decimated by direct 105mm howitzer fire. "There were enemy swarming all over those bunkers," said Specialist Four John W. Brock, "and the '105' just blew them — and the bunker — away."

Another bunker was retaken by the men of the battalion. "There were still a few NVA soldiers left," according to Master Sergeant David A. Vallee. "They threw in frags, and when those didn't do the job we went in and shot them."

Overhead, ARA (aerial rocket artillery) and the Air Force were in constant action. Air strikes and ARA filled the night with "beautiful sounds," in the words of one Skytrooper, and C-119 "Shadow" ships illuminated the night with their flares. Even though all their flares had been expended, and despite the heavy ground-to-air fire bursting around them, the "Shadow" pilots continued to circle the area using their landing lights to provide the needed illumination.

It was 6:15 a.m. before the enemy had had enough and broke contact. Fifty-three NVA were left behind inside the perimeter, and as Delta Company, 2nd Bn, 7th Cav swept around the LZ that day, they found another 22 enemy bodies.

Mongoose, 'Cobra': Pals

BY SP4 Richard Craig

TAY NINH — "Charlie" was determined to penetrate Tay Ninh West, the sprawling home of the Cav's 1st Brigade.

He slowly low-crawled toward the perimeter, his eyes to the front and side looking for signs that his presence might have been detected. As he neared the inner strands of barbed wire, he held his breath while two GIs walked in front, unaware that he was lurking a few feet from their position.

Then, with a burst of speed, he dashed through the flightline and toward the operations bunker. Charlie had passed the first hurdle. The tired old veteran drove on to complete his mission.

To the shock and disbelief of the men of Battery A, 2nd Battalion, 20th Aerial Rocket Artillery, he did.

In what is probably one of the most bizarre surrenders of the Vietnam war, Charlie crawled into the operations bunker, and lay there with a look of resignation on his face, calmly awaiting his fate.

"Charlie" is a very tired old mongoose.

"I was sitting by the radio when I thought I heard a noise behind me," said Sergeant Robert E. Westfall, "so I turned around, and there was this creature in the middle of the floor looking up at me. I started yelling to the office for someone to come and help me figure out what to do."

Just then, Specialist Four Robert M. Ferri and Private First Class Michael E. Gaul burst into the room.

"I looked at Bob, and I could see he was staring at the floor with a dull look on his face," said PFC Gaul. "So I followed his eyes to the floor, and there it was, just lying there."

Immediately a quarrel broke out, as the men tried to determine just what the creature was. PFC Gaul thought it was a skunk. SGT Westfall was certain it was an anteater with a short snout. Someone else thought it was an aardvark.

Just then, the voice of authority walked in. Sergeant First Class George R. Thompson knew what it was the minute he saw it. "It's a mongoose," he said.

Greatly relieved that his identity had been discovered, Charlie let out a hefty sigh.

The men soon decided, after a short period of debate, to let Charlie have a home, right there in the operations bunker. Charlie was so happy you could almost hear him crying.

"Right after he came to us," said SGT Westfall, "we noticed that he looked sort of sick. He'd come over to me and yank at my shoelaces until I got him water. And the only thing he'd eat was crackers and milk."

Concern soon turned to alarm as Charlie began going outside more and more frequently for fresh air. It was obvious that something had to be done, and the men wasted no time in rushing Charlie to the 15th Medical Battalion for the treatment he needed so urgently.

The doctor could hardly control his emotions as he broke the news to the apprehensive Skytroopers.

"Men," he said, "you have a very sick mongoose on your hands. Frankly, I don't think he's going to make it."

With heavy hearts and a fistfull of medication, the men brought Charlie back to the operations bunker.

Realizing that his friends were upset, and not wanting to cause them undue anguish, Charlie quietly expired in the arms of SP4 Ferri on the way back to the unit.

Charlie was a good old mongoose, and his acceptance by the 1st Cavalry's Aerial Rocket Artillery (ARA) unit marked a milestone in mongoose-cobra relations. For even if it is a Huey Cobra attack helicopter unit, it did learn to accept a mongoose as an equal partner.

Today Charlie's final resting place can be seen as you ride through the battalion area. Quietly and unceremoniously, the men have renamed the spot "Mongoose Hill."

229th Business Cards Tout 'Foxhole Service'

TAY NINH — Just like "Have Gun—Will Travel," the television western, the Skytroopers from Company B, 229th Assault Helicopter Battalion have their own business card.

Major Olen D. Thornton, commander of the unit, got the idea of printing the cards from a Skytrooper in his company. "When I came into the unit in December some of my men had these cards," said MAJ Thornton. "One of the officers in the company had a friend who owned a printing press. We sent him a letter and had over 2,000 of the cards made."

Now the commanding officer hands them out to every new member of the company he interviews. He also give the new Skytroopers some extras to give out to their 'customers'.

"We're proud of the job that we are doing," said MAJ Thornton. "And we like to advertise it. We get a charge out of handing them out and so do our 'customers'."

The business card advertises their "foxhole delivery service" at any time of the day, and rice paddy deliveries on call, with foggy peaks by appointment only.

Like any other business listed in the yellow pages of a telephone directory, Co B, 229th AHB is ready and willing.

The Big Gun
A super wide-angle lens makes this self-propelled 175mm gun from Battery C, 6th Battalion, 27th Artillery appear very formidable.
(U.S. Army Photo By SP4 Terry Moon)

Insurance	Page 2
Patrol	Page 3
Point man	Page 3
Pictorial	Pages 4-5
Reunion	Page 6
Wiffle	Page 7
Friendship	Page 8

My super wide angle lens shot of the long 175 mm howitzer was on the front page of the *Cavalair*. The whole barrel was on the negative, they cropped off the top at the photo lab. *Win some, lose some. All four of the angles I took of the 175 mm with the super wide lens would be published.*

Jun 11 - This morning, I wrote captions for prints from other photographer's notes, and logged in several rolls of film. *Now, if the photo lab could only catch up.* I received additional compliments on my combat assault pictures. Major Coleman had shown the photos to several people. *I tried to do the best job I could, it was satisfying to be appreciated.*

More of CA prints had arrived from the lab. They had also been released to the media. Unfortunately, the lab quality was subpar. I was a celebrity now with the General Staff. I presumed Major Coleman had plans in the works for me to photograph more of this type of assignment.

Tonight, I had greenline guard, but only a 12-2 a.m. shift. The sergeant of the guard was in our bunker pulling a shift. *A two-hour shift was much better than a three-hour shift.* Later as I actually slept in the bunker, a not too distant rocket attack didn't awaken me.

June 12 - I slept off guard duty for only a few hours in the morning, since I had miraculously slept in the greenline bunker from 2 to 7 a.m. Then, I rode out into the field with the base camp defense force, D 1/12, referred to as the "Palace Guard." They found last night's rocket launch site. I was interested to see from where the NVA fired the incoming rockets.

DIVARTY had two surveyors who could immediately analyze a rocket impact crater. The rocket had a rod down its center that remained imbedded in the ground after it exploded that showed its angle and direction. The gutsy surveyors would be out searching for craters while more incoming was exploding, and the rest of us were hunkered down in our bunkers. They could determine direction and distance with sophisticated instruments and charts. They would immediately radio the information to the artillery battery on base. The gunners would then pound that area with artillery rounds. This launch site was 11 km northwest of the base. There wasn't much to see at the site. They showed me a charge can from a 107 mm rocket. I visualized how easy it was for the NVA to haul in pieces of the heavy rockets, on bicycles. They assembled them near our base during the night, fired them, and quickly disappeared. Fortunately for us, these rockets were not accurate.

June 13 - The editors had planned to send me on a combat assault with C 2/5 at 9 a.m., but I couldn't find a ride to LZ Ike (25 km north of Tay Ninh) in time. The third wave of CA troops had already left when I finally arrived. Maybe that was lucky, because today was Friday, the thirteenth.

The weather had cooled off, mid 90s in the daytime, and high 70s at night. I felt cold if it was below 80.

Jun 14 - I shot several routine awards ceremonies in the morning, then worked on my R&R tan at lunchtime, and was slightly sunburned. *The sun must be stronger here.*

I received a poem in the mail from Sally, "I Like You" by Sandol Stoddard Warburg. It was just like her. I showed it to some of the guys and one of the clerks typed several copies with carbons. Everyone thought it was impressive.

Our office had a huge party tonight, everyone came in from the Brigades. We had loads of fun. Bill Ellis sang his songs (photo at right). I shot Polaroids of the frivolity, and many group shots of buddies. I gave them out and heard the familiar words, "Thanks, Flash."

CHAPTER NINE GREAT RESPONSE TO MY CA PHOTOS

Jun 15 - This morning, I photographed the opening ceremony for the dedication of a new road, from Phuoc Vinh north to Song Be, built by our 8th Engineers. FNG writer, Tom Benic worked with me. Major Coleman had him transferred to PIO from the orientation center at Bien Hoa, and saved him from being a grunt, for which he was eternally grateful. He had a masters degree in journalism from Northwestern University. Major Coleman had staff members at the replacement center looking for experienced journalists. Tom was an excellent choice.

An ARVN officer displayed a map of the new road, (photo above). After several speeches, hundreds of people lined both sides of the road, and a local dignitary cut the ribbon. The diminutive ARVN color guard with their white leggings, and band (photo above right), marched down the road as the band played "Dixie." It was bizarre, almost comical. A large convoy followed, like a parade. We shot our photos as the trucks and armored vehicles rumbled by, finishing in half an hour. At lunchtime, I continued to work on my R&R tan.

My super-wide shot from the front of the 175 mm gun was in the current *USARV Army Reporter*. Major Coleman was happy. It also appeared in the previous *Cavalair*.

I had greenline guard this evening on bunker 33. The stress was always there. The NVA could show up at any time, but it was quiet. Another hospital tour, with Brig. Gen. Meszar was planned at 10 a.m. the next morning.

Jun 16 - I had just returned from guard duty at 7:30 a.m., and almost made it into bed when they told me the general's schedule had changed. He would leave in half an hour. I quickly grabbed the Graflex XL camera and filled my pants cargo pockets with Polaroid film packs. Then I hurried to the VIP pad, about a half-mile away. The general arrived a few minutes thereafter.

Great Response to my CA Photos

The pilot banks sharply as we arrive at 93rd Evac Hospital in Long Binh.

It was the same tour as last week. First, we visited the 93rd Evac Hospital in Long Binh, then the 36th Evac Hospital in Vung Tau. I found the same spirit and courage as before. Most of these guys just wanted to return to their units. The tour was shorter this time. I napped in the Huey on the flight back. We arrived in Phuoc Vinh at 1 p.m. Then, I made a chart of our photo activities for a briefing Major Coleman would present to the General Staff in the evening.

Jun 17 - On the third order of my combat assault prints from the photo lab, I finally found some extras for myself. Plans were in full swing at home to take care of details for my July 15 R&R in Hawaii. Meanwhile, I diligently worked on my tan.

(U.S. Army Photo By SP4 Terry Moon)

Killer Snake
A deadly Huey Cobra 'air mails' rocket and minigun package to Mr. Chuck during an abortive enemy assault against Camp Gorvad.

Two FNG photographers showed up today, the first ones through regular channels since my arrival last November. Major Coleman had "discovered" a couple of others. These guys would depart to a brigade right away.

My photo of a 2/20 "Blue Max" Cobra firing rockets, taken during my motor drive camera tests, was in the current *Cavalair* (see photo at left).

Jun 18 - I had an artillery job planned today, but was ambushed by KP. They grabbed me at the last minute. *I hate when that happens!* Today, KP was different. In the afternoon, I rode in a three-wheel Lambretta (similar to a golf cart) as two Vietnamese farmers collected garbage in a truck from the several mess halls on base. They operated a 200-pig farm nearby. I must have been there in case they needed extra help, but ended up not doing much. *It wasn't as bad as it sounds.*

PIO's company, 15th Admin (forward), was moving to Bien Hoa, except for PIO (information office) and JAG (legal). We would stay in Phuoc Vinh, and become part of the Division Headquarters Company. Major Coleman was already planning to move the photo lab to PV as a few nearby buildings would be vacant. *What a great idea!*

Two more new photographers arrived today, these FNGs would also be assigned to brigades that were still understaffed. The PV office continued to run smoothly.

A low aerial photo of LZ Dolly as we arrived, two 155 mm howitzers are visible, along with a defense bunker.

Jun 19 - Today was the first part of the 1/30 artillery job for the upcoming quarterly magazine, now known as *FIRST TEAM Magazine*. First stop was picturesque, hilltop LZ Dolly, 40 km west of PV. *I had my own E/82 LOH, just like a VIP.* I photographed the different parts of the 155 crew's firing sequence, while trying to protect my ears. Unfortunately, heavy overcast and rain made photos difficult. There would be better days.

Later, we flew northwest to LZ Jamie, where it was raining harder, (photo below right). We picked up a PIO writer, and returned to PV at 6 p.m. I arrived at the office about ten minutes before it rained like hell.

Jun 20 - We heard this morning that LZ Ike (78 km, northwest of PV) was attacked last night. A company-sized unit from the NVA 1st Sapper Battalion tried to cut through the concertina wire. Perimeter guards from 2/8 heard the cutting and spotted the sappers with a starlight scope. The LZ's mortars then fired illumination rounds. A bangalore torpedo (a long tubular explosive device designed for clearing barbed wire) blew out a section of the perimeter wire. Under additional flares, several sappers were spotted and claymores were detonated. The NVA fired over sixty mortar and RPG rounds at the LZ. Thirty-seven NVA were killed. Fortunately, American casualties were light.

Great Response to my CA Photos

This photo of the crests was the finished product from the Summer 1969 FIRST TEAM Magazine.

Another routine day for me. I photographed several awards, and a company change of command ceremony in the morning.

In the afternoon, I took photos of the several unit crests, on a most appropriate background, one of our precious green towels. I had diligently collected the pins from all the battalions in the division. I used a tissue paper tent around the crests with flood lights shining on each side for diffused lighting, to remove glare from the shiny metal. It would be for a two-page spread in the next magazine.

Jun 22 - Today, I had two different hospital tours. In the morning, I flew to the large 320 bed 24th Evac Hospital in Long Binh, (photo at right), and 36th Evac Hospital at Vung Tau with Brig. Gen. Meszar, shooting Polaroids of him with the wounded soldiers. A few of the guys at Long Binh were in bad shape, waiting to be airlifted to a hospital in Japan. Most of the others were in good spirits. There were only five 1st Cav skytroopers at the Vung Tau hospital, and the tour went quickly. I returned to PV before lunch.

After a quick snack at the mess hall, I had another tour, this time with a twist. Commanding General Roberts was at 25th Infantry Division Headquarters at Cu Chi, so I had to meet him at the 93rd Evac Hospital in Long Binh.

A Medevac Huey arrives at the 15th Med pad in Phuoc Vinh.

The only way I could arrive in time was to fly on a MedEvac Huey taking a patient to the hospital. I called 15th Med and they had a flight leaving in twenty minutes. I hurried and caught the flight. The grunt wasn't severely wounded, was happy to be alive, and bound for the hospital. We talked on the half-hour trip. He noticed the big camera, was interested in photography and asked me the usual question, "How did you get this job?"

I gave him my condensed, well practiced, answer. Upon arrival, the nurses quickly wheeled him into the hospital, while I waited on the helipad.

The CG arrived about twenty minutes later. I followed him around like I always did, and shot Polaroid pictures of the general with the wounded skytroopers. This time he awarded Bronze Stars for Valor, after his aide read the citations. The courageous stories were amazing.

When he came upon an apparently uninjured patient, the CG asked, "Soldier, why are you here?"

The skytrooper smiled, stood up, and proudly exclaimed, "I've got Malaria." No picture for him. The disease could be prevented with medication, and it took gross negligence to catch Malaria. Just before we left, the nurses wheeled in the wounded guy that had accompanied me on the flight. I took the photo as the general awarded him a Purple Heart medal. We exchanged smiles and a thumbs up as I left.

Next, we flew to the 12th Evac Hospital in Cu Chi (25 km northwest of Saigon). The CG paused to speak with his aide outside, so I walked inside. I heard spirited trash talk between the few 1st Cav skytroopers, and most of the others in the room from the 25th Infantry Division. It stopped abruptly as the general entered. He spent time talking with each Cav soldier, presenting medals, and it moved quickly. I remained in the ward for a minute organizing my gear after the CG left. The trash talk resumed where it had left off.

I ran to catch up as the Huey engine whined, and the rotor spun faster, and had just jumped on when they lifted off. It rained most of the afternoon. Weary from the fast-paced pressure of shooting Polaroids for the generals, I napped in the Huey on the long flight back to PV.

Exciting news for me today. I received the actual orders for my R&R in Hawaii, July 12-18. Wow, only nineteen days to go, and, 133 days left until I would leave for home.

Jun 23 - The admin clerks told radio announcer Dave Van Drew, admin clerk Larry Adams and me to fly to Bien Hoa to appear before the E-5 promotion board. *Hooray!* We were overjoyed to be promoted, but we couldn't find a flight, usually an easy task. Finally, after lunch, Dave and I found a ride in a LOH. Upon arriving at Bien Hoa, we hurried to the 15th Admin area. We checked-in, and found they had not received any word or paperwork for us. *What! We thought we were going to be promoted, but not today. I couldn't believe it. What a bummer! Had the papers been lost? Perhaps in PIO's transfer from 15th Admin, to Division Headquarters, or was there a villain?* We caught a ride back to PV, by way of Lai Khe. We never saw Larry.

132 Great Response to my CA Photos

Jun 24 - I had a 7 a.m. job at the division chief of staff's office, but it was cancelled after I arrived, Oh well, I was still depressed from not being promoted.

At 1 p.m., I went on a VIP Tour with a New Mexico radio executive, a friend of Vice President Spiro Agnew.

Later, I listened to AFVN-FM radio on Ron Doss' stereo with his new earphones. The sound was amazing, my head was filled with music.

After dinner, Major Coleman entered the press/photo office with a big smile, waving a newspaper. He showed me my medic photo from the combat assault on the front page of the latest *USARV Army Reporter*. (See photo at right.) He was delighted and slapped me on the back.

"The CG will love this," he said, almost laughing. I received numerous congratulations during the next few days. It was always a big deal for the whole division when our pictures made it into the larger publications, but to be on the front page was extra special.

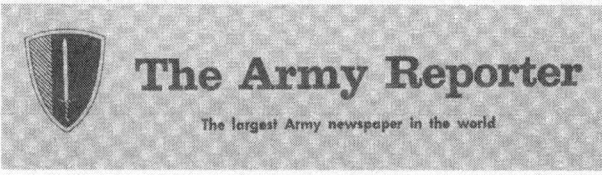

Later, an overflow crowd fit tightly in and around the TV bunker. Roars of laughter and assorted guffaws invigorated the quiet evening. *Laugh-In* was hilarious, you bet your sweet bippy. *It was pleasant to have a brief escape from the reality of where we were, and what was going on around us.*

Jun 25 - It was a long, busy day. A promotional tour was arranged by Major Coleman and Commanding General Roberts for Marilyn Genz, a TWA senior flight attendant. For the last three years, she had worked the somber flights to, and the jubilant flights from, Vietnam. She wore a smock covered with unit crest pins from all over Vietnam. Returning grunts had shared many stories with her. Maj. Gen. Roberts met Marilyn on one flight, they talked, exchanged letters and he arranged the tour. She had also worked out of Hawaii on R&R flights. We had interesting conversations, as mine would begin in seventeen days.

A mortarman at LZ Ike showed Marilyn how they figure direction for shooting the mortar.

An A 1/77th 105 mm artillery crew gave her a briefing on how they did a fire mission at LZ Jamie.

In the morning, we toured the Phuoc Vinh base camp, with stops at 15th Med, 8th Engineers, and a visit to a greenline bunker with the 2/12 base defense force. After lunch, we took a long flight to LZ Ike for a mortar demonstration. The team went through the entire sequence, from aiming to firing. Next, our Huey flew to LZ Jamie for her to witness firing of a 105 mm howitzer. The skilled 105 crew presented an impressive demonstration of teamwork. She enjoyed her time with the wisecracking artillerymen. We spent about an hour and a half at each LZ. It rained lightly several times, which minimized the dust from the helicopters. Motion picture photographer Haddon Hufford and new PIO Lieutenant Allison, the escort officer, accompanied me. I also shot a few photos with Marilyn's twin-lens Yashica D camera. I ran around as we covered interesting activities. I was fascinated with how they aimed the mortars, having been on the wrong end of mortar fire. We were scheduled to do more of the same the next day. I crashed early in my bunk, and slept well.

June 26 - Day two of the TWA tour started early. First, we flew to LZ Betty (19 km southwest of PV) where a tear gas grenade was accidentally set off. Everyone was affected, except Hufford and me, as we were upwind. Marilyn was a good sport, so we setup a gag picture with a gas mask.

She tiptoes through the mud at LZ White. If it hadn't rained she would have been sandblasted by the Chinooks.

Next, we flew to muddy LZ White, where she talked with several 2/8 grunts who had just returned from the field. From there, we made a short hop to hilltop LZ Dolly, to examine a display of captured weapons. Nearby, we listened to the entertaining music of a 2/5 grunt folksinger. The spectacular view of Nui Ba Den Mountain dominated the LZ's western horizon. A festive lunch followed at Lai Khe, where the 2nd Brigade Headquarters Staff presented her with a "Chieu Hoi" T-shirt.

Just before we arrived at Phuoc Vinh, something went wrong with our Huey. We learned later the throttle stuck and over-revved the turbine engine, a freak malfunction. A maintenance crew would later run tests on it. Colonel Foy Rich, Division Aviation Officer, had been our pilot for the morning. At PV, a new pilot and Huey flew us to Quan Loi, where Marilyn had a 3rd Brigade operations briefing, while Hufford and I briefly visited our PIO guys. Later, we rode to the 11th Armored Cavalry Headquarters, where we photographed her on an armored personnel carrier.

Nearby, there had been a cobra crash. The rotor had hit a revetment (a barrier that protected parked helicopters), flipped the cobra over on its side, and somehow fired several rockets into an unoccupied plantation house, putting big holes in the thick concrete and brick walls. Groups of guys were standing around it talking and pointing. One of our photographers would be called to photograph the scene for Aircraft Accident Investigation Board.

We flew south to show her a B-52 strike, but as usual, it was too hazy, and dangerous to fly close to the blasts. Our Huey needed fuel so we stopped at nearby Dau Tieng, east of Tay Ninh. After the long return flight, the tour ended at PV.

Two goodie packages arrived today, but I didn't have time to open them. Greenline guard for me tonight. I quickly gathered my gear and went to Bunker 33. We had the most violent rain storm any of us had ever experienced. It was brutal sitting on top of the bunker getting blasted by the powerful gusts while trying to see beyond the wire. I was totally soaked and freezing. My poncho caught the wind a couple of times, and it blew me off the bunker. Tree branches were tossed into the wire, setting off trip flares. The squall lasted several hours. It was total misery as we stayed in the bunker and didn't get any sleep. We hoped the NVA had more trouble with the weather than we did.

Jun 27 - I collapsed into my bunk, and woke up after lunch. It took a while to wash the mud off my guard fatigues and gear. Then I dried them with the fan.

The first four of my combat assault pictures were featured in this week's *Cavalier*. Page one had grunts jumping out of the Huey, on page three the medic rushed to help. Page six had the Hueys arriving at LZ Rock, and the dramatic mail call shot was on page eight. People I didn't know would see my camera and name tag now, and tell me they liked my photos in the *Cavalair. It always made my day.*

No longer would we pull greenline guard duty, as short-timer grunts would take over this vital task. *What a great idea!* I had the dubious distinction of being the last one from PIO to pull greenline guard duty on one of the most miserable, worst weather nights we ever experienced.

Great Response to my CA Photos

Jun 28 - I left early and went to LZ Grant with Brig. Gen. Meszar for a Presidential Unit Citation presentation to Battery B, 1/30 Artillery (155s). Battalion Commander Lt. Col. Wilson met us at 6:30 a.m. It was almost too dark for photos, but I had fast black and white film and it handled the low-light situation.

In the evening, I took photos of several awards at the CG's mess. It had become a fun job as General Staff members made comments and asked questions about my photos in the *USARV Army Reporter* and the *Cavalair*. As usual, excellent food was served, top quality steaks with all the trimmings. I had a loaded plate with my kitchen friends. *I remembered the first time I was here with my predecessor, Fred. He was right when he told me. "This is a great job."*

Jun 29 - KP today, but the mess sergeant was gone, so it allowed me to catch up on office work for a short time after lunch. It was much cooler today, the high 80s, and of course, it rained every afternoon. Meanwhile, I had caught a cold. Being totally soaked in the howling wind on guard duty would do it to anyone. I walked to the medics, they gave me two medications, checked my immunization record, and gleefully gave me a couple of shots.

For the second straight week, one of my pictures, the fully loaded grunt from C 1/8 CA was in the *USARV Army Reporter* (photo at right).

Jun 30 - Ron Doss, our staff artist, now had his stereo components set up, so we were able to play records. I lent him money to help buy the Pioneer speakers at the PX. *What a great investment!* When electronic equipment went on the shelf at the PX in Phuoc Vinh, it was snapped up immediately. It was exciting to have real music that we could all enjoy.

Jul 1 - I caught an early flight to Bien Hoa for a VIP tour with three gorgeous girls. *Wow! Can you believe this?* From there, we flew to several LZs. Former Miss California, Marsha Bennett, was clad in a jaw-dropping gold mini dress. *That revved up everybody.* Olympic Gold Medal swimmer Donna DeVarona, a sharp girl, was tall and muscular. Former Miss Indiana, Arlene Charles (Charley), looked stunning in a casual purple dress. Guys scrambled to see the girls, whistles and hoots greeted their arrival. All day, it was only an escort officer and me, touring with them, and their wisecracking DJ announcer. No one paid much attention to him. We left on a Huey headed for the first of three LZs.

    The girls thoroughly enjoyed their tour and we had a great time. When they realized I could answer most of their questions, they asked me more. Donna asked insightful questions. At the LZs, I shot numerous pictures, but I was probably in hundreds of photos taken by other guys. Grunts were climbing anything to get a better look. Countless times during the day, I heard, with various expletives,"You lucky SOB, how did you get this job?" Everyone smiled and laughed, an amazing day! *A brief reminder of the distant world we used to know and how anxious we were to return.*

    A big package of cookies from Grandma Miller arrived in the mail, a tasty ending to a fantastic day.

138   Great Response to my CA Photos

Marsha and Donna at Bien Hoa

Charlie riding with me in a jeep

July 2, 1969 — THE CAVALAIR — Page 3

Army's Largest To Split
15th TC Bn Decentralizes

PHUOC VINH — Quietly, efficiently and without fanfare the Army's largest battalion — the 15th Transportation Battalion — is being phased into a conventional-sized unit.

Concurrently, the division's aircraft maintenance concept is being dramatically altered from a centralized to a completely decentralized system. Moreover, even as this massive alteration of maintenance posture is being conducted, THE FIRST TEAM is continuing its assigned combat missions while still retaining a high aircraft availability rate.

Organization

The man credited with organizing this massive shift of personnel and equipment is Lieutenant Colonel Albert W. Schlim, whose most recent position in the division was Deputy Assistant Chief of Staff (G-4) for Aircraft Maintenance. It was in this capacity the final planning of the shift to decentralized maintenance was accomplished. But it was as commander of the 15th Transportation Battalion that LTC Schlim began the serious planning steps that were to place him in the curious position of presiding over the liquidation of his empire.

According to LTC Schlim, the 15th TC Bn will be reduced from a 1,500-man, four-company unit to a two-company unit, with the bulk of its maintenance forces allocated into 19 maintenance detachments. Each company-battery-troop sized unit will receive a specialized direct support maintenance detachment.

The batteries of the 20th Artillery, for example, will receive a detachment that specializes in Cobra maintenance; while one of the air troops of the 1st Squadron, 9th Cavalry will need a detachment that could maintain Hueys and LOHs as well as Cobras.

The personnel for these detachments largely will be peeled out of the organic resources of the 15th TC Bn., but according to LTC Schlim, some personnel augmentation has been or will be needed. The major input into the division has been in the realm of tools, tool kits and publications.

Some of the line items represent more than meets the eye. The new shop set, which LTC Schlim said contains some new and exotic maintenance equipment not now in the 1st Cav, has an inventory list of component parts that totals 50 typewritten pages. These shop sets are now on hand in the division and will be assigned to each maintenance detachment when it is activated.

The activation of each detachment and the concurrent reorganization of the 15th TC Bn., is to be effected over a carefully planned time phase schedule, LTC Schlim said. The first units affected are the companies of the 228th Assault Support Helicopter Battalion, which were to have received their maintenance detachments during the first week of June. The bulk of the personnel and equipment assets for this phase will come from the existing Company A, 15th TC.

Phases

September 30 there are a total of seven phases.

At that time, the 15th TC will have two companies that will provide backup maintenance for the detachments that are unable, for whatever reason, to handle a high volume of business. In addition, each of the companies will provide direct support maintenance for the divisional units that own aircraft, but do not have them in sufficient numbers to justify a separate maintenance detachment.

By the time the transition has been completed, the division's direct support maintenance personnel picture will have shown an increase of 195 spaces, or a total of 1,625 men devoted to keeping the birds of THE FIRST TEAM flying.

The concept of decentralized direct support maintenance had its inception at Department of the Army about three years ago, LTC Schlim said, and gradually has moved down through the echelons to field units. The 1st Cav actually is the last major unit in Vietnam to effect a changeover, he said, but THE FIRST TEAM is the first to make the transition while fully engaged in combat operations.

The 101st Airborne Division (Airmobile) also has "transitioned" into the decentralized concept, he said, but it was able to do it while attaining its aircraft and aircraft maintenance assets during its organization as an airmobile division.

Four Objectives

When LTC Schlim began serious planning toward implementation of the decentralized concept, he received solid guidance from the division command group. The implementation had to meet four objectives:

1. It had to be set up on a time phase plan.
2. There had to be a minimum delay between detachment activation and effectiveness.
3. There was to be no degradation in aircraft availability rates.
4. There was to be no degradation in direct support maintenance.

The division's maintenance officers will closely analyze the operation of the concept during the summer and early fall. Then, LTC Schlim said, a position paper will be forwarded to USARV maintenance elements, listing the division's recommendations for any alterations that may be needed to make the basic concept more effective.

(U.S. Army Photo By SP4 Terry Moon)

Ridin' Shotgun
A shotgun-wielding Skytrooper from the 1st Battalion, 8th Cavalry leads his comrades into battle near Xuan Loc.

(U.S. Army Photo By SP4 Terry Moon)

Contemplation
A Cavalryman from the 1st Battalion, 8th Cavalry stops for a brief moment and takes a pensive look at the war before going on with his mission.

First Shirt Offers Free Frosties

BLACKHORSE — If you have more than nine years of service in the 1st Cav, you've got a free, tall, cold beer coming.

A First Sergeant with the 3rd Brigade is offering that thirst quencher to the man who can top or equal his time with the 1st Cav.

The chilled nectar of hops will be given by First Sergeant Normand A. Madore, "first shirt" for Headquarters and Headquarters Company, 3rd Brigade.

When he finishes this year's tour of Vietnam with the Garry Owen Brigade, 1SG Madore will have completed 10 years with the Cav and 30 years in the Army.

And he's not finished yet.

With 29 years of service to date, 1SG Madore said, "I'm thinking of making a career out of the Army."

First Sergeant Madore was first assigned to the division in 1952 when it was in Japan. "That was some time before the Cav became airmobile," he recalled.

"The airmobile concept is a tremendous thing," he said. "Young men in the Cav today don't know what it was like in the old Cav. You used to have to walk to the hill and then climb it. Now you've just dropped on top of it."

1SG Madore was with the 5th Cavalry in Japan until 1955.

After a few months, the 5th Cavalry and there 1SG Madore rejoined his unit. For the next eight years he alternated between Korea and Ft. Dix, N.J.

In 1957, in honor of his Cav tenure and enthusiasm, he was named "Mr. 1st Cav."

Altogether, he spent 72 months — six years — with the 5th Cav in Korea. That brings his total 1st Cav time to nine years. He's working on his tenth year now.

First Sgt Madore will accept challenges to his Cav tenure from any active duty soldier now assigned to the division.

If you think you can collect that cold beer, 1SG Madore can be found at HHC, 3rd Bde.

Cries Of 'Incoming' Change To 'Timber' For Blackhorses

By Sp4 George Vindedzis

LAI KHE — Quiet nightfall settled over the basecamp of the 2nd Brigade at Lai Khe. Wind rustled gently through the trees overhead.

Suddenly the silence broke. Snap, crack, smash — incoming?

Not really. Only incoming trees.

As it true of many of the basecamp areas of the Cav, the 2nd Brigade is located in the midst of what was once a rubber plantation. This one, however, is different. An experiment in growing a new type of hybrid rubber tree was undertaken and the plantation was eventually closed down when it became obvious the experiment failed. The trees, without warning, sometimes snap off at the base and thunder to the ground — or, in some cases, onto the nearest tent. Various attempts to bind up the trees have not yet succeeded.

Like most problems encountered by the men of the 1st Cav, what looks like a disadvantage is turned to good use. The men of Headquarters and Headquarters Company are becoming experts in tree climbing, tree cutting — and in learning to predict where the next tree will collapse.

So, along with the other hazards in Vietnam, there is now the added incoming-tree. After all, it's a hardship tour.

Jul 2 - Five more of my pictures were in the current *Cavalair*, including the skytrooper with the shotgun riding on the skid, the fully loaded grunt (photo above). Another wide-angle shot appeared of the 175 mm howitzer, from the

140   Great Response to my CA Photos

back (photo to the right). Captions kept me busy on the several TWA tour photos for promotional release.

A letter arrived today from Sally, the Hawaiian R&R plans were almost completed. The date change from the eighteenth to the twelfth was a slight glitch, but she adjusted. The hotel reservations and the rental car were set. She had friends there, and they would help us make the most of our short time. Enclosed in the letter was a picture of herself in a bridesmaid's dress, with a note on the back, "This is not a hint." *But, it was.*

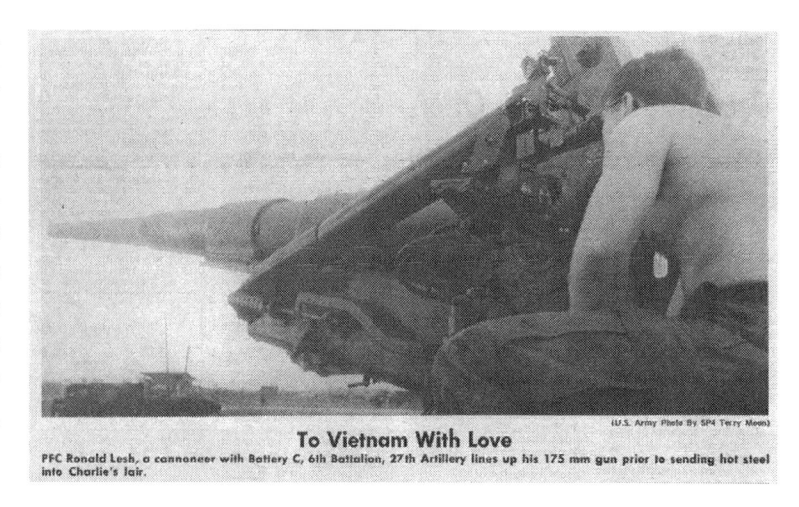

To Vietnam With Love
PFC Ronald Lesh, a cannoneer with Battery C, 6th Battalion, 27th Artillery lines up his 175 mm gun prior to sending hot steel into Charlie's lair.
(U.S. Army Photo By SP4 Terry Moon)

Jul 3 - Two routine awards ceremonies started my morning. A couple of guys recognized my name tag and said they liked my photos in the *Cavalair*. This happened frequently now, and it always made my day. One of the guys added, "By the way, how did you get this great job?"

What! It didn't rain today, how strange.

Defensive bunkers on the perimeter of LZ Dolly as we arrive.

Jul 5 - Not much was scheduled, so I found a flight out to LZ Dolly. On arrival I talked with several artillerymen and grunts. One recognized my name tag and said, "You took the shotgun picture, right?" I smiled and nodded. "I'll be right back," A minute or so later he proudly showed me his shotgun, and said, "I ride in on combat assaults just like your picture." After an hour, when a ride became available, I returned to PV. It was a fun break from the office.

Ron Doss received his record albums in the mail today, including The Moody Blues, Jimi Hendrix, Traffic, Creedence Clearwater Revival, and others. Of course, that called for a party. I set up the slide projector with a red filter over the lens, made a cardboard disk with a hole cut in it and taped it to the blades of a fan. We had our own flashing, red strobe-light. Everyone loved the psychedelic vibe, with more solo dancing than usual. Ron Doss had his own dance, somewhere between crawling on the floor and doing push-ups. He called it "The Gator." It fit well with "Born on a Bayou," by CCR. The new music was welcome, and a great time was had by all.

Jul 7 - A VIP tour for Representative George Cleveland of New Hampshire was my morning assignment. We flew to LZ Wescott between Quan Loi and Song Be. I photographed the member of congress talking with the grunts, as he toured the LZ. They showed him how to shoot an M79 grenade launcher. Thankfully, no one was hurt. Meanwhile, Brig. Gen. Meszar puffed on his cigar, (see photo at right).

A high aerial photo (to the right) of LZ Wescott taken on a good day, as Nui Ba Ra Mountain, near Song Be, loomed in the distance through the haze.

It continued to rain most of the time. We departed for a long flight southwest to LZ Grant. Uncomfortably close, green tracers from antiaircraft fire streaked by our Huey along the way. We weren't hit, but there was no place to hide. At LZ Grant, the congressman only had a briefing, and having seen the close tracers earlier, we assumed he wanted to return to a safer area.

When I returned to the office, Sgt.1st Class DeGard had set up a flight for me in the gunner's seat of a Blue Max Cobra gunship. He did helpful and fun things like this for us. I walked over to 2/20, climbed in and the pilot closed the canopy over us. The gunship was so quiet inside (see photo below right). The pilot pulled some stunts, trying to scare me. I expected this, it happened frequently, but it was an exhilarating ride. The DIVARTY staff appreciated my setting up the magazine story on the 155 howitzers. They were my friends, and I often caught rides with their E/82 Hueys and LOHs.

Jul 8 - After one award ceremony in the morning, I processed work orders and logged in film during the afternoon. There were administrative duties included besides my shooting pictures. This also was an enjoyable part of my duties. I saw most of the shots taken by the photographers. I could shoot photos during the day and catch up on the administrative stuff in the evening. It was like two separate jobs. Phil did a large amount of work, and preferred to be busy.

Jul 9 - I endured KP again today. My promotion should come through soon. As a Spec. 5, I would no longer have KP.

142 Great Response to my CA Photos

Page 6 — THE CAVALAIR — July 9, 1969

At LZ Jamie
Clear Head Keeps Skytroopers Alive

By SP4 George Vindedzis

LAI KHE — Three men of Company E, 2nd Battalion, 7th Cavalry lay silently alert on a lonely LP (listening post) as their eyes scanned the darkness.

Suddenly one of them spotted movement and called the CP (command post) for permission to fire. Permission was granted, but as the men scurried for cover behind a mound of dirt, one of them accidentally set off a trip flare and the enemy slipped away into the darkness.

The three men, pinned down by enemy mortar fire, lay silently and prayed as the explosions sent shrapnel zipping over their heads. Then a blanket of stillness again covered the dark jungle as the firing ceased.

"I had made it through the mortar barrage okay," said the 20-year-old Skytrooper, "but the other two men were hurt pretty badly. I called for permission to come in but they said someone had to stay out there to watch for the enemy."

At first light the cavalryman spotted men on patrol and beckoned to them for assistance. After they got back to the 2nd Brigade LZ, the two wounded men were MEDEVACKED and PFC Respress learned that the trip flare that accidently ignited had served as an early warning signal for the men of the LZ.

Later that morning Major General E.B. Roberts, commanding general of the 1st Cav., visited the LZ. When he heard of PFC Respress' actions he presented him the Bronze Star with "V" device as an immediate impact award.

Cobra's Ammo Bay Saves Wounded Troop

TAY NINH — The heavily armed Cobra gunships are not usually associated with missions of mercy. An ingenious pilot, however, proved their versatility when he rescued a wounded man from a downed observation helicopter.

"I saw the LOH taking small arms and automatic weapons fire," said Cobra pilot, Captain Richard K. Rowe. "It was forced down in tall elephant grass about 300 meters from 40 or 50 NVA who were firing from trenches."

Warrant Officer Robert Larson, flying another LOH, landed right behind the crippled chopper. "When I got there several small fires had broken out in the area. My door gunner got off and we loaded two of the wounded men on my ship. The door gunner stayed on the ground with the other wounded man," said WO Larson.

CPT Rowe made a quick pass over the area in his gunship. "I tried to release my rocket pods but only one came off. When I landed, the remaining men quickly got over to my ship. I opened the ammo bay doors and they climbed in," he said.

The ammunition bay, which normally accommodates thousands of rounds of minigun ammunition had been emptied in the course of the heavy contact leaving an area about the size of a steamer trunk into which the men squeezed themselves.

"They hung on until I could get them to Landing Zone Ike, about two miles away," said CPT Rowe. At LZ Ike, the wounded men were transferred to a MEDEVAC helicopter and were soon on their way to the hospital.

Blues Strip Red Site, Bare NVA

By SP4 Bob Smith

TAY NINH — A number of enemy soldiers were forced to expose themselves recently by members of the infantry platoon (Blues), 1st Squadron, 9th Cavalry. The "Blues" substantially reduced Chuck's clothing inventory when they discovered a cache and bunker complex north of Landing Zone Grant.

"We found over 250 pairs of fatigues, 200 pairs of black pajamas, and more than 200 pairs of shorts and underwear," First Lieutenant Robert B. Alexander, the "Blues" platoon leader said. "In addition to clothing we found 300 spools of thread, over 50 meters of cloth, some electrical wire and one sewing machine," he added.

The 21-man platoon combat assaulted into an area about 20 miles northeast of here after 1st Squadron scout birds (light observation helicopters) discovered the complex. The Skytroopers neared their objective after a two hour push in heavy jungle terrain from their landing zone.

The cavalrymen noticed immediately that the enemy had constructed bamboo hootches with tin roofs in the center of the complex. One of the buildings stood out like a sore thumb.

"It had two floors," the unit's platoon sergeant, Staff Sergeant George B. Busch, Jr. said. "The first floor was partially below ground level. The building was made out of the same material as the other hootches, but it was heavily camouflaged and easy to pick out. The first floor appeared to be a work area and had electric lights. The second floor was a storage area," he added.

The building and its contents were destroyed by incendiary grenades. As the "Blues" pulled out of the area air strikes were called in to complete the job.

"Here I Come..."

A machine gunner from the 1st Battalion, 8th Cavalry leaps to the ground during a combat assault near Xuan Loc. (U.S. Army Photo By SP4 Terry Moon)

Wet, Cold All Part Skytrooper's Life

By CPT Peter Zastrow

LAI KHE — Company C, 1st Battalion, 5th Cavalry was scheduled to combat assault (CA) at 10 a.m. This would give them time to find a night location and set up before the afternoon rains began.

Water in the helicopter fuel delayed the CA until 4 o'clock. As the men of the company jumped off the last lift, the rains followed them into the grassy clearing.

When a company has to move from the landing zone, and the rain is streaming from the sky, there is only one thing a Skytrooper can do: get wet. When he turns his head, trickles of water roll down inside his shirt. If he tries to light a cigarette, it crumbles in his hand.

There were attempts to keep dry. One man pulled out a raincoat which helped slightly. Others made sure their gear was wrapped in plastic bags, but within half an hour, everyone was wet. The muddy trails through the bamboo grew waterlogged, and the craters left by an old B-52 strike became sizable lakes.

The packs, heavy enough when dry, grew heavier. It didn't help to stop and rest since that only meant more water and more weight.

Most of the men of Company C said that the rain felt good — even though they had just been in on the firebase and didn't need a shower yet. But jungle fatigues, even though quick-drying, can't dry when the rain is still falling.

Finally, with mud-caked boots adding several pounds, the men found a FOB (forward operations base) position. And the rain slacked off to a hard drizzle.

No longer were the men of Company C faced with the problems of keeping dry — it was too late for that. Now the problem was how to keep from getting any wetter during the night. Cutting through dripping vines and knocking wet bamboo out of the way, men tied poncho roofs to the trees, stretched out wet towels and shirts over wet leaves, and inflated damp air mattresses.

Night settled quickly and through the dark hours the slow drip of the trees sang a Skytroopers' lullaby.

Dawn, and it was time to wring out socks before putting them back on. Tee-Shirts were almost dry, but there was still the painful experience of putting on the soggy fatigue shirt. Captain Clearence W. Kehoe, out in the field for the first time in command of Company C had his RTO hold one end of his towel while he squeezed out streams of water.

Still damp, the company moved out. Soon, the sun came out and the water turned slowly to steam. Now only pockets were wet — and of course boots, since the rain had left ample puddles.

Often movement stopped as the lead platoon had to cut through the dense undergrowth. The men watched the sides of the trail, sat back on their packs, and sweated.

The company found a FOB position early. "Today," said CPT Kehoe, "we're going to set up before the rain."

Pumping 'Em Out...

Making life miserable for Charlie is an artillery crew from the 1st Battalion, 30th Artillery as they ram another projectile into their 155mm howitzer. (U.S. Army Photo By SP4 Terry Moon)

The current *Cavalair* had four more of my photos, three combat assault shots, including the M60 machine gunner who jumped early out of the Huey, and I caught a photo of him in midair, and a 155 crew in action from LZ Grant (photo above).

My name tag continued to be recognized. I received compliments about my photos in the newspapers. The "How did you get this job?" question was asked frequently. I loved it. The shotgun picture was popular, and many proud grunts carried shotguns, it was like a brotherhood. I would find when I walked around an LZ, a grunt would see my name tag and tell me someone wanted to meet me. He would bring a friend with his shotgun to shake my hand. One grunt showed me the "Duckbill" choke on his shotgun. It would scatter the shot in a horizontal pattern, making it much more effective. *I thoroughly enjoyed my newfound "fame."*

Jul 10 - My record albums arrived in the mail today, The Rolling Stones, The Yardbirds, The Lovin' Spoonful, and The New Christy Minstrels, to name a few. Now we had a wider variety of music. Of course, that called for a party. *But, I have a much more important reason to celebrate. Tomorrow, I leave for R&R.*

Jul 11 - I caught an 8 a.m. prearranged flight to Bien Hoa, with a suitcase borrowed from Chuck Spicer. I stayed at the photo lab and would report to the R&R center at 7 a.m. the next day. Filled with anticipation, sleep was elusive.

Jul 12 - I left early, and reported to the Bien Hoa R&R center. I started processing out for departure. This was well planned and it went smoothly. I waited, along with many others, in the photo to the right. Finally, we caught a bus to Camp Alpha at Tan Son Nhut Airport. The 707 took off at 6:55 p.m.

Jul 12 - We crossed the International Dateline, so today was still the twelfth. Upon arrival in Hawaii, we went to the terminal and found our bags. In a brief orientation, the staff informed us of the rules that we had to follow. Then we walked down an aisle between hundreds of screaming women looking for their soldiers. There were hugs breaking out all around me. Finally, I saw Sally and enjoyed my own hug. She had a hotel room for us at the Outrigger on Waikiki, so we went there, talked for a while, and shared quality time together. The R&R rate was $17.50 a night. She said she had been listening to Sinatra's "Fly Me to the Moon" for the last week.

Jul 13-16 - Sally and I drove around the coast of Oahu, stopping numerous times to admire romantic views and take short walks. I had bought a camera for her and had a wonderful time teaching her how to use it. A long walk along Makaha beach was delightful. Unfortunately, it was the wrong time of year to see the giant surf at Waimea Bay. The big Kahana Park on the other side of the island was our next stop. We saw the Crouching Lion near the Polynesian Center and made it out to Koko Head. It was fun to walk on some of the famous beaches, one in the moonlight. Other evenings, we saw shows at some of the hotels, including a Tommy Sands rock show and a romantic Lou Rawls show. The Don Ho "Tiny Bubbles" show was in the International Market Place.

The time went by too quickly, and was a blur. I called home three times from Hawaii, and talked to everyone in the family, including several friends that were at the house. It was an intensely emotional few days. Sally and I talked about our future. I still had more than three months to serve in Vietnam before returning home for a six-week leave. Then I would report to my next duty station which could be anywhere in the U.S.

Jul 17 - I bought Sally a beautiful Hawaiian dress and she bought me a matching shirt. She continued to have fun taking pictures with her new camera. We were acquiring a taste for passion fruit soda.

Jul 18 - Sally looked lovely in the new dress she wore when I had to leave, it was still a depressing moment. Returning to Vietnam was one of the toughest challenges I had ever faced. She cried a lot and I almost did also, a total emotional reversal from the arrival here six short days ago. A dark cloud enveloped us, and stayed with me until I woke up as the plane prepared to land.

144   Great Response to my CA Photos

GI Combat Toll Drops as War Lull Continues

By JO2 DAVE WARSH
S&S Staff Correspondent

SAIGON — U.S. combat deaths in Vietnam have held at a six-month low for the second week according to figures released Thursday by the U.S. Command.

Officials said 148 GIs died on the battlefield last week, three less than the week before and the fewest since the week ending Jan. 4, 1969, when 101 Americans died during a post-Christmas lull.

But the deaths brought to more than 37,000 the number of American dead in the eight-year war; about 43,000 when deaths that did not result from battle are included.

The latest figures compared with an average of about 240 deaths weekly for the first six months of 1969 and confirmed the existence of a "lull" in the level of fighting in Vietnam.

Last week 1,612 Americans were wounded.

Despite the low level of contact between opposing armies, knowledgeable sources still look for renewed fighting in parts of Vietnam.

In the vital 11 provinces surrounding Saigon, Allied defenses continued to shift slightly, adjusting to intelligence reports on Communist movements.

Singled out for special attention were two areas in the III Corps 10,000 square mile military district around the capital and one on the northern edge of Mekong Delta.

Well-informed sources have repeatedly identified the provincial capital of Tay Ninh City, 50 miles northwest of Saigon, as the Reds' chief objective. Another suspected trouble spot is the An Loc — Loc Ninh region 60 miles north of the capital and only a few miles from Communist bastions across the Cambodian border.

A third possible objective is Chau Doc, upper Mekong Delta city about 115 miles west of Saigon in IV Corps and barely two miles from the Cambodian border.

Nearly a full regiment of North Vietnamese soldiers — the 273rd — has been reliably reported moving into IV Corps, where military operations have traditionally been left almost entirely to the native Viet Cong.

Militia camps including Chau Doc along the Cambodian border, advised by U.S. Green Berets, are bristling with reconnaissance activity.

But officials discount low-level intelligence reports that the Communists hope to sieze a major community — Tay Ninh or An Loc or Chau Doc — and hold it for as briefly as 48 hours to declare it the seat of the new "provisional revolutionary government" of the Viet Cong.

The officials believe the Communist forces — if indeed they succeeded in taking a city in the first place — would be quickly ousted. They think it unlikely the Viet Cong would risk such an embarrassment as finding their "government" suddenly without a capital.

These same analysts consider it more likely that the Communists will again move into an "action phase" — or rash of overnight shellings and sporadic ground assaults — perhaps before the end of July.

The sources believe the Reds' ability to carry through any offensive has diminished. They say the intensity of the June 5-6 action phase, when 100 GIs died in 48 hours, was about half that of the May 11-12 high point, when 208 Americans were killed.

But the sources credit the Communists with the ability to extract at least the toll taken by their June wave of attacks.

Report Full N. Viet Division, 60 Russ Tanks Invading Laos

VIENTIANE, Laos (UPI) — A full division of North Vietnamese "mountaineer" troops behind 60 Russian tanks was reported pouring into northern Laos Thursday. Laotian commanders said the situation was deteriorating rapidly.

The National Assembly convened in Vientiane in an atmosphere of crisis.

Some Laotian officials said the North Vietnamese might be part of an overall scheme in which the Pathet Lao, Laos' equivalent of the Viet Cong, would try to establish a provisional revolutionary government.

There were reports of new fighting around Muong Soui, a Laotian stronghold which fell to North Vietnamese and Pathet Lao forces 2 1-2 weeks ago. Military sources said at least 500 pro-government neutralist troops had thrown down their weapons and deserted in the past three weeks.

Gen. Oudone Sananikone, the Laotian chief of staff, said the North Vietnamese division—up to 12,000 men—had entered Laos and was approaching the strategic Plain of Jars.

The Russian tanks were identified as amphibious PT76's, a model which has been seen in South Vietnam.

Oudone quoted Gen. Vang Pao, commander of Laotian forces in the northern provinces, as saying that his troops were no match for the modern Communist weapons of the fresh mountain units moving into the area.

Viets Kill 50 Reds; GIs Repulse Attack

By SPEC. 5 ERIC JOHNS
S&S Staff Correspondent

SAIGON — Vietnamese troops killed 50 Communist soldiers in clashes about 50 miles southwest of Saigon Wednesday and GIs repulsed several Viet Cong sappers who tried to break into their brigade base camp on Vietnam's central coastline, military officials said.

But ground fighting occurred only sporadically elsewhere, with no American deaths reported by U.S. military spokesmen in Saigon. Fifteen enemy indirect fire attacks were reported in the 24-hour period ending at 8 a.m. Thursday.

Twenty-seven Reds were killed in the Mekong Delta fighting during scattered afternoon contacts with infantrymen of the ARVN 7th Div. in Vinh Binh Province. Friendly casualties were light.

Early Wednesday morning, Americal Div. soldiers killed six Reds as they repulsed a light attack on their 11th Light Inf. Brigade headquarters near Duc Pho, about 100 miles south of Da Nang.

Radar picked up movement around the base, called Landing Zone Bronco, about 2 a. m., and gun crews lashed out with more than 900 rounds of mortar fire. The sappers, who apparently infiltrated the area as farmers, got close enough to toss grenades at perimeter bunkers, but only two GIs were lightly wounded in the 30-minute probe.

Spokesmen said 10 of the 15 rocket and mortar attacks reported caused casualties or damage. Two shellings were aimed at U.S. troops, but neither caused casualties.

NVA Beat, Hurt GI

By SPEC 4. RON MINNIX
S&S Staff Correspondent

SAIGON — A wounded American prisoner held captive by the North Vietnamese may have been clubbed to near death rather than allowed to fall into the hands of rescuers, according to reliable sources.

Spec. 4 Larry D. Aiken, rescued from Communist troops July 10 after being held prisoner for two months, remained in very serious condition Thursday.

He had not regained consciousness at the 91st Evac. Hospital in Chu Lai seven days after his rescue.

Stars and Stripes correspondent Bill Elsen reported Thursday from Chu Lai that knowledgeable sources now believe Aiken was struck in the head with a rifle but when — because of a previously broken leg — he was unable to travel. He was apparently clubbed repeatedly, shattering the skull and sending bone fragments into the brain.

Communist guards watching Aiken realized that Allied forces would soon discover their hideout and before fleeing hit Aiken over the head to kill him, rather than tipping off their location with a gunshot, sources speculated.

Ex-VC Spots His 2nd Cache

SAIGON (S&S) — A former Viet Cong who led American and Vietnamese soldiers to a 1½-ton enemy arms cache Monday did it again Tuesday.

After pacing off several steps from a Viet Cong landmark, the Communist defector pointed to a hide-away containing 48 mortar shells, 82 hand grenades, 10 rocket-grenades and assorted other explosives.

Love Those Copters

"Skytroopers" of the 1st Air Cav. Div. pay close attention while a buddy calls out names during mail call on a break at a division firebase. The unit's famed helicopter "airmobility" means more to the GIs than lightning strikes at the Communists—it insures that letters from home arrive more quickly.
(USA Photo by Spec. 4 Terry Moon)

Airman Outwits Enemy

Reds Down Helo, Pilot Is Up 'n' Away

SAIGON (Special) — Communist riflemen downed a U.S. Army light observation helicopter with two rounds Monday afternoon, but found the pilot to be a bit more elusive.

WO Glen A. Maxson, a 4th Inf. Div. artillery aviator, was flying solo near Pleiku in the central highlands when the Reds opened fire.

"I was about 25 to 50 feet above the trees when suddenly I heard a hit," he said. "I'm not sure, but I think it was fire from an SKS (rifle)."

A second bullet snipped the fuel line, and Maxson braced himself as he tried to guide the LOH to a safe landing. The helicopter rolled onto its side the instant it hit the ground, but Maxson was uninjured.

"I stayed in the craft for about a minute making a Mayday call," he said. Then he abandoned ship and raced for cover in the nearby bamboo.

But four or five North Vietnamese soldiers spotted him and started shooting, so Maxson decided it was time to put as much ground between me and the helicopter as possible.

"I looked around as I moved out and I heard them talking when they were firing at me, but I never saw the enemy."

Then he faced another problem. With daylight fading quickly, five American choppers passed overhead without seeing Maxson.

"After I went two kilometers, I stood off to the side of a trail and when a plane was overhead, I moved into the open," he said. "I shot my pistol three times, and a copter finally saw me."

The 4th Div. helicopter, commanded by 1st Lt. James A. Johnson, landed immediately and was greeted by a much relieved Maxson waving his hands over his head.

"I was on the ship as soon as it touched ground," he grinned. "I was never so glad to see an aircraft."

6   Pacific Stars & Stripes
Saturday, July 19, 1969

July 19 - We landed on Guam to refuel. As the plane slowed down on the airstrip, I could see dozens of ominous looking flat-black B-52s parked along the runway. *This was where our thundering "arc-lights" originated.*

Late in the afternoon we landed at Tan Son Nhut, then I took a bus to Bien Hoa and trudged up the hill to the photo lab. *In my continuing fog of depression, at least I could loiter in the air conditioning.*

At the lab, I picked up a *Pacific Stars and Stripes* newspaper and discovered my mail call photo on page six. It had a prominent credit line. That lifted me out of the fog. I was now eager to return to the office, but it was too late for a flight back to Phuoc Vinh, so I stayed the night at the lab.

CHAPTER TEN I GO TO THE FIELD WITH 2ND BRIGADE

July 20 - I caught an early Huey to PV. Congratulations from all around when I arrived at the office. A sign on my desk read "Welcome Back, Flash!" There was a copy of the *Pacific Stars and Stripes* open to my picture with a note on it that read "Out Fucking Standing." It had been a long time since we had a photo in S&S. This was overwhelming, *I couldn't believe it! I was on a roll, a mini-celebrity, and extremely proud of that picture.*

Not so fast, grasshopper.

In the afternoon, Major Coleman called me into his office and congratulated me on the *Pacific Stars and Stripes* photo. He said CG Roberts mentioned it at the General Staff briefing the previous evening. Then he caught me by surprise, and announced I would now be assigned to the field with 2nd Brigade. *What! I was shocked, everything had been going so well here.*

He thought every PIO photographer should spend time in the field. *I had to agree.* He wanted more photos from me like the 1/8 combat assault shots, that had been in the *Cavalair* and the larger publications for the last month. He would designate several special assignments for me during that time, allowing me the freedom to shoot more photos. *What a great opportunity.*

In a day or two, I would depart Phuoc Vinh for seven weeks with 2nd Brigade, until my Tokyo leave in mid-September when Phil would begin processing out to fly home (DEROS). My last six weeks would be back in PV as photo coordinator. *That was fine with me.* A photographer went on R&R in January and was sent to a brigade on his return, when I thought it would be me. Now it was my turn. My only absence from Phuoc Vinh was when I worked at the photo lab for three weeks last December. Phil could handle everything at the PV office with one other photographer during my reassignment to 2nd Brigade. He spent the first four months of his tour in the field with 3rd Brigade.

How could I legitimately call myself a combat photographer if I didn't do field time?

Jul 21 - Today, our astronauts landed on the moon. It was the 20th in the USA because we were on opposite sides of the International Dateline.

Damn, was it a conspiracy? They nailed me one more time for ghastly KP. This had to be the last one.

While I was on R&R, two more of my photos appeared in the *Cavalair*. A Skycrane with a 155 sling out was on page one, and a CA Huey with a machine gunner riding the skid, was on page six (see photo at right).

2nd Brigade was currently based at Lai Khe, 22 km southwest of PV, also the 1st Infantry Division base camp. Captain Peter Zastro, Officer in Charge of the 2nd Brigade Information Office was a pleasant, quiet, red-haired fellow with glasses, and a fine writer. Their main LZ was LZ Dolly, my favorite, situated high on a hilltop. I was also familiar with LZs Grant, White, Jamie and Carolyn, where 2nd Brigade operated.

Jul 22 - A strange feeling came over me as I packed my gear to leave PV. The California flag was down, and the pictures of Sally were gone from around my old desk. It had been raining hard for the last several hours. It wasn't as hot now, but the air was heavy with the ever-present humidity.

I Go to the Field with 2nd Brigade

We had a late-night rocket attack, although not close to us. Later, two nearby B-52 strikes were spectacular and I could feel my cot shaking. I had seen the B52s at their base on Guam, and now they were high above us.

Jul 23 - The rain continued, and I couldn't find any flight to Lai Khe. Captain Zastro called and said they also couldn't find any flights to send photographer Ed Koehnlein to PV. He would work with Phil until his DEROS in early September. Eddie was a grunt with a camera, and had been at 2nd Brigade for more than ten months. He was out with grunt units more than any of our other photographers. I didn't know how he would handle the structure and discipline of the PV office. However, Phil would help him. Paul's attitude had improved. He was shooting photos for writers' feature stories, and continued to take photos for CID, and AAIB. Phil could call on him to help.

Two of my photos were in the current *Cavalair*, the B 1/30 Presidential Unit Citation award on page one, and a 1/8 CA machine gunner riding the skid on page eight. Also, the two-day tour with the TWA flight attendant invited by CG Roberts was the center spread with several photos. I couldn't believe they used the gas mask picture.

All this waiting was a real drag. I was eager to start this new chapter of my Vietnam experience.

An aerial photo of Lai Khe, on the lower right is 1st Infantry Division Headquarters.

Jul 24 - I took the regular Carabou flight to Lai Khe. The three 2nd Brigade PIO people were waiting for me, Captain Zastro, George Vindedzis, a writer from Alaska, and John Dixon, a radio reporter from Tempe, Arizona.

We started the long walk to the office. What to my wandering eyes should appear? The unbelievable sight of the Kwiki Freeze soft-serve ice cream shack. We went to the end of the line, and I almost drooled as the each guy passed by with his ice cream. The PIO guys laughed as each of us devoured a luscious chocolate sundae.

Unfortunately, the generator for our area blew up a few nights ago and we didn't have any power, so I wrote my letters by candlelight. Our hooch was totally sandbagged with ammo box frames, providing much more incoming protection than PV, and we were nowhere near the greenline. This place was older, as it had been a Big Red One (1st Infantry Division) base for a long time.

The Lai Khe PX was much larger than the one at Phuoc Vinh (photo at left). Australians were selling cars that would be waiting at your local dealer, when you returned to the good old USA.

"Step right up, mate. You know you always wanted that Mustang."

The main road at Lai Khe, a long walk to the PX, above, or the airstrip from our office in the 2nd Brigade area.

148   I Go to the Field with 2nd Brigade

Jul 25 - Leaving early, George, John and I caught a Huey to LZ Grant. From there, I flew out with D 1/12 grunts and took photos of captured ammo and supplies about 4 km north of the LZ. A giant "X" of destruction was made by two crossing B-52 strikes, each one a long straight line of giant craters.

Numerous items were stacked on the side of a huge bomb crater, 40 feet across, and 20 feet deep. They found several odd items I didn't usually see, antitank mines, and what looked like 37 mm antiaircraft ammunition (in the box). Many mortar rounds, RPGs, belts and cases of 51 Caliber ammo were also displayed. *It always bothered me to see any antiaircraft guns or ammunition, because I flew frequently.*

There were large amounts of various bicycle parts in the bottom of the crater. The NVA hauled all their supplies and equipment in from Cambodia on bicycles. This was a sprawling bunker complex, but there wasn't much that remained. Many items from it were scattered throughout the area by the huge explosions. *I can't imagine what it was like for the nearby NVA when this hit.*

A 1/12 Skytrooper walks down "Route 66," at the 1st Cav's LZ Grant

The mud was unbelievable at LZ Grant. The skytroopers prepared their defensive positions, as one shaved. The bunker on the right had a recoilless rifle in it.

After flying back to LZ Grant in a logbird, I photographed 2nd Brigade PIO radio reporter John Dixon as he interviewed 105 mm artillerymen, (see photo above). It didn't take long for us to walk around the entire LZ. Later, it rained hard, so we stayed inside a bunker until we caught our Huey back to Lai Khe at 3:30 p.m.

Back at the office, we heard of several attacks on 3rd Brigade units near Quan Loi last night, but no further details were available.

Jul 26 - Midmorning, I shot Polaroid photos of several officers at 2nd Brigade Headquarters. Later, after another delightful visit to Kwiki Freeze, I wrote captions for yesterday's LZ Grant photos, as I listened to local Radio KLIK, 1550 AM. I munched Hersheyettes from a sundry pack, and drank an ice-cold RC Cola.

Jul 27 - The 2nd Brigade area of operations changed dramatically, a big deal for us. They were relocating the war personnel to Song Be (LZ Buttons) about 70 km northeast of Lai Khe. Today, all of our plans were cancelled. Some of the grunt battalions were transferred to different brigades to make this massive move easier. Division intelligence was expecting the large 5th VC Division of regular NVA troops to come through that area. The bad guys were trying to sneak down the seam between II Corps and III Corps to attack Bien Hoa and Long Binh. That meant 2nd Brigade would be much further east than before. In that area, it would be necessary to construct several new LZs. Major Coleman must have known this was coming when he sent me here. He called tonight and wanted me to photograph the construction of the first new fire support base southeast of Song Be first thing the next morning.

Jul 28 - Up at 5:30 a.m., I quickly caught a ride in a Huey, as several were flying to Song Be. After a brief stop, I arrived at the new LZ well before 8 a.m. The new site was flat, empty ground, busy with many skytroopers who had recently arrived by helicopter. Heavy weapons grunts from 2nd Battalion, 5th Cavalry were setting up several mortars for defense. The NVA could attack at any time. This would be the new home of the battalion. The construction of LZ Mary, 13 km southeast of Song Be, had begun in the notorious red clay.

Early in the morning, these E 2/5 mortarmen quickly set up their 81 mm mortar as the construction of the new LZ was beginning on empty flat ground.

A Chinook brings in a slingout load to the site of LZ Mary.

Engineers appeared to be everywhere. It looked chaotic, but somehow organized. The large bulldozers came in two loads, the tracks and blade came in first, carried by a Chinook. Then a Skycrane brought in the large dozer body and lowered it onto the tracks that had been carefully positioned, as the engineers guided it on (see photo above). They assembled it quickly and immediately started clearing the area. Later, the bulldozers created the four-foot high earthen berm around the LZ perimeter. That would provide cover from small arms fire during a ground attack.

Engineers sort and prepare the huge timbers for the large bunkers

Smaller bulldozers came intact, on slingouts under Skycranes similar to the one in the photo above. Several vehicles, including a deuce-and-a-half, were delivered to move construction materials around the LZ. The engineers had these materials assembled ahead of time in an "LZ kit" at one of the base camps. It could be transported quickly to the new fire support base site taking about 25 Chinook sorties to bring in the whole "kit."

Chinooks came in a steady stream, first bringing backhoes to dig the Tactical Operations Center (TOC), Fire Direction Control (FDC) for the artillery, the medical bunker, and the below ground level ammo storage pits (you don't want ammo exploding on level ground). There were loads of huge timbers for the frames of the large bunkers. Chinooks continued hauling in concertina wire, culverts, PSP, C-rations, water, numerous sandbags and other construction materials.

In the middle of my busy afternoon, hunger kicked in. I usually carried a couple of cans of C-rations with me in one of my pistol belt pouches, but those were devoured earlier. When I asked, the grunts filling sandbags directed me to a small box of loose C-ration cans that had obviously been picked over. It was in the center of the photo to the right. Most of them were lima beans & ham or fruitcake. Finally, I found two cans of apricots to go with the fruitcakes. *Bon Appetit*.

Constant activity continued around the LZ. Many grunts filled sandbags, strung wire around the perimeter, and built defense bunkers into the berm. It was well organized. Apparently, most of these guys had done this before a few times. The organization, cooperation and teamwork impressed me.

The dozer clears debris while the backhoe digs the hole for the tactical operations center (TOC)

Grunts unpacked the concertina wire that they would string around the perimeter of the LZ.

Sandbag fillers take a well deserved break near the end of the very long day.

It was a fast moving, extremely busy day. At least two full grunt companies, about 200 skytroopers, had worked hard. By evening, the new LZ looked secure as my LOH gained altitude, (see photo above). The berm, the defensive bunkers, and the wire were complete. It looked fully defensible. It hadn't rained at all today, *a miracle*. It was much closer, and easier, for me to find a flight to Phuoc Vinh, rather than Lai Khe.

Fatigue hit me hard as I trudged the half mile to the PIO office at PV. It took a while to wash off the red clay. We saw a movie in the evening, "The Producers." It was hilarious, but weird. Sleep came quickly to me in the guest bunk in the back of the press/photo office.

Lt. Col. Andre Broumas, CO of 8th Engineers goes over other job plans before we left for LZ Mary.

Jul 29 - Rising early, I walked over to the skybeaver pad, and caught the 8th Engineer's C&C Huey with my friend, Lt. Col. Broumas, for the flight to LZ Mary. The clouds were low and heavy. With the limited visibility, we had to skim over the treetops. Twice we managed to get lost. *Scary*. Once we hit a tree with the skid. The normal half hour trip took well over an hour. I discussed what I had photographed the previous day with Lt. Col. Broumas. He gave me a briefing on what I would see today, helpful for planning my photos.

Artillerymen begin building the pit for their 105 howitzer.

158   I Go to the Field with 2nd Brigade

LZ Mary wasn't as busy as the preceding day. The perimeter wire and bunkers were completed. Three 105 mm howitzers were being set up by their crews. The teamwork was efficient and impressive. They did this a couple of times a month. Numerous grunts were filling sandbags for interior bunker (hooch) building with the large half-round culverts.

Early morning delivery of culverts for more hooch building.

It seems like there are never enough sandbags, skytroopers take a break from the never ending job. You can see the partially covered culvert behind the grunt on the left, and a fully covered one on the right; they sleep in those at night for protection from incoming rockets and mortars.

Writer Al Persons, and photographer Ed Koehnlein, flew up from PV, arriving about 1 p.m. Eddie didn't say anything about how he liked PV, but then Eddie rarely said much. Most of the construction was completed, and more artillery would arrive later. Al would do a couple of stories and Eddie would take photos for him.

I had already shot several rolls of film, so I took advantage of a LOH flying back to PV. I washed off the red clay again and listened to records on Ron Doss' stereo in the press office, "Days of Future Past" by the Moody Blues and "Are You Experienced" by Jimi Hendrix. After a few beers with the guys, I cruised to the guest bunk in the back of the press office and crashed.

Jul 30 - I caught the regular 10:20 a.m. Carabou flight to Lai Khe, returned to the office and picked up the last three days of my precious mail. After an extended visit to Kwiki Freeze, where I enjoyed two sundaes, then trudged back to the office and captioned my several rolls of LZ Mary film. Today I had only 102 days to go.

Jul 31 - Captain Zastro woke us up early as we had to clean up the office for an inspection, *what!* We quickly cleaned the room and it looked okay. I had to leave about 8:30 a.m. to photograph a psychological operations (PSYOPS) mission. The Huey broadcast Chieu Hoi messages over a loudspeaker encouraging NVA soldiers to defect, and dropped safe passage leaflets over a few suspected NVA unit locations in thick jungle near LZ Mary. (See photo to the right.) There weren't many photo opportunities. It was slightly more than a three hour Huey ride. They said the NVA might shoot at us, but the enemy decided to stay hidden. *A wise decision.* I was back in Lai Khe by noon, so I went to the PX and the post office (APO).

The front and back of one of the Chieu Hoi leaflets dropped today

Aug 1 - This morning, I took photos of 1st Infantry's Huey gunships. It was the first time I had seen one. After lunch, Captain Z had fantastic news, I was to go to Phuoc Vinh for my E-5 promotion board appearance. *Hooray! It's about time.* However, I was wary, my promotion paperwork was messed up last month. When I first arrived in country, my orders were specific but the clerks still couldn't figure out where I was supposed to go. It was gratifying to finally appear before the board. I found a Huey flight quickly.

Stopping at PV whenever possible, it was always uplifting to be back with my friends, and, of course, the music.

160   I Go to the Field with 2nd Brigade

Aug 2 - I arrived early at 7:30 a.m., and appeared before the E-5 Promotion Board at 11:30. They asked me numerous questions. My confidence was high, as I had filled an E-5 slot since February 2. The photo operations I directed as photo coordinator, had run smoothly even though we were understaffed. The *Cavalairs* and larger publications ran several of my pictures. I hoped the board was impressed.

The PIO guys here at Phuoc Vinh were angry, the new Division Headquarters Company Commander had made several new "harassment" policies that made no sense in a combat zone. A mandatory 7:30 a.m. formation ticked off everyone, and they had to be in full uniform at all times, along with other annoying rules. KP came up much more often. *This bullshit would't last.*

Today, I had 99 days to go, and they now called me a "two-digit midget."

A LOH leaves Phuoc Vinh, just like I did today.

Aug 3 - I caught the regular Carabou 10:20 a.m. flight to Lai Khe. It rained so hard, that we couldn't land. That forced us to return to PV, where it wasn't raining. From the Carabou on the airstrip, I quickly ran over to 2nd Brigade Aviation to see if they had any flights. When I asked, the controller immediately yelled into his mike, "Hold it, I have a passenger for you." He pointed to a LOH turning around. *Perfect timing.* We flew to Lai Khe, by way of Bien Hoa, at low altitude, and I took some photos of the airbase. Nearby, we saw a bombed out village. *I wonder what happened there. I learned later it had beens the last stand of the local Viet Cong forces.* It was exhilarating flying in LOHs, the sports car of helicopters. The left front seat was my favorite place. Back at the 2nd Brigade information office, a welcome load of mail awaited me.

Aug 4 - 2nd Brigade S-1 (personnel) needed some photos taken in the morning. Later, I caught the only flight available, a LOH, to PV for PIO clerk Chuck Spicer's farewell party. Chuck was my friend, another Californian who had drawn one of the portraits of Sally. He was helpful as he shot a few photo assignments for us when we were in a pinch. Chuck danced the night away, (photo at right). All of us were happy for him, but he would be missed.

Bill Ellis and some of his friends supplied the music. In the photo to the right Bill was singing, to his left was artist Ron Doss, writer Eugene Christianson, Paul, and Bill's grunt friend Terry. Radio announcer Dave Van Drew hid his face below Bill's guitar neck. The back of Chuck Spicer's head was in the center. Major Coleman lurked in the background.

The information office staff was larger now with many new people, including some I didn't know. Major Coleman even joined the fun. I took some photos. *Just call me "Flash."*

Aug 5 - Rising at 5 a.m. in Phuoc Vinh, I caught the 2nd Brigade Aviation Command and Control (C&C) Huey to LZ Mary. My new assignment was to photograph company commanders and their RTOs in the jungle. A warning light came on as we were hovering, so "no go." Unfortunately, no other rides were available to LZ Mary or Song Be, so I flashed my USARV Press Card and flew back to Lai Khe on the regular 10:20 a.m. Carabou flight. I returned to a stack of mail, including my *Psychology Today* magazine.

I would try again tomorrow to get to LZ Mary. *Patience, grasshopper.*

Aug 6 - "You can't get there from here."

Up at 6 am, I rode crammed in a jeep with John Dixon and five other guys to the airstrip trying again to fly to LZ Mary. We found a Huey bound for Song Be, but its assignment was changed once we were seated inside. After a short search we found another going to LZ Mary, but it struggled to take off and shut down with mechanical trouble. We jumped out and walked around the area until we spotted a third Huey. It was going to Tay Ninh, 70 km west, then to Song Be, so we hopped in with our equipment. When we arrived in Tay Ninh, (aerial photo of Tay Ninh base above), after discussions between other officers and our pilot, the flight plan changed and we were kicked off. Tay Ninh was the home of the 1st Cav's 1st Brigade and a brigade of the 25th Infantry Division.

162   I Go to the Field with 2nd Brigade

The 1st Brigade VIP Center at Tay Ninh, known as the "All the Way Hilton."

We gave up trying to fly to LZ Mary and took the long walk to 1st Brigade PIO. We visited with them and they found a ride for us to the "terminal" at the airstrip. Flashing our press cards, we signed our names on the Carabou flight list to Phuoc Vinh. That was our best chance, since there weren't any flights to Lai Khe from Tay Ninh. We were numbers 22 and 23 on the list, a Carabou only carries 19 people. *Stuck in Tay Ninh, it just wasn't our day.*

We had a few hours, and being lunchtime, we hiked to the 25th Infantry PX and ate some delicious cheeseburgers. Next, we strolled to the 1st Brigade VIP center (photo above) where we met comedian George Gobel, (photo at left). We had a pleasant chat with plenty of laughs, and the entertainer told us he was thoroughly enjoying his tour. He showed interest in my photography and asked several questions. Shortly, some officers arrived to escort him to his show.

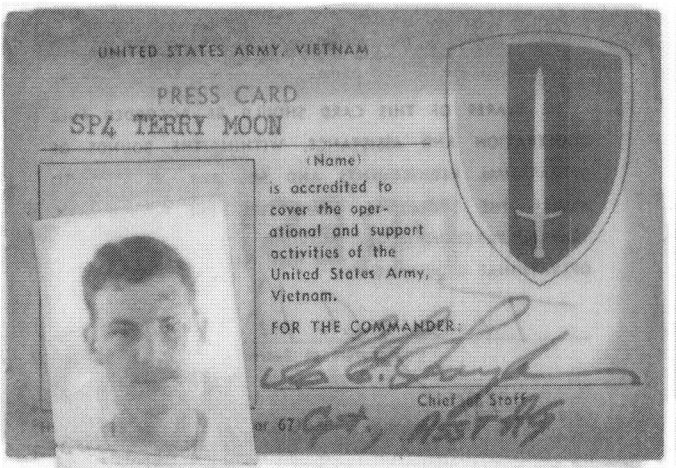

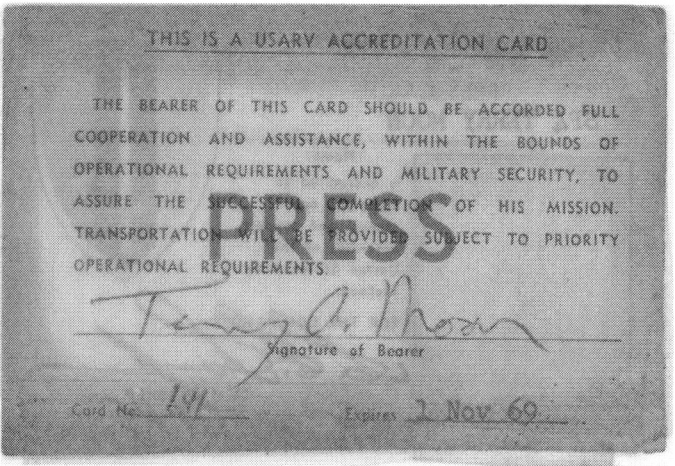

We walked back to the airstrip "terminal," and heard them announce 1-17, 22 and 23. Wow! Our press cards, (see above), had authorized priority for us. We thought we would be stuck here overnight. The flight arrived in PV about 2 p.m. and we took the long walk to 227th AHB where we caught a courier Huey to Lai Khe that arrived about 3:45 p.m. We trudged back to the office. Having walked around three large base camps, Tay Ninh, Phuoc Vinh and Lai Khe with all our stuff, we were exhausted. I received a goodie package from the family, containing snickerdoodles and brownies. It was extra welcome, today. For the second straight day, I didn't make it back to LZ Mary.

The August 6 *Cavalair* had Tom Benic's and my photos of 15th TC helicopter maintenance from Bearcat as the center spread, (see photo above).

Low angle aerial photo of LZ Mary on a good day

Aug 7 - I finally made it to LZ Mary today. After being bumped off one chopper, I caught a second one a short time later. My assignment from Major Coleman was to photograph company commanders, and their RTOs (radio operators) out in the jungle. I usually hung around with them anyway. Today, LZ Mary was a swamp. We always dreaded the nasty, gooey, slippery red clay mud.

I flew out on a Huey log bird to a grunt company, A 2/5, a couple of kilometers east of LZ Mary, located in heavy jungle. The "Landing Zone" where the logbird landed was a small hole in the jungle. The door gunners had to watch the tail rotor as it came close to the trees as we landed. I jumped out immediately, stepped into the jungle and took the photo above. Later, they told me the hole in the jungle was created by cutting down several trees with C-4 explosives. It wasn't raining, what a relief.

I photographed the Company Commander, Captain Peeler, talking to his men and directing defensive positions. Also, he was on the radio along with his RTO, and during a break, he read mail in the deep jungle. Earlier my camera caught the skytroopers carrying their supplies from the log bird. Out with grunt units before, I always stayed with the company commander and the RTO, so I knew what was going on and didn't interfere with their mission.

Familiar with how they worked, I quickly shot plenty of photos. I flew back to LZ Mary on the next logbird that brought in more grunts. Later, I caught another Huey back to Lai Khe. It was crammed with people and equipment. We flew to Song Be where two guys jumped off and two others climbed aboard, then to Quan Loi where another guy left. Next the long flight to Tay Ninh, where everyone exited but me. *What a weird flight plan.* Finally we left for Lai Khe, and arrived at 5:15 p.m. *It was a productive day, my timing for finding flights was excellent, but one time I caught the local when I wanted the express.*

Aug 8 - Major Coleman gave me an assignment to shoot the communications center on top of Nui Ba Ra (east of Song Be). I couldn't get a flight (of course) up to the mountain, so I would try again later.

The entire 2nd Brigade PIO crew would fly to Phuoc Vinh for the monthly PIO party tomorrow evening.

Aug 9 - The four of us flew to PV on the daily Carabou flight. Later in the day, Sgt. 1st Class DeGard gave me my long awaited Spec. 5 promotion orders. I received many congratulations. *Hooray! Our party was now my party. It should have been sooner, and no more ghastly KP.* Plenty of music filled the office. I fired up the psychedelic red strobe light, and did some dancing on my former desk. There were toasts to "Flash." With everyone here from all three brigades, there were new faces that joined in the celebration. I even received a letter from Sally today postmarked November, 1968.

"Congratulations Flash." I was so happy here with my long awaited promotion.

The magazines should have been here by now. Major Coleman called Tokyo to see what the problem was, and he was told they would arrive any day. Many of my photos should be in it.

Aug 10 - I went to Bien Hoa, celebrating my Spec. 5 promotion, then caught a ride to the Long Binh PX where I bought items for myself, including a Jimi Hendrix album *Electric Ladyland*. My flight back was delayed two hours so I didn't arrive in Phuoc Vinh in time to fly back to Lai Khe.

We played the new album on the stereo and particularly enjoyed one song, *All Along The Watchtower*.
There must be some kinda way outa here...

Aug 11 - My only chance for a ride to Lai Khe today ended when my pilot was stung by several yellow jackets as he arrived at PV. After he landed to pick me up, he jumped out of the LOH, ran around frantically, waved his arms, and then rolled on the ground. Immediately, he was taken to the medics. I walked back to the office. The guest bunk in the back of the press/photo office was now like my own.

It was conversion day for our MPC (money). They checked everyone's money, trying to stop drug sales and black market operations. *If you had too much cash, you had some serious explaining to do.* I had to change my old bills for new, different MPC. My wallet bulged with $11.05.

Tonight at PV, heavy firing erupted three or four bunkers away from us on the greenline, and it lasted about an hour. I hadn't heard that for a while, as Lai Khe had been quiet.

Aug 12 - Early we heard that several attacks occurred over the Cav's area of operations last night besides the one near us. The largest was at Quan Loi, a three pronged attack led by elite NVA sapper companies. A massive rocket and mortar attack accompanied the sappers. The sappers penetrated the base perimeter, and two defense bunkers were overrun. Many of the greenline bunkers at Quan Loi were staffed by clerks, mechanics and other support workers, similar to our former role here at Phuoc Vinh. *This was terrible, our worst nightmare. This could have happened to us anytime we had been on guard duty.*

Sappers broke through the wire and fighting broke out inside the base. This time an NVA rocket destroyed a Cobra gunship on the ground. American casualties were five killed and 51 wounded, fifty-five dead NVA were found, along with many blood trails leaving the area. They also captured a sapper.

LZ Becky (northeast of LZ Carolyn and 7 km south of Cambodia), LZ Grant, and new LZ Caldwell (28 km southeast of Song Be) were also attacked. Many more NVA were killed in the morning, as helicopter scout teams found them retreating to the safety of their Cambodian bases, for a total of 460 KIA. Twenty Americans died in all the actions across the Cav's area of operations. This was the largest number of NVA attacks the Cav had seen in one day since the Tet offensive of 1968. It was a sad day for all of us.

With all this activity, I was immediately sent back to Lai Khe. They quickly took care of my MPC exchange. See the photo of an MPC nickel above.

Captain Zastro was sent to Quan Loi to help handle the large numbers of journalists arriving after the big attack. I would handle duties at 2nd Brigade PIO. Later, I had to provide transportation for a CBS News team to Quan Loi. Of course, the 1st Cav didn't have any flights available at Lai Khe. So I asked our friends at 1st Infantry Division (Big Red One) to fly the team to Quan Loi and they took care of it.

Aug 13 - I tried to fly to LZ Caldwell (east of Song Be) but it was raining violently, and no flights were available. Running around looking for a flight left me totally soaked. Again, my heavy duty plastic bags saved my cameras. Back at the office, I changed out of the wet clothes. I always had extra towels. The afternoon went well as I carefully dismantled a newly received goodie package containing my favorite cookies. This weeks *Cavalair* had a Cobra photo by Chuck Spicer on the front page. A PIO clerk, he was very popular. Sgt. 1st Class DeGard took him out on a photo 'assignment,' before he left. We would send a copy of this *Cavalair* to his home in the USA. He would love it.

Aug 14 - Stuck at the office, no flights, no calls, no mail, just an empty day. This weeks *USARV Army Reporte*r had two 1st Cav photos. One was more than six months old, a creative sunset silhouette of a greenline tower by Paul, from before he arrived at Phuoc Vinh. The other was from one of the new 3rd Brigade photographers. PIO had many new, and talented people.

Aug 16 - Today was "the day of the Chinook." Up at 5:30, I took the long flight to LZ Mary on a Huey logbird.

What, I couldn't believe it! They were tearing down the LZ. A new one further east was under construction in an area where they found an NVA supply route. Skycranes and Chinooks kept hauling things away. *What a hell of a scene.* It hadn't rained for several days and what had been a terrible mud hole a week ago, was now a swirling dust storm, fanned by the numerous helicopters. The 2/5 grunts had packed up and were leaving. Among the chaos, I photographed the engineers as they destroyed the Medic bunker, Tactical Operations Center and Artillery Fire Direction Control bunker.

An E 2/5 mortarman smiled as he left LZ Mary with his mortar tube, his M16, and his precious guitar.

Blackhats (field air traffic controllers) guided in the Chinooks. They kept what looked like total chaos, orderly. Another good example of the teamwork I had consistently observed. I took photos of an A 1/77 105 mm howitzer sling out under a Chinook, and a C 1/30 155 mm howitzer sling out under a Skycrane as they departed. Later, I caught the E 2/5 mortar platoon leaving, as we were sandblasted by the Chinooks, (see photo below).

It quickly became too dusty for photos with the constant helicopter activity. I ran, jumped into one of the Chinooks, it lifted off and hovered for a howitzer to be attached. I photographed the 105 sling out from inside through the hole in the floor. When we arrived at the new LZ, I shot photos of the Blackhat's purple smoke marker below the dangling 105, (photo at right).

The Chinook was large enough to hold more than twenty grunts, however, visibility inside was limited. I saw a narrow slit out the back, over the raised ramp, and there was one small round window on each side.

Arriving at PV before lunch, it felt like I had been in a Chinook for an entire day. They were claustrophobic, and extremely noisy with the big, whining driveshaft directly overhead between the two large rotors. Today was by far the most time I had ever spent in a Chinook. My ears were ringing, and my ear plugs didn't help. *No wonder they called them "shithooks."*

As I arrived, heavy rain blasted Phouc Vinh. I quickly ran about 300 yards from the Chinook area (see photo to the right, on a good day) to a 2nd Brigade Aviation helicopter that was flying to Lai Khe. I was soaked and looked like hell as the red dust covering me became wet. It looked like thin, rusty blood. The rain continued at Lai Khe. Still thoroughly soaked, I ran from the airstrip a couple of hundred yards to the 2nd Brigade PIO office. By then, most of the red clay was washed away. Again, the plastic bags saved my cameras. I arrived in time for supper, and after I changed into a dry uniform, I ate my first meal of the day.

170   I Go to the Field with 2nd Brigade

I had taken many unusual, what I thought were interesting pictures, but I was never able to see them, a drawback of being at a brigade. As photo coordinator, I saw most of the photos that came through the office from the photo lab.

Aug 17 - I wrote captions for the five rolls of film shot the previous day. How strange to have photographed the construction and the destruction of LZ Mary in a three week period.

Patience, grasshopper, LZ Mary would rise again.

Aug 18 - Captain Z sent me to Phuoc Vinh on the scheduled Carabou flight to deliver my film. Of course, it was too late for a ride back to Lai Khe, so I stayed in PV and listened to music.

The much anticipated summer *FIRST TEAM Magazines* had finally arrived. Numerous photos in it were mine. Every member of the 1st Cavalry Division would receive one, about 20,000 copies.

I also received good comments from Major Coleman on my CO in the field pictures for a major article in the next magazine. Other photographers were also working on this. He mentioned I would have another special assignment in a few days.

Aug 19 - I flew back to Lai Khe on the regular Carabou flight with several copies of the Summer 1969 *FIRST TEAM Magazine*. (Cover photo at right). It was forty-four pages, with eight articles. A major effort went into this from everyone in the office.

The door gunner story was first with four of my photos and a Ron Doss painting. Next, the Cav unit crests that I shot on the appropriate green towel background. Phil Blackmarr's great An Tuc Dispensary story followed, with several of Phil's creative pictures. The ceremony photo was mine. Thereafter, a maintenance story by Tom Benic, along with two of my color photos. Almost a full page for my shot of the mechanics working on the LOH rotor head with the dramatic clouds in the background.

Next an eight page pictorial of uncredited photos "humping through III Corps." This was followed by the 1/30 artillery story I organized and photographed. Al Persons and Dave Wolfe wrote the story. My super wide shot of a 175 mm howitzer that looked extremely long, was on the first page. Then, a sequence of 155 howitzers firing from LZ Grant on the next two pages, followed by a Skycrane carrying a 155 and a Chinook with a 105. A Ron Doss painting of a girl filled the next page.

Al Schlosser's Kit Carson scout (NVA defectors helping us) story was next with Eddie Koehnlein's photos, followed by Joe Kamalick's story on the blackhats (airborne air traffic controllers) with some photos by Paul. Finally, Steve Haldemann's Cordon and Search story with five of my pictures. The maintenance and artillery photos on the Table of Contents also were mine (see next page). I was proud of my contribution to our quarterly publication.

Volume 2, Number 2   Summer 1969

THE FIRST TEAM

CONTENTS

Page 2 — Grace Under Pressure
Ernest Hemingway once defined courage as "grace under pressure." In this article correspondent Richard Craig compares the Cav doorgunner to a Spanish matador and staff photographer Terry Moon captures the spectacle in full color.
Story By Richard Craig
Photos By Terry Moon

Page 6 — Cav Heraldry
Displayed in this feature are the distinctive crests of the individual units of the 1st Air Cavalry Division.

Page 8 — An Tuc: 1 Part Medicine, 2 Parts Compassion
Nestled in Vietnam's Central Highlands, the An Tuc Dispensary has become more than just a medical clinic. Under the auspices of the 15th Medical Battalion, this hospital is today a showcase of American-Vietnamese relations.
Story and Photos By Philip Blackmarr

Page 12 — From Trucks To Transistors
Maintenance may not be glamorous, but no one is more essential to a modern fighting division than the highly skilled mechanic. In this article staff writer Tom Benic salutes the men who keep the "mobility" in airmobility.
Story By Tom Benic

Page 17 Humping Through III Corps: A Pictorial Essay

Page 25 — The Yank Of The Lanyard, The Roar Of The Gun
Artillery's job is to bring "smoke" and "steel" on the enemy. Within the Cav, the artillery is known as the infantryman's best friend.
Story By Al Persons and Dave Wolfe
Photos By Terry Moon

Page 30 — Flight To Freedom
Editor Al Schlosser lived with the Kit Carson Scouts at their training center, where he conducted this interview with NVA defector Tran Quoc Hong.
Story By Al Schlosser
Photos By Ed Koehnlein

Page 34 — The Man In The Black Flannel Hat
Like the Pathfinders of old, Cav Blackhats guide adventurous men into virgin territory. These Skytroopers are usually the "first in and last out" of a new landing zone.
Story By Joe Kamalick
Photos By Paul Sgroi

Page 37 — Anatomy Of A Cordon And Search
The cordon tactic—encircling and capturing guerillas and their supplies—is an integral part of Allied strategy in Vietnam. In this story a cordon operation is chronicled by editor Steve Haldeman and staff photographer Terry Moon.
Story By Steve Haldeman
Photos By Terry Moon

Front cover by Mike Miller   Back cover by Paul Sgroi

COMMAND GROUP: MG E. B. Roberts, Commanding General; BG William E. Shedd, Assistant Division Commander (Operations); BG Frank Meszar, Assistant Division Commander (Logistics); MAJ J.D. Coleman, Information Officer.

THE FIRST TEAM is published quarterly under the supervision of the Information Office, 1st Air Cavalry Division, APO SF 96490 and is an authorized publication. Opinions expressed herein are not necessarily those of the Department of the Army. Letters to the editor should be addressed: Editor, THE FIRST TEAM, c/o Information Office, 1st Air Cavalry Division, APO SF 96490.

The magazine was distributed with a record of four Bill Ellis songs. The cover art of the record was painted by Ron Doss from a color Polaroid print I took of Bill on a greenline bunker. (See record cover at right.)

Aug 20 - Quan Loi was attacked again last night. We had a practice alert at Lai Khe and quickly ran to our bunker. Then we had some *real* incoming. Lai Khe radio (KLIK 1550) went into red alert mode and played a strange Jimi Hendrix song, *'Third Stone from the Sun'* over and over and over for about 45 minutes. *Creepy.* No one wanted to leave the safety of the bunker to turn it off. It was the only incoming I experienced at Lai Khe. We didn't hear of any casualties.

More favorable remarks from division on my company commander in the field photos for the next magazine. Great. I hadn't even seen them. *I never did see all of them.*

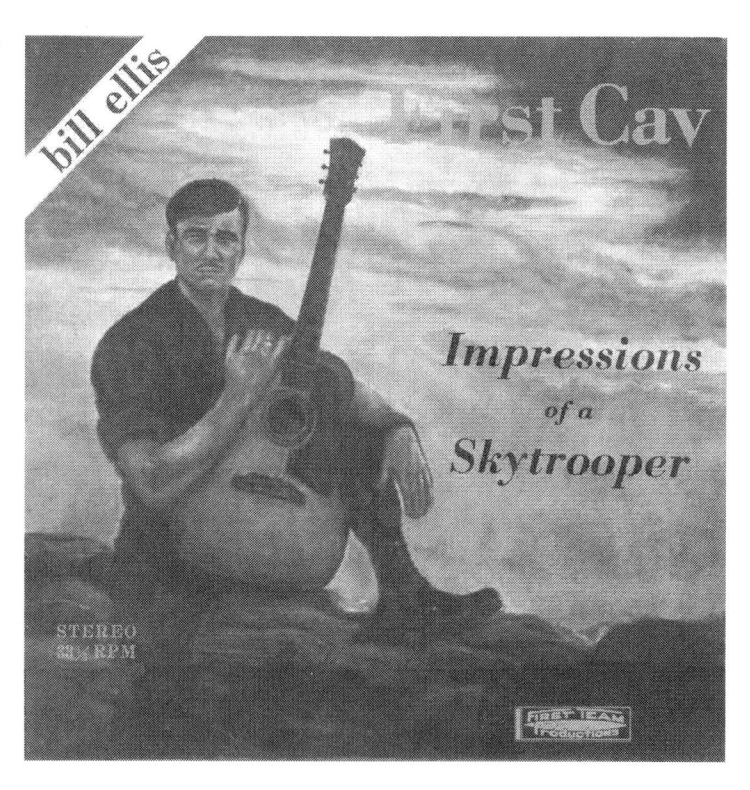

The sign in front of the 227th AHB area at Lai Khe. The small sign underneath reads: "This area is secured for your convenience with our compliments" (signed) The Cav.

Huey Gunship prepares to leave Lai Khe on a mission. It belonged to the 1st Infantry Division that shared the base with 1st Cav's 2nd Brigade.

A Huey of the 229th AHB leaves the 227th VIP pad at Lai Khe

D 227th Cobra, known as "The Experience," with respect for Jimi Hendrix.

Aug 21 - Today, at Lai Khe, I took photos of our D 227th Cobra Gunships. Interesting names and artwork gave them extra character: *Arizona Gambler, Gunslinger, The Leprechaun, Hellfire, The Montana Mercenary, The Experience, and The Phenix.* I hadn't been out long before it started to rain heavily, so I would try again the next day.

We had a good laugh this evening, as we watched AFVN-TV news. PIO writer Tom Benic had snuck into the background of a CBS News report from Quan Loi. I didn't notice if it was Don Webster or Burt Quint mumbling into the microphone. Tom was right behind him doing the "Hi Mom" thing. Many guys tried to do this, but he was the first to succeed.

I received a letter from my friend Allan in Korea, saying his leave had been denied. He was too valuable, and they couldn't spare him. *We would have had a great time in Tokyo. What a bummer.*

Aug 22 - I took more photos of the D 227th gunships. Arizona Gambler was one of the first Cobras that arrived in Vietnam for the Cav. A big snake between the words of its name made it look menacing, (see photo to the left).

Major Coleman had told me a couple of days ago, that I would have another special assignment tomorrow at Song Be, (also known as LZ Buttons).

Aug 23 - Up at 6 a.m., I caught a helicopter at 7 a.m., and was in Song Be at 8 a.m. Roving 1st Cav writer Tom Benic was working with me. He had written many page-one stories for the *Cavalair* since his arrival about two months ago. We were briefed by the 5/7 Battalion Commander Lt. Col. Thomas Healey. Our mission would be to search for NVA supply trails on the other side of Nui Ba Ra Mountain.

I grabbed a ride with D troop, 1/9, a jeep mounted unit called the "Rat Patrol," (see photo at right). Tom accompanied the recon platoon of E Company, 5/7. They would be escorting an ARVN infantry company riding out in trucks for a sweep around the base of Nui Ba Ra Mountain, east of LZ Buttons.

The M60 gunner on one of the jeeps watches as we swept around the base of Nui Ba Ra mountain.

Some roads were barely passable, but most appeared okay. The dense trees close to the road kept everyone alert for a possible ambush. The ARVN soldiers rode in trucks behind us (see photo above). They started a sweep through the jungle between the road and the backside of the mountain (from the Song Be base), along with the 5/7 recon platoon.

The jeep had to cross a two-foot deep creek at one spot. I jumped out first, crossed on the large board before they hit the water, and took a photo of them splashing through. The gunner nearly fell in.

How Did You Get This Job? 177

We arrived at our waiting point and were joined by another platoon of grunts that had been airlifted in, minutes before. The jeep guys told me they were "Blues," a 1st of the 9th infantry platoon, (see photo above).

We dismounted from the jeeps and headed into the jungle to set up an ambush. The ARVN company was sweeping toward us through the dense jungle between the road and the mountain. We left them about eight kilometers back. Anyone running from them would be caught in our ambush.

At the beginning, I took one shot of the grunts crossing a rice paddy, and took a shot of a grunt as we entered the jungle, (see photo at right). Arriving in the deep jungle, we moved around in ankle deep water. I was cautious and extremely careful not to get in the way, limiting what could be photographed. An NVA presence was suspected in this immediate area.

It was too dark for photos in the deep jungle. The random brilliant streaks of sunlight created more contrast than film could handle. I stayed close to the RTO as the ambush was set up. Unable to see very far, I was unsure of the full size of the ambush, I suspect there were more grunts involved than the ones I had seen. They moved quietly

178   I Go to the Field with 2nd Brigade

to their positions through the shallow water of the jungle floor. They all knew exactly what they were doing. *Not me, what the hell was I going to do. I only carried a 45 pistol!*

An excruciating half hour, *it seemed so much longer*, as we listened intently for the approach of the NVA. Finally, the ARVNs contacted us and no NVA were ahead of them. *What a huge relief.* The NVA probably had tunnels and bunkers to hide in along the way. We saw no signs of supply trails where we had been, however, the ARVNs had seen several on their sweep. They would follow up on that soon.

The trip back to base, around the mountain was faster than before. Vietnamese people along the road waved and said, "Hello," as if watching a parade. We returned to LZ Buttons about 3 p.m. Commanding General Roberts was at the Tactical Operations Center discussing strategy with 5/7 Battalion Commander Lt. Col. Healey and several 2nd Brigade intelligence and operations officers.

A Long Range Recon Patrol (LRRP) team had spotted a 100-man NVA force, not far from where we had been earlier in the day. The response began, a company of 5/7 was air assaulted into that area to find the enemy. *What a drag, I only had a few shots left on my last roll of film so I couldn't join them and photograph the operation.*

When a LOH quickly appeared leaving for Quan Loi, I grabbed it. Then I had to wait for a ride back to Lai Khe because the helicopters were busy with all the activities.

Hueys and Cobras were firing up with one just lifting off (down toward the end) and some already leaving Quan Loi. The first two Blue Max Cobras had pilots and gunners. The first Huey's nose bore the crossed swords of 1/9. A large NVA force had been spotted, and the response had begun.

I took my last few shots of several 1/9 and 227th Hueys and Cobras firing up and leaving, (see photo above). As I waited at the airstrip "terminal," some of the guys recognized my name tag and said they liked my pictures from the *Cavalair* and the new *FIRST TEAM Magazine*. That always made my day. Of course, someone asked me "How did you get this job?"

Shortly before 8 p.m., I caught a Huey back to Lai Khe. It was dark. I dragged myself back to the office after 9 p.m. I had only been there a few minutes when the phone rang. It was Captain Kallunki, Acting Information Officer, (Major Coleman had accompanied Bill Ellis back to the US for the 1st Cav Association Convention). Through the weak connection, he sounded angry, and I assumed something bad had happened. He said, "Get back up here right away and clean up this mess. General Roberts is very upset with us." He wanted me to return immediately to my old job as photo coordinator at the PV office. *I guess they now realized that I did more to keep the office running smoothly than they thought, because it was fine when I left. I had only been gone from that job for less than a month. How could it have gone to hell so quickly?*

Chapter Eleven

They call me back early as Photo Coordinator

Aug 24 - Today, I never made it out of Lai Khe. The transportation situation was terrible, and there were only a few flights available. *Being back at my old job in Phuoc Vinh couldn't happen soon enough.*

Later, through the grapevine, I heard that PV photographer Paul had been banished by the commanding general from division headquarters. He should never have been given the chance to shoot a job for the CG. In June, when he first arrived at PV from 3rd Brigade, Major Coleman told me to watch him. He had been a problem there, and I had never assigned him an important job. He was given all the Criminal Investigation Division and Aircraft Accident Investigation Board assignments, and I assumed he enjoyed them. With a terrible fixation on dead NVA, he had many pictures of burned and mangled bodies. Phil said he showed some gruesome slides to everyone while I was away.

This was the ideal situation for Paul to mess up. I was gone. the acting press officer had sent Phil to the photo lab for a few days, so he was gone. Major Coleman was gone. New Press Officer, Captain Tom Kallunki was now acting information officer. Captain Jim Ryan, the former press officer, had just moved up to Quan Loi to be 3rd Brigade Information Officer. That allowed Paul to be acting photo coordinator. An amazing set of circumstances. This only lasted a few days. Paul was very near his departure (DEROS) date. When I returned, they had exiled him somewhere, and I never saw him again. *This was an embarrassment to the information office and the reason they called me back early. I never learned all the details of these problems, I heard of some missed assignments, and he may have said something disrespectful to the CG.*

If they had allowed Phil to run the place while I was gone, these problems would not have transpired. Phil had always done a great job, covering for me many times when schedules were messed up.

Aug 25 - Again, no flights for me to Phuoc Vinh. Captain Z and I went to Radio Lai Khe (1st Infantry Division, KLIK 1550) and gave them a Bill Ellis record (it came with the summer *FIRST TEAM Magazine*). They played all four songs right away. Many calls came into the station saying they liked Bill's music. We headed back to the office, stopping at Kwiki Freeze one more time. *I would certainly miss the ice cream.*

Captain Z wrote a very clever, over-the-top home town news release on my promotion and sent it to the *Vista Press*.

I thoroughly enjoyed my time at 2nd Brigade, when flights could be found to my various destinations. Much time was wasted because helicopters were not always available. The freedom to photograph what I wanted was satisfying, but not seeing proofs or prints of my photos was a problem. At Phuoc Vinh, my routine was photographing assignments during the day and doing the administrative tasks in the evening. The resumption of my old job would be welcome.

The photo to the right showed my desk after my return, with pictures of Sally. The large coffee can was a goodie package, and to the left on the desk was the Graflex XL camera with the Polaroid back.

Aug 26 - Made it to PV today and I settled back in at my old desk. My California flag was again hanging from the rafters. I returned to my old friends and routines, as if I had never left. However, some of the office paperwork was messed up, and it took days to straighten everything out. It was great listening to the music on Ron Doss' stereo.

Phil learned his next duty station would be an air defense brigade in Chicago. He had three weeks left, it wouldn't be the same here without him. Some new people had joined the office team, and we were no longer understaffed.

Aug 27 - Today, both of my jobs were cancelled at the last minute when I had already arrived. I talked with some of the people I knew at Division HQ, and 227th, and they were pleased to see me back on the job. The people at the different units had talked to one another, and informed me there had been recent problems and missed photo assignments.

Aug 28 - I took advantage of being back as photo coordinator, and went on the 11 a.m. courier flight to the photo lab at Bien Hoa. I snuck away to the huge Long Binh (II Field Force) PX in a LOH with a pilot I knew. I bought some records there, including a brand new Creedence Clearwater Revival album, *Green River*. I also bought booze: Johnnie Walker Black, Chevas Regal, Bacardi, and Cutty Sark ordered by several guys at PIO. I brought a duffel bag with towels to wrap the bottles so they could be carried safely. Back to Bien Hoa, I picked up the packet from the photo lab, caught a flight to Phuoc Vinh, and arrived about 4 p.m.

When we first played the *Green River* album, the song *Bad Moon Risin'* came on, and since my last name was Moon, everyone looked at me and laughed. We played it several times, and the laughter continued. I was now known to all as Bad Moon Risin', my second *Nom de Guerre*.

Flying in a Snake . . .

(U.S. Army Photo by Sp4 Phillip Blackmarr)
A "Killer Snake" pilot of the 2nd Battalion, 20th Artillery (ARA), bares the snake's fangs as he sights a target and strikes. The photographer took this shot from the front seat by holding up a mirror, then printing the picture backwards. Loaded rocket pods can be seen to the left.

An unusual creative photo by Phil graced the front page of the *Cavalair*, (photo above). He flew in the gunner seat of a 2/20 Cobra gunship and used a mirror to photograph the pilot.

Aug 29 - I flew to the Bu Dop Special Forces Camp north of Quan Loi, near Cambodia, on the 8th Engineers C&C Huey as I accompanied Battalion Commander Lt. Col. Broumas, one of my favorite people. My job was photographing the construction of an airstrip extension so C-130s could land. This was for a magazine story on the engineer's projects.

Incoming mortar rounds struck throughout the day, but no one was hurt. The engineers had to fill in many craters in the airstrip. I took some photos of surveyors, (see photo at right), and a grader doing finish work.

As we descended out of the clouds on the way back to Quan Loi, our Huey was hit by 51 caliber antiaircraft fire. The pilot took immediate evasive action. One round went through the bottom of the Huey, hit the pilot's armored seat and deflected back into Lt. Col. Broumas' galvanized water cooler. It was sitting right in front of me. It jumped back toward me, water went all over the floor and there was smoke.

I was so fortunate that large water cooler was there. I was sitting behind it on the bench between Lt. Col. Broumas and Sgt. Maj. Salazar. The colonel was trying to see where the shooting was coming from, but we were still very high (1500 feet). We limped into Quan Loi, which was not far away. There was a ragged hole in the floor of the Huey under the pilot's seat, (see photo above), and a massive dent and jagged holes in the heavy Igloo galvanized steel water cooler, (see photo at right). Lt. Col. Broumas patted me on the back and said, "We were all very lucky today, but especially you." We waited at the 8th Engineers C Company while a maintenance crew thoroughly checked the Huey. We caught a ride back to PV in a Chinook.

I wasn't going to think about this incident any longer, the "what if" thoughts would mess up my mind. In this environment, close calls happened frequently. I had already been lucky several times.

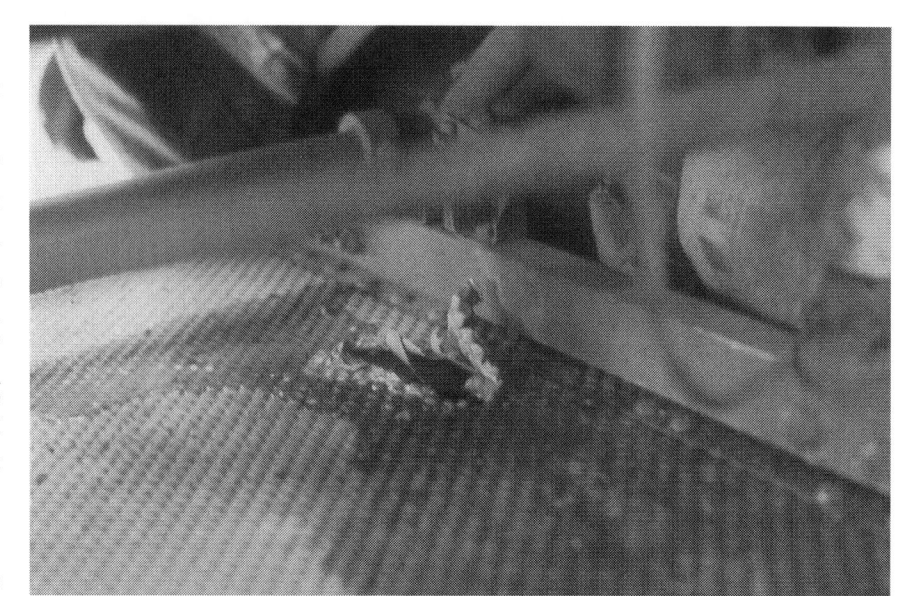

Aug 30 - Up early, I put the events of the past day behind me and flew back to Bu Dop with the engineers. First, we stopped at LZ Thunder III, near Lai Khe. Then to Quan Loi, where we stopped for fuel at the POL point, and as was his custom, Lt. Col. Broumas had everyone on board do pushups. We finally arrived at Bu Dop. I took more photos of the engineers and of the first C-130 landing on the new extended airstrip. Later, I shot the unloading of a huge tractor, and other equipment.

The first C130 into Bu Dop as it leaves from the newly constructed airstrip.

LZ Buttons was our next stop where the 2nd Brigade engineer company had a memorial service for a buddy killed a few days before. They had the boots, the M16 with its bayonet stuck in the ground, and the helmet on top. It was a very dramatic and sad scene, (see photo to the right). After that, we went to the top of Nui Ba Ra Mountain, where engineers were working on the communications station. I finally fulfilled the assignment I had received two weeks ago to photograph the facility. There was a good view of LZ Buttons below. A wild ride back to Phuoc Vinh followed, some of these pilots were hot rodders. They tried to scare us by hitting trees with the skids.

Later, I went to the PX with two other guys to buy soft drinks and beer for our party this evening. Our "truck" only had second gear. We had to push it to back up or to get it moving forward, that was why there were three of us. It rained hard as we crept back to the office. Nobody knew who the truck belonged to, so we couldn't get it fixed through normal channels. I didn't know what the party was celebrating, but we didn't need a reason!

184 They Call me Back Early as Photo Coordinator

Aug 31 - As the day began, I accompanied Brig. Gen. Meszar on a tour of the 93rd Evac Hospital in Long Binh (photo at right). I took polaroids as the general presented medals, mostly Purple Hearts, and talked to the wounded 1st Cav soldiers. I was grateful that now there were fewer wounded guys than during my previous visits. I was always amazed at the high spirits and courage of the wounded skytroopers. Most of them couldn't wait to get back to their units. *Nothing less than the best possible job from me for these guys!*

Sep 1 - Late in the morning, I photographed several 15th Medical Battalion awards with Commanding Officer Lt. Col. Joe McNancy. The medics were special, highly trained people with extremely stressful jobs. After the ceremonies, at their invitation, I stayed for an enjoyable lunch. They remembered my medic photo from the papers.

We had a party at the office in the evening. Phil invited four Red Cross girls. Quite a change from our regular parties, much quieter. Everyone just wanted to look at real, live, American girls because it reminded them of home. Phil had a favorite.

Sep 2 - Early, my assignment was a safety award presentation at Lai Khe with Brig. Gen. Meszar. We returned about 11 a.m. Later, I shot an award ceremony for the 545th MP Company at Phuoc Vinh. They were out in their formation when a violent cloudburst struck and drenched the unfortunate MPs. The rain was amazing, sometimes it seemed like an inch an hour. *It was so heavy it pounded you down.*

Sep 3 - There were 2 a.m. incoming rockets and a ground attack on the greenline about 200 yards away from our office. We heard sporadic small arms fire and exploding claymores until one of our Cobras above us fired its minigun and several rockets. It was quiet after that.

It was announced that Ho Chi Minh, the leader of North Vietnam had died. We wondered how this would change the war.

Lt. Col. Broumas, CO of the 8th Engineers, had told me if additional pictures were needed for the magazine article, I could fly to more of their projects in his C&C Huey today with his planning team. I told Major Coleman I was going with Lt. Col. Broumas to finish up the magazine story and started the long walk to the Skybeaver pad. The photos for the job, so far, went through my mind and I thought about what was needed to finish the article. One of the places on their agenda had already been photographed. There were plenty of things I could do at the office. Just a few days ago I had flown with them for two entire days. My photos of new LZ Mary construction could be used if needed.

I was momentarily distracted by the "octopus" hollow metal tube with one end blown open that remained from a recent incoming rocket. I paused, seeing it lying beside the road near where it detonated during the night. A bad omen? I changed my mind about going, turned around and returned to the office. There would be plenty of photos for the magazine article.

In the middle of the afternoon, I heard Major Coleman shouting, "Where's Terry?" I stood up as he burst into the press office. He rushed over and hugged me. He had difficulty speaking. "The 8th Engineer C&C Huey crashed today. Lt. Col. Broumas and everyone else on it were killed," he said breathlessly. "I thought you were on it."

I should have been. I collapsed into my chair. He said some other things, but I didn't comprehend any of it, as my mind was numb.

Thinking back, before I left the office this morning, I told Major Coleman I was flying with the engineer's on their C&C Huey, but he had already left the office when I returned.

I was in shock. I just sat there for a long time. Everyone left me alone.

There was a powerful, strange, dreadful feeling that overwhelmed me, as I tried to comprehend the situation. I learned later it was called survivor guilt. I was supposed to have been with my friends, but I wasn't. Now they were all dead, and I was still here. Why? It took a while for me to get over this tragedy. I had flown with them so many times. What really caused me not to go today? Random luck had saved me again, or was it, as a few friends suggested, divine intervention.

Sep 4 - Famous journalists, Horst Faas and Peter Arnett, arrived the previous day and stayed in the press office. The following morning, they flew out to LZ Ike (25 km NE of Tay Ninh). Arnett wrote a partly fictitious story about drug use among troops, and a guard dog warning the firebase of enemy attacks. *Pacific Stars and Stripes* ran this story with a photo of the dog barking at the gate of the LZ, implying that the dog warned the LZ of attacks. The fact that the attack came after midnight was never mentioned. *Arnett had completely ignored the heroics of C and E companies of 2/8 during an attack on the firebase. He wasn't interested in reporting the war. He had his own agenda. Major Coleman had trusted him to be an honest journalist, and Peter Arnett had stabbed him in the back. CG Roberts had been skeptical in the first place, the shit hit the fan through the chain of command and Major Coleman was almost fired. Typical of the new agenda driven media, truth no longer mattered to them. They weren't reporting what we were doing. They were looking to fuel the antiwar sentiment in the USA. When Major Coleman cut back media access to our operations, they screamed "cover-up." This went on over several days, but I'm putting it all here, as I was still in a funk from yesterday.*

Sep 5 - "The night the sky exploded."
First, we heard the siren at 3 a.m., then the sounds of incoming rockets nearby. Suddenly, a brilliant flash lit up everything and a thunderous blast shook the building. I was already on the floor wearing my helmet and flak jacket. This was an automatic response, I didn't need to think about it. Debris pounded the roof hard. We all ran for the bunker. Several more rockets hit, none of them close.

A 122 mm rocket impacted high on a rubber tree on the other side of the press/photo office from our building, about seventy feet from us. There wasn't much left of the tree, (see photo at right). A large piece of the rocket was embedded in the ground behind the front building. The office roof looked like it had been hit by a giant shotgun blast, and inside, was a total mess. Shrapnel was scattered over the floor with jagged pieces sticking in our tables and desks. Ironically, a copy of Norman Mailer's book *Armies of the Night* had a ragged hole through it. Tom Benic's typewriter was hit, but nothing else was damaged.

My area was covered with leaves, splinters and shrapnel. There was a large hole in the roof over my desk, (see photo to the right). *We were lucky we weren't in there when the rocket hit.* The tin roof was totally replaced before lunchtime by the PA&E construction crew of Vietnamese contract workers. *A grim reminder, I still have 65 days to go.*

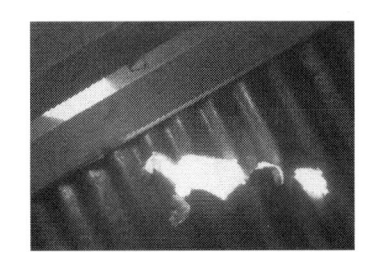

Sep 7 - I shot photos in the afternoon of George Jessel, a celebrity from another era, and other entertainers at the EM club. Next, a 13th Signal Battalion award ceremony. It rained hard on the way back, fortunately, a helpful MP gave me a ride in his jeep.

Sep 8 - It was a pleasant day for me with several routine assignments. Many of the people I worked with on these jobs were happy to adjust schedules for us. A big help to Phil and me. We enjoyed a movie in the evening *Thoroughly Modern Millie*. It was more upbeat than the one we saw last week, *Sweet November*.

Sep 9 - My assignment today was photographing several awards for the LRRP team members. They really earned these medals, the information the six-man teams found on the enemy as they did their gutsy reconnaissance was invaluable. After the lengthy ceremony, a guy, with the unmistakable look of an FNG, approached me and asked, "How do I become a photographer with the information office?"

I replied. "Go to the information office building in the rubber trees, see Major Coleman, the information officer, and have an extremely good resume."

It didn't take long, Major Coleman had Jim McCabe, the FNG, transferred quickly to PIO and he was assigned to my old spot at 2nd Brigade, now based at Song Be.

Greenline bunker 35, behind the press/photo office.

Sep 11 - About midnight, the greenline bunkers behind the office began heavy M-16, M-60, and M-79 fire, and someone was shooting back. Quickly, the Nighthawk Huey and Cobra arrived from DIVARTY. We could see the big searchlight come on from the Nighthawk Huey and both choppers fired their miniguns. Silence followed. The greenline bunkers were now staffed by short-timer grunts that really knew what they were doing. In the morning, they found several dead NVA outside the wire. We could see a few of them from behind the office. We all chipped in and bought a case of beer for the guys on each bunker for a job well done.

This morning, I shot several award presentations in the CG's office and the chain of command portrait of our new Assistant Division Commander, Brig. Gen. George Casey in front of his Huey (photo to the right). *He was intense, very sharp, and impressed everyone. I could tell he would be a great general. He would become the next 1st Cav CG in May of 1970.*

Later, I went to the airstrip and shot photos of LRRPs practicing rope extractions, where a Huey trailing a long, dangling rope would fly by, the LRRPs would grab hold and ride safely away. *Amazing, this was so fast and scary.* It was a challenging subject for a camera with all manual controls. About the time I figured how to shoot it, they stopped doing it. I also shot photos of C-130s with the long 400 mm lens (see photo next page).

Sep 12 - In the morning, I photographed 227th AHB pilot awards and promotions. There were nods and smiles as I knew some of these pilots. Later, I went to division artillery (DIVARTY) and photographed 2/20 Blue Max Cobra maintenance as they removed a rotor head. Next to 1/9 Cobra maintenance with an unusual shot of a mechanic brushing the "teeth" of a Cobra.

Phil Blackmarr entertains the skytroopers and six armed 155 rounds at an LZ during the tour. The grunt on the right is wearing a "chicken plate."
Photo by Captain Jim Ryan

Sep 13 - I missed a big tour today celebrating the 1st Cav's 48th birthday, as I was unable to find a flight. This rarely happened. Phil left on an all-day entertainment tour of fire support bases, Jamie, Ike, Grant and Buttons, playing his violin along with the singing and guitars of Bill Ellis and Captain James Ryan (our former press officer, now 3rd Brigade IO). *I wanted to go on this tour, and don't know how I messed it up.*

Instead, I shot a special presentation by Phil's favorite red cross girl in the commanding general's office, and a show with a Vietnamese rock band "singing" American pop songs at the EM club, (*Cavalair* page at right).

Some of the guys in the club audience recognized my name tag and told me they liked my pictures in the *FIRST TEAM Magazine* and the *Cavalair*. I always appreciated that. Again, the same old question popped up, "How did you get this job?"

Later, I prepared for my Tokyo leave where I planned to buy camera gear and stereo equipment. *I would be the kid in the candy store and could save so much money buying it there.* One of the office guys bought my old Pentax Spotmatic camera. I would buy a new one in Tokyo.

Sep 14 - Today, the D Troop 1/9 jeep guys that I had spent a day with three weeks before, were ambushed in the same area, near Song Be, where I had been out with them. A bad scene, there were several casualties. *You never knew what could happen on any given day. This could have been the day I went with them. Heroics in this battle resulted in a Congressional Medal of Honor for Sergeant Donald Skidgel, one of the D 1/9 jeep gunners.*

188   They Call me Back Early as Photo Coordinator

In the morning, I made another courier run with the packet to the Bien Hoa photo lab. Also with me was the notorious duffel bag full of towels for wrapping the booze bottles purchased from the Long Binh PX. The guys appreciated this, and it was not abused. We had our monthly party in the evening with steaks and beans. The PIO guys from the brigades had arrived during the day. A couple of the photographers would stay in Phuoc Vinh and cover for me while I was on leave.

Sep 15 - It rained hard the entire day. Some of the new brigade photographers helped cover jobs today, showing respect which I appreciated. We now had a larger staff. Major Coleman was planning to audition photographers to take over my job when I departed in early November.

Phil only had a few days left, but he didn't have the normal short-timer paranoia. As always, he was efficient, quiet and completely calm.

Radio announcer and short-timer, Dave VanDrew, took his leave in Tokyo last month. He had good information that would help me make the most of my time there. I could also have items shipped home for free from the huge Ginza USO PX.

Getting my finances in order, I would leave PV the very next day for my Tokyo leave. I can't believe this is finally happening.

Sep 16 - I said good-bye to Phil, he would leave for home tomorrow. It wouldn't be the same here without him, we worked together so well for so long.

I flew to Bien Hoa early to process out on leave. At the R&R center, a fire direction control computer operator from 1/30 Artillery, Donn Rojeski, introduced himself. A University of Nebraska graduate, he recognized my name tag, knew of my pictures in the newspapers, and the 1/30 magazine story. Donn also was going to Tokyo to get stereo and camera equipment. We would go together.

As I assembled my necessary leave papers, I couldn't find my shot record. *Panic! This was a BIG problem. No shot record, no leave, or, would they possibly give me all the shots again?* Not to worry, Donn just happened to know the 1st Cav medical officer here at Bien Hoa. We went to see him and he knew I had been given all the shots so he kindly made a new shot record for me. *What a relief! We get by with a little help from our friends.* Both of us took care of our leave paperwork and walked back to the photo lab. Donn enjoyed a tour. He had many questions. The entire operation was much improved since I had worked there last December. We sipped cold cokes and watched TV with the lab guys.

Sep 17 - Up early, we left at 6:30 a.m., and strolled to the Bien Hoa R&R center and finished processing out on leave. They had told us earlier that we would depart for Japan from Cam Rahn Bay, *Wrong!* We boarded a bus to Tan Son Nhut Airport, just north of Saigon (photo at right) about 10:30 a.m. On standby, they called us sooner than expected, we were cleared to go at 5 p.m., boarded a World Airways 707, and left for Tokyo at 8:15 p.m.

Sep 18 - The plane landed at Yakota AFB, Japan at 2:30 a.m. Donn and I took a bus ride to the Camp Zama processing center for a briefing, rented a room for the bargain price of 50 cents, and rested for a few hours. A bus took us to the Ginza USO in downtown Tokyo, where we made a hotel reservation at the Asia Center Hotel in the Akasaka section of Tokyo. It was necessary to go to the Sanno Hotel to cash our money orders, and change dollars into Yen. My $1400 was nearly half a million Yen. Our hotel was only a block away.

Donn and I held on for dear life during an unbelievable wild ride in a taxi (photo at right) back to the Ginza USO. *These drivers were crazy, missing accidents by inches. This was far beyond an E ticket ride.*

Then to the huge PX next door, where I bought a Sansui stereo amplifier, two big Pioneer speakers and had them shipped home, free of charge. We walked around the large Ginza area visiting numerous camera shops. The sales people were very courteous and helpful, and they all spoke English. I bought a Mamiya C-33 camera with 55, 105, and 180 lenses, a prism finder, and a grip. It was a large, heavy, true press camera. I also found a great deal on a black Pentax Spotmatic camera. Having sold my old Pentax before I left for more than I paid for the new black one, I bought a cool Seiko watch with the difference. *I would wear the watch for the next forty years.* Then to our hotel, where we finished unpacking and secured the camera equipment.

We took another taxi to the Sands Club in the Stars and Stripes Building where we had a steak dinner with the 1st Cav Tokyo newspaper production team, Al Persons and Dave Wolfe, along with Dave's wife Kathy. It was great to see these guys again, I had worked closely with each of them earlier back at Phuoc Vinh. They put together the *Cavalair* newspaper here in Tokyo every week. At 10 p.m., we went back to the hotel. *We had a great view of Tokyo Tower out of our window.*

Sep 19 - Up at 9:30 a.m., we went to the Ginza USO PX and ordered the remaining camera equipment on our lists. Walking along Ginza, (see photo at right), we took pictures, stopped at several stores, and toured the Bridgestone Art Museum.

Along the way, I bought a slick Tamron 80-250 zoom lens, *I couldn't wait to use this back in Vietnam. I could take photos with this that I was unable to take before.*

On to the Sands Club, we enjoyed a seafood dinner, followed by a loud rock band. We had another heart-in-your-throat surreal taxi ride back to Asia Center Hotel. *It was even more scary at night.*

190   They Call me Back Early as Photo Coordinator

Here I am on Tokyo Tower with my new black Pentax, new Seiko watch and a Japanese Pepsi.

Sep 20 - Up at 6:30 a.m. we walked to the Akasaka Tokyo Hotel to take a taxi to the Ginza USO. My arms were aching from constantly bracing for anticipated crashes in the taxi cabs. We took the full day Tokyo bus tour, where we saw Tokyo Tower, the Buddhist Shrine, and the Imperial Palace. After lunch, the Shinto Shrine, a pearl farm, and the National gym from the Olympics. Our tour guide had been a Japanese soldier in World War II, an interesting fellow. Someone asked him about the war, and he replied, it was like a bad dream.

That evening, we leisurely strolled from our hotel to a nearby Japanese League baseball game, Atoms versus Dragons. There were a couple of American players. Japanese fans were politely quiet, we ate crunchy (rice?) snacks and drank local beer. After the game, we rode in a taxi with our eyes closed to the Sands Club for cheese burgers, the American thing to do. Then back to the hotel where we crashed at midnight and slept well.

Sep 21 - Back to the Ginza USO PX for more shopping, I bought a record changer, a lens for my friend Allan in Korea, a zoom lens for my brother Dennis and had them shipped.

Several Japanese school girls tried speaking to us in English, with many giggles. (photo below right), as we walked around the Ginza area. We returned to the Sands Club for dinner, then back to the hotel to pack.

Sep 22 - Donn and I left the Asia Center Hotel and went to the Sony building where we purchased gifts, and I bought a canvas tote bag. We ate Japanese food and drank Sake at a small restaurant near the Akasaka Sanno Hotel, where we also watched Japanese TV, *Mission Impossible* and *Bonanza*. It was tough to handle Hoss Cartright speaking Japanese. Back to the hotel for our stuff, then another life-threatening taxi ride to the Ginza USO where we caught a bus to Camp Zama and rented a room.

Sep 23 - Up at 8:45 a.m., for the Hakone National Park tour in the rain. A spectacular view of Mt. Fuji should have been there, but not today. I watched a speeding bullet train as it overshot the station and had to back up (photo at right).

We rode a bus back to Camp Zama, arriving at 6 p.m. I bought several rolls of medium format 120 film for my new C-33 camera at the big Zama PX. Both of us carefully packed our new camera gear for the flight. After dinner at the cafeteria, we went back to the R&R lounge, checked our bags and were given boarding passes.

Sep 24 - We arrived at Yakota AFB around 5 a.m. after a long rainy bus ride. Our 707 took off at 6:45 a.m., with never a glimpse of Mt. Fuji the entire time we were in Japan. I slept during the flight. We arrived at Tan Son Nhut Airport at 12:30 p.m. and caught a bus back to Bien Hoa, arriving at the photo lab about 4 p.m. Donn and I had a tough time hauling all our stuff up the hill from the R&R center to the lab. Neither one of us were in a hurry to return to PV.

Tomorrow, I would check on my next duty station, since there would be a year and a half remaining for me in the Army after I left Vietnam.

Sep 25 - The lab guys helped Donn and me take his luggage down to the airstrip for the flight back to PV. Then I walked to 15th Admin to learn where my next duty station would be. Of course I had to wait, but finally they told me they would send it to me in a day or two. My return to Phuoc Vinh would be early tomorrow. *It will be great fun to use my new camera equipment. Only forty days left for me in Vietnam.*

I posed in a LOH with my new zoom lens, wishing I had bought it sooner.

CHAPTER TWELVE
SHORT TIMER FOG AND PARANOIA, LEAVING WITH A FLOURISH

Sep 26 - Leaving the photo lab early, I caught a Huey to PV. Phil had gone home, and I would miss him. We had worked together daily since February. Major Coleman brought in many new experienced journalists. He spared some of them the agony of being grunts, and created a highly motivated, talented team. A couple of photographers were here helping me as they waited for their assignment from Major Coleman.

Our artist, Ron Doss, spent a few days out in the field with a 3rd Brigade grunt company. He would turn that experience into artwork for future *Cavalairs,* and the next *FIRST TEAM Magazine.*

Sep 28 - After several assignments today, I was quickly back into the routine. My first stop was technical maintenance at the 13th Signal Battalion, then photos of Division Artillery communications equipment. These were close-up flash photos of technicians working on bulky electronic equipment.

Tonight, was Brig. Gen. Meszar's last night at the CG's mess. In February, I had photographed his arrival, and had been on several hospital tours with him. I took Polaroid pictures of the general staff activities and received compliments from some of them. They asked what I had photographed lately, and what good stuff I bought in Tokyo.

Sep 29 - In the morning, Brig. Gen. Meszar's farewell ceremony at the VIP pad was my assignment. It was a large ceremony with the band and all the flags. I used the new, heavy, twin-lens C-33 camera, (see photo at right). I worked with one previously at the *Vista Press* newspaper. The photo lab guys would love the larger negatives.

Oct 1 - Only one job for me today, a change-of-command ceremony at 13th Signal Battalion where Lt. Col. Archibald took over from Lt. Col. Cook. These ceremonies were so familiar to me. It was almost like being on autopilot.

I had two photos in the latest *Cavalair,* CG Roberts with a presentation to Phil's favorite Red Cross girl on page one, and a Bu Dop engineer photo of a Skycrane carrying a bulldozer on page eight.

Only a few small attacks had occurred since the NVA suffered the overwhelming defeat on August 12. *I hope they wait another month for their next attack, by then I would be gone.*

"We couldn't get cokes the last few days. Oh well, war is hell." I lamented as I drank Kool-Aid. A *Vista Press* newspaper arrived in the mail with my letter published in editor Russ Dietrich's column. I wrote to him every three or four weeks and he would then run my letter in the newspaper.

Oct 2 - Great news! My next duty station would be, Ft. Myer, Virginia, The Signal Support Photo Lab at The Military District of Washington D.C. I would report there on my next birthday, January 5, 1970. Everyone in the office agreed, that it would be a great assignment. *I will see if I can persuade President Nixon to let the 1st Cav chase the NVA into their safe havens in Cambodia.*

My Division Artillery Nighthawk job was rained out, so we would try again the next day.

One of the 3rd Brigade photographers, Bill Ahrbeck, who had arrived at PIO in June, photographed an interesting demonstration several weeks ago at Quan Loi. The photos ran as the center spread of the *Cavalair* last week, (see photo next page). The morning after the August 12 attack on Quan Loi, a sapper gave himself up. All his comrades had been killed during the attack. A demonstration was arranged for him to show us how sappers operated as they tried to penetrate our greenline defenses. That was extremely interesting to everyone.

Wearing only shorts and his satchel charge back pack, the sapper carried wire cutters and an AK-47. Trip flares were tied off and claymores were disarmed easily, as he methodically moved through the greenline wire. Soon, he emerged inside, ready to blow up something. Impressive! The demonstration would help us strengthen our defenses. I had talked at length to Bill Ahrbeck at one of our parties at PV and during a visit to Quan Loi, where he mentioned the sapper job. In the jungle, he also had taken several excellent "grunt portraits" that had been in the *Cavalair*.

The DIVARTY Nighthawk team over the Song Be River near Phuoc Vinh.

Oct 3 - Today, I flew with the DIVARTY Nighthawk team, a Huey with a minigun in the middle of the door and a huge searchlight with a starlight scope mounted in the door gun spot. (See photo at the right.) It was from E/82, Division Artillery's flight support battery, accompanied by a Cobra gunship from Battery B, 2/20 Aerial Rocket Artillery (photo below). On several nights, we had seen the team flying outside our greenline. They were extremely effective countering ground attacks, and we were thankful they were out there watching. The Huey flew low at night around our base looking for signs of NVA activity using the starlight scope. When they saw something, they lit it up with the giant searchlight, or threw out a flare. Then the Cobra flying high above rolled in and blasted the area. The minigun on the Huey was also ready to deal out destruction. I shot the team together over the Song Be River as we shadowed them in a LOH (photo previous page).

Cobra Gunship from 2/20 Aerial Rocket Artillery provides most of the firepower to the Nighthawk team.

My new 80-250 mm zoom lens was outstanding! Took several shots of the Nighthawk Huey showing the starlight scope, searchlight, and the minigun. Then I rode to Bien Hoa in the Huey. The Cobra flew amazingly close, creating a nice shot of the gunship over top of the starlight scope (it was mounted in the door gun position) and its operator, (see photo above).

Both pilots were goofing off and ascended to 5500 feet where it was freezing cold. The Cobra dove (see photo at right, the Cobra is on the left side) and we followed in the Huey reaching 125 knots. It really rattled the chopper, and was more than scary. I thought it would rip the rotor right off as they pulled out of the dive, another macho maneuver. *Some pilots got a rise out of scaring passengers. I experienced this pilot behavior frequently. This was one of the worst.*

When we returned to Division Artillery, I stopped at 1/30 to see my Tokyo leave friend Donn Rojeski. Although busy, he would join us at PIO later. He arrived at 3:30 p.m., we talked and I gave him some photos. Staff Judge Advocate (legal) next door had a party so we enjoyed steaks, chicken, and beans, along with a few refreshing, cold Budweisers. An uplifting, pleasant evening was enjoyed by all.

Oct 4 - Only a few routine assignments today. At times, I was the only photographer available to shoot jobs. We now had a busier schedule, and Phil was gone. Brigade photographers were rotating to PV filling in for Phil, and Major Coleman would chose one or two soon to stay in PV. Former grunt Dean Sharp impressed me the most.

I think short timer fog and paranoia are creeping into my head. Activities, like flying, that had been routine, seem more dangerous to me now, because as of today, I have one month to go.

Oct 5 - The shit house fragging.

I was the only one in the office when Criminal Investigation Division guys (CID) came looking for a photographer. An unusual crime had been committed in the base defense force area, where a grunt battalion had just rotated in from the field. Apparently, a grudge also came in with the grunts. Someone had crept up behind a four hole shit house and dropped a frag (fragmentation grenade) under a guy sitting on the hole by the door. A cutoff 55 gallon drum was under each hole, and the back of the structure was open on the bottom so the drum could be removed and the waste burned. For some reason, the guy jumped out the door before the frag exploded and the entire structure was destroyed. I photographed what remained. It looked similar to destruction from a tornado, as nothing was still standing. However, no one was hurt. The CID guys were laughing, but I failed to see the humor. It looked like attempted murder to me. Some of the guys back at the office also thought it was funny. Later, CID promptly picked up the pictures and I never saw them. No further information was made available.

Statistics showed the 1st Cav had a much lower crime rate than any other combat division. Here again, it was due to the pride and cooperative team spirit.

Tom Benic's Army-Navy game Promo setup. That's Tom with the pipe and the Cav patch, Office NCOIC Roger Ruhl is in front of Tom, and the guy with the boonie hat is the grunt assigned to the bunker. This is from the November 26 Cavalair.

Oct 6 - In the morning, I photographed several routine awards ceremonies. Later, PIO writer Tom Benic and I set up a promotional shot for the Army-Navy football game. We put a TV and a "Go Army" pennant out on picturesque greenline bunker 36. Included were a couple of guys who watched wearing helmets, flak jackets and carrying M16s. In the foreground, we spiced it up with an M60 machine gun and ammo belts. *It looked great! This would become the most successful promo photo that we had ever released. It ran in almost all Army publications, and it even ran in the LA Examiner and several other US newspapers.*

Giant Skycrane helicopter hovers while Battery C 1/30 artillerymen attach the 155mm howitzer for it's trip from LZ Wescott to LZ Vivian (between Quan Loi and Song Be) It is on it's way in photo below.

Oct 7 - Up early, I caught a flight to LZ Wescott, northeast of Quan Loi. *A strong, new feeling of apprehension about flying had crept into my mind.* My assignment was to photograph C Battery, 1/30 Artillery moving three of their 155 howitzers to LZ Vivian, about 12 km to the North. It appeared that the rainy season was over. It was extremely hot. I kept getting sandblasted by the Skycranes and Chinooks as I ran around taking photos.

I took numerous shots of Skycranes hauling 155s, and artillery crews setting up at the new LZ. Within minutes, the guns were ready for a fire mission. *The half-hour flight back to PV seemed much longer. My flight anxiety was growing.*

Aerial view of 155 crew setting up their new pit at LZ Vivian.

The 155 howitzer is anchored down in preparation for firing

1st Cav's 1/30 Artillery crew members fill sandbags in the foreground as the 155 howitzer is set up at its new home at LZ Vivian, near Quan Loi. The skytrooper on the radio is coordinating the arrival of additional equipment while more of the artillery crew arrive on the Huey in the background.

I wished I had bought this zoom lens much earlier, as it made it easier to take better photos. These pictures would be a Cavalair center spread and also run in Pacific Stars and Stripes in late November.

Oct 8 - I stayed in the office most of the day and did the weekly output report while relaxing in the sun on top of our bunker. In the afternoon, I walked over to a job with 8th Engineers. They were building an M16 rifle range with bulldozers. A sad scene for me at the 8th Engineer Headquarters without Lt. Col. Broumas' enthusiasm and humor. I had assigned engineer jobs to others for weeks to avoid going there.

One photo in the latest *Cavalair* was mine, the engineers memorial service at LZ Buttons, with the M16, the boots, and the helmet. *How ironic, the tragic engineer Huey crash was only a few days after I had taken this picture on August 30. That day was the last time I saw Lt. Col. Broumas and his crew.*

PIO writer Tom Benic had an interesting story to accompany his center spread photos from the latest *Cavalair*, (see above). He had been working in a joint operation of ARVN Regional Forces and 1st Cav grunts along with two former NVA troops that had defected, called Hoi Chanhs by the Vietnamese. The former NVA were leading the Cav-ARVN RF soldiers to their old unit's base camp in the thick jungle near Song Be. The two former NVA soldiers broke into a run down a trail, so the RTO and Tom followed them. Several minutes later, they came to a clearing with bamboo "Hooches" and stopped. Tom and the RTO looked around and realized they were the only ones there with the former NVA. The RTO radioed the company commander, "Captain, where are you?"

Ace Cavalair reporter Tom Benic did such a great job, in December he was selected to join the prestigious Pacific Stars and Stripes staff.

"We're coming, staying off the trail. Who is with you?" replied the Captain.

"Only the newspaper guy, and the NVA." responded the RTO.

Tom was very fortunate that no NVA were in the clearing. The rest of the Cav and ARVN RFs arrived about ten minutes later. After searching the area, they did find a sizable cache of weapons.

The weather was in transition. It was extremely hot during the day and rained at night. The oppressive humidity remained constant.

Oct 9 - In the morning, I took a portrait of Commanding General Roberts behind his desk with my new C33 camera, a tripod and the big floodlights. They sent a jeep for me and all my gear. This was an elaborate production compared to the single flash we usually used. It went smoothly, he seemed to enjoy the session. *In fact, it was fun for both of us. He was almost too nice to be a general.*

The Nighthawk prints arrived and they looked terrific. Major Coleman liked several of the shots and wanted to send them to all the publications.

Oct 10 - I shot E/82nd awards with Commanding Officer Major Joe Davis, then later, some maintenance photos. They were Division Artillery's air wing, and I often rode in their choppers. *They would love the Nighthawk pictures.*

Oct 12 - A large group photo of SGMs was my assignment for Division Command Sergeant Major Kennedy. He gave up harassing me about my mustache long ago. Later, I shot several awards for my friends at 227th Assault Helicopter Battalion.

The engineers wanted prints of all my LZ Mary construction pictures, as they planned to quickly reopen it.

Oct 13 - Spec. 5 Terry Moon won the PIO football pool last week. *Yes, as the guys said, the Bad Moon had risen.*

Oct 14 - My job today was taking photos of Chaplain's activities, first at the main chapel (photo above right), and later at Division Artillery (DIVARTY). I also photographed Chaplain Hosutt with Battery A, 2/19 Artillery at Phuoc Vinh. Thereafter, we took a coffee break and talked about cameras, it seemed like everyone had a question.

Oct 15 - The Phuoc Vinh "Palace Guard," 2/8 under Lt. Col. Fred Lindsey, had an award ceremony. Later, I photographed Nighthawk maintenance at E/82nd as the crew disassembled the Huey's minigun, (photo at right).

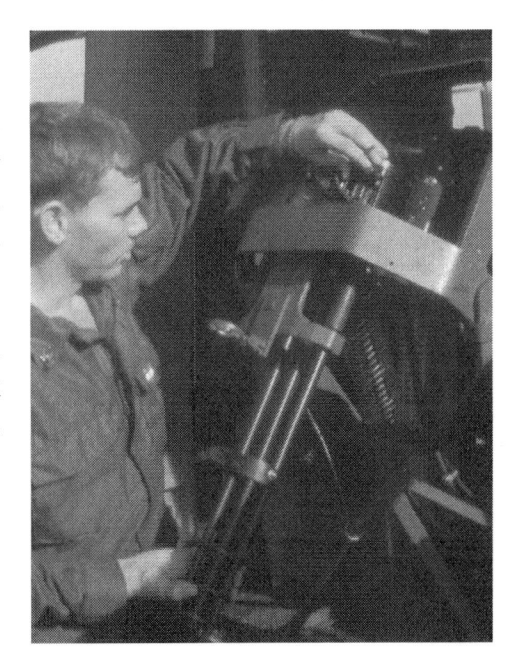

I had two photos in the latest *Cavalair*, a Troop C, 1/9 Cobra getting its "teeth" brushed (photo at right) and Brig. Gen. Meszar's departure ceremony, both on page one.

It had been more than a month since we had any incoming or a ground attack. Phouc Vinh was overdue. We used to have attacks every couple of weeks.

Oct 16 - Late this morning, I shot the Division Artillery (DIVARTY) Change of Command Ceremony. Col. James A. Munson passed command to Col. Morris J. Brady. The band played and the flags rippled in the light breeze and hundreds of skytroopers stood at attention.

I accompanied Major Coleman to the ceremony. He had a superb story about Col. Brady dating back to May 1966. Then Lt. Col. Brady was 2/20 ARA commanding officer, and a Huey gunship pilot. He had defended the surrounded B 2/8 grunt company commanded by then Captain Coleman. The gunship hovered above the pinned down company and stopped a VC assault in a mountainous area of the central highlands. The grunt company had taken heavy casualties, but with radio directions from Captain Coleman during a driving rainstorm, the heavy fire from the gunships of Lt Col. Brady and his wing man, forced the VC to back off long enough for reinforcements and more ammunition to be airlifted in. Major Coleman, for his heroics, was awarded a Silver Star, the third highest medal for valor. He was well respected throughout the division.

62% Less NVA With Cobra...

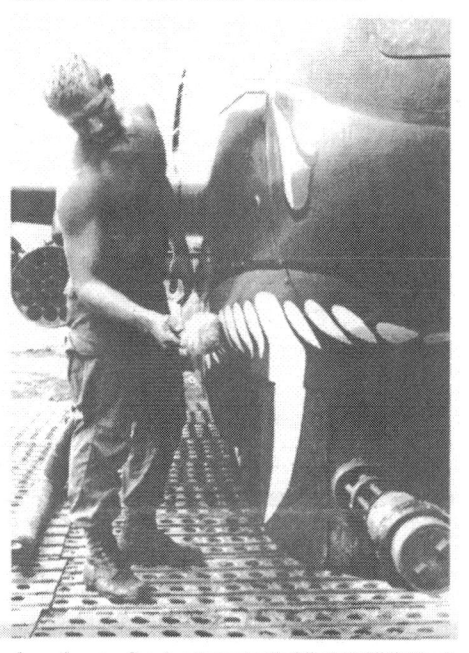

(U.S. Army Photo by SP5 Terry Moon)
Taking a king-size toothbrush to the teeth of a Cobra, Specialist Four Duane Grenz of Troop C, 1st Squadron of the 9th Cav shines the ship as part of the preventive maintenance program.

A C123 lands at the Phuoc Vinh and is framed inside the gateway to the 1/9 area.

Oct 17 - An early job for me, photographing a Troop C, 1/9 awards ceremony. These guys earned a ton of medals. Around their area, the officers wore the Stetson hats and carried swords. *They really were crazy.* Somehow, my own pictures of them were lost. To the right is one from the *Cavalair*. They had an "attitude," and didn't like photographers, or writers. When I flew with the 1/9 scout team, the pilot threatened to "throw my ass out" of his LOH, but when I accompanied the D Troop jeep unit on a mission, they accepted me as one of their own. The 1st Squadron, 9th Cavalry was the most decorated and took more casualties than any other battalion sized unit during the entire Vietnam war.

Oct 18 - General Ralph Haines, US Army Pacific Commander toured Quan Loi and several LZs. It would be my all-day assignment. We flew to reopened LZ Mary (D 5/7) southeast of Song Be. *The rebuilt LZ looked different, and I was pleased it had risen again.* Next, a quick flight north to LZ Judie (2/12), then to Quan Loi. He toured the 6/27 175 mm Artillery Battery (photo at right) and had lunch with the 11th Armored Cavalry Regiment.

A stop followed at the 11th ARVN Airborne Division base at LZ Jackie, 28 km northeast of Nui Ba Den. This fire base was totally South Vietnamese. The ARVN soldiers of this elite unit were much smaller in stature than the Americans (see photo below). Finally, we visited 1st Brigade's LZ Ike, 25 km northeast of Tay Ninh. This was a brief stop, and I only took a few photos. We returned to Phuoc Vinh by 3 p.m. *I managed to keep my rising flight anxiety under control, it was inconsistent, sometimes overwhelming, sometimes absent. Flying in a LOH was never a problem.*

US Army Pacific Commander Gen. R. E. Haines, 1st Cav Commanding General E. B. Roberts and 1st Cav 1st Brigade Commander Col. Joseph E. Collins are led by leaders of the 11th ARVN Airborne Division on a tour of LZ Jackie, northeast of Tay Ninh.

Short-Timer Fog and Paranoia, Leaving with a Flourish

The following was the itinerary for General Haines' tour. The Phuoc Vinh base camp was also known as Camp Gorvad, named for the 2/12 Battalion Commander Peter Gorvad who was killed by a rocket at LZ Grant last March.

Confidential

DEPARTMENT OF THE ARMY
HEADQUARTERS 1ST AIR CAVALRY DIVISION
APO San Francisco 96490

AVDACS   18 October 1969

Itinerary for GEN Ralph E. Haines Jr., CINCUSARPAC, plus 4

PERIOD OF VISIT: 200730 - 201500 October 1969

TIME	EVENT	TRANS	RESP INDIV/UNIT
0730	Arrive Camp Gorvad	UH-1	USARV
0730-0815	Morning Briefing		CG
0815-0830	Coffee Break		CG
0830-0900 ~ 930	G2/G3 Update Briefing		G2/G3
930-955 0900-0925	Enroute to FSB Mary	UH-1	CG
955 1055 0925-1000	Briefing, Tour FSB Mary		CO, 2nd Bde
1100 1110 1000-1010	Enroute to FSB Judie	UH-1	CG
1110 1140 1010-1040	Briefing, Tour FSB Judie		CO, 2nd Bde
1140 1200 1040-1055	Enroute to Quan Loi	UH-1	CG
1200 1055-1100	Enroute to Hqs 6/27th Arty (II FFV Arty)	M-151	CO, 3rd Bde
1100-1115	Briefing, Hqs 6/27th Arty		CO, 6/27th Arty
1115-1125	Tour A Brty 6/27th Arty		CO, 6/27th Arty
1125-1135	Enroute to 11th ACR	UH-1	CG
1235 1135-1230	Lunch w/11th ACR		CO, 11th ACR
1330 1230-1300	Briefing, 11th ACR		CO, 11th ACR
1410 1440 1300-1330	Enroute to FSB Jackie	UH-1	CG
1440 1330-1400	Briefing FSB Jackie		CO, 3rd Bn, 2nd Bde 11th ARVN ABN DIV
1500 1400-1415	Enroute to FSB Ike	UH-1	CG
1415-1435	Briefing, Tour FSB Ike		CO, 1st Bde
1435-1500	Enroute to Camp Gorvad	UH-1	CG
1500	Depart Camp Gorvad for USARV	UH-1	USARV

Oct 19 - Early today, I flew to Cu Chi, Bien Hoa, and Bearcat, an extremely safe flight plan, with Division Chief of Staff, Col. Robert M. Shoemaker. He would be the Cav's next assistant division commander, replacing Brig. Gen. Meszar, and would soon receive his brigadier general star. *He struck me as another impressive leader. The Cav had many outstanding officers.*

Sunday afternoon everyone was off, so several of the office guys walked with me to the 227th helicopters. A couple of them shot photos as I sat in the left seat of a LOH, holding my camera with the zoom lens. We had a great time, with nonstop wisecracks and jokes.

Some of the office staff now did the administrative tasks, and the new photographer did most of the jobs. *Just fifteen days to go as I slowly phased myself out.*

I really enjoyed flying in LOHs, and I had to have pictures of me in my favorite spot.

After numerous applicants, Major Coleman had finally found his grunt photographer. Spec. 4 Dean Sharp had been a grunt for two months with Charlie Company, 1/5. He became his battalion's unofficial photographer and sent photos to PIO. Major Coleman liked what he saw and had him transferred. Previously, he had accompanied me on a few jobs, and obviously knew what he was doing. Assigned to the Phuoc Vinh office, he would also spend time with the grunts and handle occasional special assignments that Phil and I had previously photographed.

Oct 20 - I was unable to avoid flying on a VIP tour to Quan Loi and several LZs. My short-timer paranoia was severe, with terrible flashbacks of our Huey being struck by antiaircraft fire. We were flying in the same area where the engineer Huey was previously hit. No photos were taken with my own camera on this trip or notes written about what I did. *I must have functioned totally on autopilot because the actual job photos came out fine. There was no logic to this fear, flying was no more dangerous now than it had been before, but this emotion was powerful at times.*

Oct 21 - I photographed a 227th AHB awards ceremony. There were 28 medals presented, so they kindly stopped and waited for me to change film before they continued, as we used 20 exposure rolls. I chose one or two jobs per day for myself, and other photographers did the remainder.

Oct 22 - I shot LRRP Awards again. Our special forces, their recon was invaluable and they were well respected. Later, I took a few nearby aerial photos for 191st Military Intelligence Company, they pointed, I shot. *This was so brief my anxiety never surfaced.*

208 Short-Timer Fog and Paranoia, Leaving with a Flourish

What! No incoming at Phuoc Vinh for almost six weeks. Amazing. I'm so paranoid, I expect it every night now. I took advantage of my authority as photo coordinator to be selective with my jobs. Having control of what I did subdued my anxiety for these last several days.

Oct 23 - I had a 7:30 a.m. job and another at 3 p.m., both routine awards. My short-timer fog was so bad I didn't remember where I had been. On another extremely hot and humid day, the hours dragged by. *Time was beginning to slow down. In eleven days I would leave Phuoc Vinh and begin my journey home.*

Oct 24 - Today, Major Coleman and I went to division headquarters where I took the General Staff photo. Col. Shoemaker, with the cast on his foot, was the new Assistant Division Commander. Major Coleman (on the left) briefed them before I took about twelve pictures. It was always difficult to take one picture where the entire staff looked good.

Oct 25 - I photographed an awards ceremony at Headquarters Company, 228th AHB, the Chinook battalion, and picked this job because I hadn't been there in several months. It was a long walk to the opposite end of the base. I received a ride for most of the way, as usual, everyone wanted to help.

Later, Brig. Gen. Casey gave a tour of Phouc Vinh to an Air Force general, perhaps one of his old friends. It was relaxed and casual. I tagged along and took a few photos.

Oct 26 - I walked to CG Roberts office for a Bronze Star presentation. After the brief ceremony, he smiled at me and pulled a copy of the October 24 *MACV Observer* newspaper out of his desk drawer and showed me my Nighthawk photos on page eight (photo on next page). He was delighted and congratulated me on this one. It was a great feeling to be complimented by the commanding general. He searched for our photos as he carefully scanned the larger publications (*MACV Observer, USARV Army Reporter,* and *Pacific Stars and Stripes*). I had several pictures published in the papers over the last few months.

Page 8   The OBSERVER   October 24, 1969

The Deadly Duo

Story by Captain Gerald Sharpe, USA
Photos by SP5 Terry Moon, USA

'Charlie' Strikes; Nighthawk Bites

PHUOC VINH (USA) — A hail of bullets and rockets streaking down a beam of light are only part of the "Nighthawk" surprise waiting for Charlie when he decides to invade the darkness in the 1st Cavalry Division's area of operations.

"Nighthawk" is a division artillery team composed of two helicopters — a Huey from Battery E, 82nd Artillery, and a Cobra gunship from the 2nd Battalion, 20th Aerial Rocket Artillery's Battery B.

The firepower available to this team include two 7.62mm mini-guns, each capable of spewing 4,000 rounds a minute; a 40mm grenade launcher, which can deliver 150 grenades in 30 seconds; and 76 2.75-inch rockets.

The Huey is equipped with a powerful infra-red light and scope, which turn night into day for the chopper's keen-eyed target detection crewman, Specialist 4 Harold Boatz. Also at his disposal is a night observation device which needs only starlight to operate effectively.

The "ultimate finder," though, is a 50,000-watt searchlight which not only serves as a locator but also as an enemy position marker.

Nighthawk's specialty is giving close support to an infantry unit in a night defensive or ambush position.

The moment an infantry squad spots enemy movement around its position, word is flashed to Nighthawk. Within seconds, the pilots are briefed and the positions marked with a light that can be seen only from the sky.

With the target sighted, Warrant Officer John Snowgren, piloting the Huey, banks to the left while co-pilot Warrant Officer Ronald Baker informs the Cobra pilots circling above of the sighting.

As the searchlight beam hits the ground, the Skytroopers below relay their positions in reference to the light before the Huey's radio crackles: "Nighthawk Two, this is Dodge Six. You are clear to engage."

On the mini-gun, Specialist 4 Stanley Cook pours a constant stream of fire and lead down into the small beam of light. Moments later, the Cobra releases a burst of mini-gun fire and a salvo of rockets from pods tucked under its sides.

The light goes dark, but infrared scopes continue to probe the target area for an assessment of damage.

"Mission Completed" for Nighthawk means the enemy has been caught and stopped in the darkness — before he can strike at Cav unit positions on the ground.

Before the mission, SP4 Harold W. Boatz inspects the heart of the Nighthawk's detection system, a combination Starlight Scope (top) and 50,000-watt searchlight.

Scope and searchlight replace machine gun in search ship.

A mini-gun stands ready beside the target detection equipment.

Brig. Gen. George W. Casey, 1st Cav Assistant Division Commander speaks to the ARVN unit that guarded the strategic Song Be River bridge, after he awarded medals to unit members.

Oct 27 - Brig. Gen. Casey flew to the Song Be bridge, south of Phuoc Vinh, and presented medals to ARVN soldiers who had bravely defended the strategic river crossing from a large NVA attack. I took several photos with the bridge in the background (see photo above). The general didn't actually fly his Huey like the other generals did. He was on the radio most of the time, and the copilot's seat was like his office.

Major Coleman told me the *USARV Army Reporter* was planning to run a full page of the Nighthawk photos, and *Army Times Magazine* would also run the story. These photos had been so successful that Major Coleman wanted a similar photo story with our E-82 LOH, 2/20 ARA Cobra hunter-killer scout team. The 1st Cav scout teams really excelled at finding the elusive NVA, and my assignment would be to show the process in photos. *After what CG Roberts told me yesterday and with the timing of this, he may have suggested it to Major Coleman. I always wanted to photograph the scouts, now I have the equipment to handle the difficult job.* It *would mean flying treetop level with the vulnerable scout team. With less than a week to go, I would certainly be pushing my luck. Oddly enough, I felt comfortable, and hadn't experienced any anxiety flying in a LOH.*

Oct 28 - I went to the 2/20 Blue Max gunship battalion with Brig. Gen. Casey for a large ceremony with numerous awards. I had hoped to fly with the scouts today, but the general's visit delayed it until tomorrow. I later photographed a reenlistment ceremony for an E/82 Huey mechanic. He received an $8000 bonus because he had a very important job that required extensive training and experience.

For the last several days I had packed various items to mail home, so I wouldn't have as much to carry. My camera equipment alone would be heavy.

Oct 29 - When I arrived at 2/20 and E/82 to photograph the hunter-killer team, all their choppers were tied up. With some finagling, and a little help from my friends, I found E/82 LOH and B 2/20 Cobra gunship pilots being briefed for a nearby search mission. Another LOH was available just for me. First, I took a photo of the gunship pilot, Lt. William Dobbs. After a briefing by Operations Officer Captain Epperson, I shot several photos of the LOH gunners carefully loading ammo for their M60s. They wore harnesses and sat on the floor with their machine guns in their laps and legs dangling (see photo above). I ran out in front of them and photographed the team ready for takeoff, (see photo below).

212 Short-Timer Fog and Paranoia, Leaving with a Flourish

I quickly put on my "chicken plate" body armor, climbed into the left seat of the other LOH and away we went. We flew beside the team. I photographed the two helicopters together several times. As we came to the search area, I took photos looking down on the other LOH skimming over the jungle canopy. The LOHs flew erratically to avoid being easy targets as they were only about sixty feet above the ground. That caused me to make constant adjustments with my cameras. *I couldn't have taken those photographs without my new zoom lens, and thoroughly enjoyed this great photo opportunity. I was totally focused on the job.*

At treetop level, NVA trails were easy to spot. When visibility allowed, the disturbed vegetation showed up well from the air. It required sharp eyes.

One of the gunners in the other LOH saw something, tossed a smoke grenade marker and called in the Cobra. The gunship fired several rockets, that opened up the area. We went in to check and spotted some bunkers. I could see what looked like reinforced doors, probably blown-up roofs, made of bamboo lashed together like a raft. Amazing, we weren't that far from the 1st Cav base camp at Phuoc Vinh. Grunts would be brought in quickly to investigate, probably the rapid response 1/9 infantry, known as the "Blues."

The other LOH dropped CS gas grenades into the bunkers, but they failed to mention it to my pilot on the radio as we were zigzagging around to take a look. Unfortunately, we flew right through the gas that we thought was smoke. *Gasp! Cough! Intense burning filled our eyes and noses.* The experienced pilot took us straight up since he couldn't see. We stuck our heads out into the air flow, and soon were OK. Circling around so I could get photos of the bunkers, we heard shooting. The CS gas must have pissed off the NVA. The other LOH was taking fire. *Had my luck finally run out with five days to go?* They may have also shot at us, but I didn't see any tracers. The firing continued as we quickly darted out of the way while the cobra swooped in with minigun and rockets blazing. When the gunship finished his run, silence. *What a relief.*

Blues would arrive soon on the ground to check out the bunkers. We flew the short distance back to Phuoc Vinh and my pilot dropped me off. With just five days left to go, everyone respected a short-timer. I thanked the skillful pilot, Lt. Glenn Gordon. He smiled. "Did you see the tracers go by us?"

"No," I gasped and slowly exited the LOH.

I knew this would be my last ride in the nimble aerial sports car. I took off the chicken plate and was thankful it wasn't needed. I waved to the crews at E/82. They were some of my favorite people. It was starting to sink in, that I was doing exciting, enjoyable things for the last time and I would never see these great guys again.

I walked the short distance over to 2/20 Aerial Rocket Artillery and climbed into the front (gunner) seat of a Blue Max Cobra gunship. They had invited me for one more ride, since I would soon leave for home. It was quiet, like riding in an air conditioned limo. The body was extremely narrow, and I could see the terrain clearly below (photo to the right). The pilot was showing off as he tried to scare me with some aerobatic stunts. I expected this, as it had happened often, just another "E ticket" ride. When I stepped out, I thanked the pilot and the nearby maintenance crew.

Walking back to the office, I shot photos of an automatic sandbag filling machine. I could really appreciate this from my FNG days when I filled a humongous number of sandbags with a shovel. *What a great idea, why didn't they have this a year ago?*

Back to the office briefly, then at 4:30 p.m., I walked to 15th Med for a VIP visit. Staff Sgt. John Rozell was there from the An Tuc Dispensary, a real humanitarian. He had been in Vietnam for more than three years building the fine urgent-care facility. They gave medical treatment to thousands of Vietnamese. He invited me to eat at his hooch, where he did his own cooking. So I stayed there and we watched the fifth game of the World Series while we talked about being part of a great unit like the 1st Cav. His chicken and rice was delicious. He invited me back Sunday for a Vietnamese style dinner. *I would leave Phuoc Vinh on Monday.*

Oct 30 - I received a Halloween "Witch" card from Sally. It was appropriate as she had this hilarious, cackling witch character that she played once in a while. She went to the last San Diego State football game with my family. I would be there for the next home game. Several items were packed to send home so I wouldn't have to carry them. A heavy load still remained.

Oct 31 - Two assignments today, one was an elaborate flag raising ceremony at 8th Engineers. It still bothered me to go there. The tragic Huey crash still haunted me. In the evening, we had our Halloween party. I fired up the red strobe light again as it was also my farewell party. They played *Bad Moon Risin'* several times for me. Everyone enjoyed that, envious that I would leave in two days.

Nov 1 - A quasi "holiday" here, the 1st Air Cavalry Division, similar to a city with 20,000 "residents," had a sister city like relationship with the city of Columbia, South Carolina. We called it Reuben Grauer Day, since Reuben was the Mayor there. At the same time, they celebrated the 1st Cav back in their city. Office manager, Roger Ruhl, and I went to several festivities throughout the base. We took advantage of any excuse to party. I took pictures of some of the activities for an upcoming *Cavalair* full-page spread. On this tour of the base, I also said good bye to my pilot, crew, and administrative friends at 227th Assault Helicopter Battalion, also the Division Headquarters staff, including the CG's Mess cooks. *Great memories for me with these special people.*

Nov 2 - Today, I signed over my trusty 45 pistol, the Graflex XL camera, the Polaroid backs, and other stuff to my replacement, Spec.4 Leonard Fallscheer, another Californian who had also attended San Diego State. A sharp guy, with an extensive photo lab background and camera experience shooting motorcycle races. His tour began in September at Quan Loi with 3rd Brigade. The photo coordinator job would be in good hands. *He would spearhead the relocation of the photo lab from Bien Hoa to Phuoc Vinh. This had been a problem that I wanted solved long ago.* While Phil Blackmarr and I covered most of the jobs at PV, they would now have three photographers to handle it, Leonard, former grunt Dean Sharp, and Robert Conway.

My Sunday dinner was a tasty, interesting Vietnamese style meal prepared by Staff Sgt. John Rozell at his 15th Med area hooch. *This was a most appropriate last taste of Vietnam as tomorrow I would begin my journey home.*

Nov 3 - After a sleepless night, I was up early and actually ate breakfast in the mess hall which I rarely had done. *I can't believe I leave for home today.* Midmorning, Major Coleman awarded me a Bronze Star, for meritorious service and an Air Medal. *I had more than enough hours for two Air Medals.* I was washing some of Vietnam off of me in the shower when they called me to the ceremony, I quickly dressed while everyone snickered as they waited in the formation. *No Catch 22, Yosarian-like, naked stunt from me today.*

What a strange feeling. After countless handshakes and good-byes. I was happy to be going home, but sad to be leaving the information office team. Having contributed to our success, with numerous pictures in the large publications and over a hundred photos in the *Cavalair*, I felt like an important part of a superb team. I would miss the great spirit of camaraderie and cooperation from all the members of the 1st Cav that had crossed my path each day. I doubted that anything close to this experience would ever happen to me again. How fortunate I was to have been chosen for this great opportunity.

No incoming for my last six weeks here. Remarkable. *Many close calls during the year and not a scratch, someone must have been looking out for me.*

A few of the guys accompanied me to the airstrip. After the last good-byes, I slowly looked around. Remembering the day I first arrived and saw the horror of the sinister Graves Registration area beside the airstrip. All of us who arrived that day knew we could have gone home in a bag, but thankfully, few of us did. As I walked over to the waiting C130, I watched the last of several shiny new FNGs as they struggled off the plane into the oppressive heat, that today, I hardly noticed. *Good luck, guys.*

C130 taxis on the airstrip at Phuoc Vinh, I arrived on one and I departed on one.

One last look at what had been my home for the past year, then I marched up the ramp with my heavy bags, entered the oven-like, rumbling C130, sat down on the floor and grabbed hold of a rope across the cargo bay. There were no seats or seat belts here. We roared down the runway, left Phuoc Vinh and flew to Bien Hoa. I didn't notice how heavy my load was as I carried it up the hill to the photo lab, for the very last time.

Nov 4 - I walked over to 15th Admin., turned in my M-16, which had been ready many times, but thankfully, was never used, and picked up my health records, but unfortunately I would have to return tomorrow to finish processing out.

Last night, my former comrades at 2nd Brigade, now based at LZ Buttons (Song Be), were attacked by a large NVA force. Some sappers from elite NVA units breached the wire and were finally gunned down just short of the command bunker of 2nd Brigade Commander Col. Shy Meyer. LZ Ellen, 10 km West of LZ Buttons was also attacked, but defended well by C and E companies of 1/8. *My signature combat assault job had been with the great grunts of Charlie Company.*

Nov 5 - After finishing the seemingly endless forms at 15th Admin., I returned to the photo lab, packed and later mailed some of my stuff home. I would have a heavy load, even my aluminum camera case, carefully assembled and padded, weighed over 25 pounds.

Nov 6 - Major Coleman had recruited some skilled people and lab operations were improving. Having actually worked at the photo lab, I was closer with these guys than most of the photographers. A couple of them found a ride for me to the Bien Hoa 1st Cav DEROS center to begin processing out. One final example of the helpful spirit of cooperation I experienced from members of the Cav. The theme of the day at the center was "hurry up and wait." The time passed by slowly.

The latest *Cavalair* had my super-wide shot of the 175 mm gun again, the same photo that ran six months ago, and one of my Nighthawk pilot pictures was on page one. *PIO NCOIC Roger Ruhl later sent this Cavalair and many other newspapers to me.*

An aerial photo of part of the massive Long Binh complex

Nov 7 - Leaving the 1st Cav DEROS Center early, I bounced along in a bus with dozens of other smiling faces to the 90th Replacement Center at Long Binh, to prepare for our flight home. I was disappointed not to find any of my photo school friends today that had arrived with me a year ago. I was now more impatient to leave for home. Today, the jubilant group around me relaxed and laughed as they waited for a flight back to the real world.

Not so fast, grasshopper.
There were no flights out today. *What, this can't be. We were supposed to go home, now.*
The bad news got worse. Late in the evening, we heard that terrifying, all-too-familiar sound of incoming rockets exploding extremely close to us. Many panic stricken guys screamed "Incoming," as they hit the floor. We were supposed to be out of here earlier today, but we were still here sweating out an attack. *Unbelievable.* With no idea where to find safe bunkers, we hid in a concrete shower. In my haste, I smashed the brand new sunglasses I had bought earlier today. Other guys had scrapes and bruises, but no one was seriously hurt. It was beyond scary, the total irony of this was not lost on any of us and that made it much worse. *How bizarre to be killed or wounded after we were supposed to have been out of Vietnam.*

Nov 8 - After our harrowing night, we weren't laughing as much as the day before. All we wanted to do was leave. Following a short bus ride to Bien Hoa airport, with minimal delays, we boarded a 707 "freedom bird." When we finally took off the feeling was surreal, and intensely emotional. I watched Bien Hoa and Vietnam slowly disappear behind me, forever.

A "freedom bird" leaves Bien Hoa Airport on its way back to the U.S.A., as seen earlier from the photo lab.

I made it through my year in Vietnam.

I slept through most of the long flight to Wake Island. We deplaned and walked around for a while. The ocean was on one side of the runway and a light blue lagoon on the other side. *This tiny place really was in the middle of nowhere.*

Nov 8 - We lost a day crossing the international date line. We left Wake Island and flew to Hawaii. There must have been a problem with the plane. I remembered being in the terminal several hours. My mind was racing, thinking about home and the massive lifestyle changes ahead for me.

Nov 9 - It was still dark when we boarded the plane. *Reality was blurring.* I may have slept for a while. We were in the plane for quite a while before take off. *This all seemed to be in slow motion.* Finally, late in the afternoon, we flew over the Golden Gate Bridge. We could see it as we crowded around the windows. Extreme emotion boiled over, cheering broke out, a plane full of battle-hardened veterans and everyone was crying. Minutes later, we landed at Travis AFB, northeast of Oakland.

Back home in the good old USA, my great adventure is over.

By the time we deplaned, retrieved our stuff, waited for a bus, and rode the never-ending fifty miles to the Oakland processing center, it was late in the evening. I previously told Sally and my family I would call today, but never had a chance. We ultimately stayed there for the night.

Nov 10 - Out-processing seemed to move ever so slowly. I received a new, fully decorated green uniform. It took a while for them to put the insignia and decorations on it. They gave me my orders to report to the photo lab at the Military District of Washington D. C. on January 5. There were endless visits to different stations where forms would be initialed or stamped.

I called Sally. *What a lift to hear her voice!* I would see her in a few hours. Finally cleared to leave in the evening, I left in my spiffy new uniform, carrying the heavy duffel bag and camera case.

I caught a ride to Oakland airport to wait for a PSA flight to San Diego. In the terminal, I met a pleasant, professional looking man who admired my uniform, and recognized the Cav patch and the decorations. He asked questions about my time in Vietnam and was impressed that I had been a 1st Cav photographer. A National Basketball Association Referee, he was going to San Diego for the Rockets-Pistons game on the twelfth. We sat together on the plane. After a stop in LA, we were delayed so I called my parents. Conversations with my new acquaintance relaxed me. When we finally arrived in San Diego, my NBA friend accompanied me through the terminal. I finally met Sally and my folks at 3:20 a.m. November 11, Veterans Day. After hugging Sally and my family, I saw my friend was watching. I told them who he was and we all waved. He gave us a thumbs up and smiled, then he turned and headed out. *I think he had done this before.*

It was fantastic to be with my loved ones again. My mind was in emotional overload, totally overwhelmed. Everything felt so different.

Was I now a different person? How could I not have been changed by all I went through? I would appreciate all the little things that before, I had taken for granted. Back in the real world, I would begin a wonderful, extended period of lifestyle readjustment.

Epilogue 1

Page 6 — THE ARMY REPORTER — November 10, 1969

Nighthawk choppers prey on enemy

PHUOC VINH—A hail of bullets and rockets streaking down a beam of light are only part of the Nighthawk surprise waiting for Charlie operating during darkness in the 1st Cavalry Division (Airmobile) area of operation.

The surprise is packaged in the form of a specially equipped Huey chopper teamed up with a deadly Cobra.

The firepower available to this team includes two 7.62mm miniguns, each capable of firing 4,000 rounds a minute; a 40mm grenade launcher, delivering 150 grenades in 30 seconds; and 76 2.75-inch rockets in a variety of weights, warheads and fuses.

The Nighthawks patrol the division's area each night with assistance from several target detection teams, ranging from the infantrymen to sophisticated ground and air radar. When the Nighthawk team is alerted to a possible enemy location, the crew is well equipped to find whatever is lurking in the shadows near friendly positions.

A powerful infrared light and scope turn night into day for the keen-eyed target detection crewman. Also at his disposal is a night observation device, which needs only starlight to operate effectively.

Besides these two modern electronic detection systems, the crew uses the "ultimate finder" — a 50,000-watt Xenon searchlight which not only serves as a locator but also as a marker of the enemy's position.

The Nighthawk's specialty is giving close support to the infantry unit in a night defensive or ambush position. The moment that an infantry squad spots movement around its position, word is flashed to the Nighthawk.

In a matter of seconds the unit briefs the pilots and marks the positions with a light that can only be seen from the sky. Quickly, the Nighthawk begins searching the area until target detector Spec. 4 Harold Boatz picks up movement on his scope.

With a target in sight, WO John Snowgren, piloting the Huey, banks to the left while co-pilot WO Ronald Baker informs the Cobra pilot circling above the Huey of the sighting.

As the searchlight beam hits the ground, the infantrymen below relay their positions in reference to the light before the Huey's radio crackles with—"Nighthawk Two, this is Dodge Six, you are clear to engage."

On the minigun, Spec. 4 Stanley Cook pours a constant stream of fire and lead down into the small beam of light. Moments later, the Cobra overhead rolls hot and releases a burst of minigun fire and a salvo of rockets from pods tucked under its sides.

The light goes dark, but infrared scopes continue to probe the target area for an assessment of damage.

Mission completed for Nighthawk means that the enemy has been caught and stopped in the darkness before he can strike at unit positions on the ground.

A gunship underlines the team's firepower

A pilot carefully checks his Huey

Huey and Cobra depart at sunset

I was gone from Vietnam, but my photos lingered on. Information Office NCOIC Roger Ruhl sent me the Nov.10, *USARV Army Reporter* with a full page of my Nighthawk photos on page six. This one had a different layout from the October 24 *MACV Observer*.

220 Epilogue

Roger's 1969 Christmas Card is to the right.

peace on earth,
good will to men

SERGEANT ROGER RUHL
PHUOC VINH, VIETNAM

Nov 19 - The D 1/9 Rat Patrol jeep picture from August was in the *Cavalair* on page two, and one chaplain photo in the center spread was mine.

Air Cav. Swings Battery Into Action

Nov 22 - My photos of the C Battery, 1/30 Artillery move of 155 howitzers from LZ Wescott to LZ Vivian made the center spread of *Pacific Stars and Stripes*. I had many friends in 1/30, and they would enjoy the countrywide recognition as these photos showed them performing their duties. *I am sure this pleased Major Coleman and Commanding General Roberts.*

Nov 26 - My photo of Tom Benic's Army-Navy game promo was on page eight of the *Cavalair*. It also ran in the *MACV Observer*, and the *USARV Army Reporter*. It was on page one of the *Army Times* and many stateside newspapers including the *LA Examiner*.

Dec 3 - My 155 artillery move from LZ Wescott to LZ Vivian made the center spread of the *Cavalair*. A sandbag filling machine picture (on the right) was on page three and Reuben Grauer day photos filled page seven.

Dec 17 - The Cobra - LOH hunter-killer team was the center spread in the *Cavalair*. It was the best looking center spread of my pictures (with the worst name, they combined 2/20 Blue Max) and E 82 Woodpecker.) from my final big job, photographed with only five days to go.

Jan 7, 1970 - The *Cavalair* had a helicopter year-in-review center spread. The Hueys, Cobra, Skycrane and LOH were my pictures. *Somehow, I missed the Chinook.* On page seven, was a photo I took of Ron Doss' puppy "Gator" at the typewriter, (see photo at right).

Thanks to Roger Ruhl, PIO press office NCOIC, for sending me the newspapers with my pictures in them, after I left. He said I had so many photos in the publications in November and December, that no one realized I had gone home (DEROSed).

EPILOGUE 2

January 5, 1970 - My birthday - I arrived at Dulles Airport the previous day near snow covered Washington D.C. It was so cold, I had to immediately buy cold weather civilian clothes at the nearby PX.

I moved into the huge four-story brick Train Barracks building at Fort Myer, Virginia. My window overlooked part of the huge Arlington National Cemetery. The next morning, after a half-mile walk through the snow, I reported to my new duty station, the Military District of Washington Signal Support Photo Lab. When I entered the antique brick building, a huge surprise awaited. The lab chief was the same Sgt. 1st Class William Rosenmund who had been head instructor at my Fort Monmouth Photo School class from July to October of 1968. *Coincidence?*

He had practically guaranteed me an instructor position at the Ft. Monmouth Photo School, but instead, orders to Vietnam came for my entire class. I had been chosen to be part of the best unit in Vietnam, the 1st Air Cavalry. Later, I found out the 1st Cav had first choice of all skilled personnel arriving in Vietnam. Here in D.C. I was assigned to one of the best photographic jobs in the entire U. S. Army. *Sgt. 1st Class Rosenmund had prestigious jobs at Army photo school and Military District of Washington photo lab. Although he always denied it, he may have influenced my Army unit assignments. I always had the feeling someone was looking out for me. It had all worked out well.*

Happy Birthday to me, I am now in DC. I have a friend here you see, it's a great place to be.

I was in awe of the history in D.C., the White House, the Pentagon, the Capitol, the Lincoln, Washington and Jefferson Memorials, and Arlington National Cemetery. Also, I would photograph the colorful military ceremonies with President Nixon and many international dignitaries at the White House.

It looks like my great adventure isn't over after all.

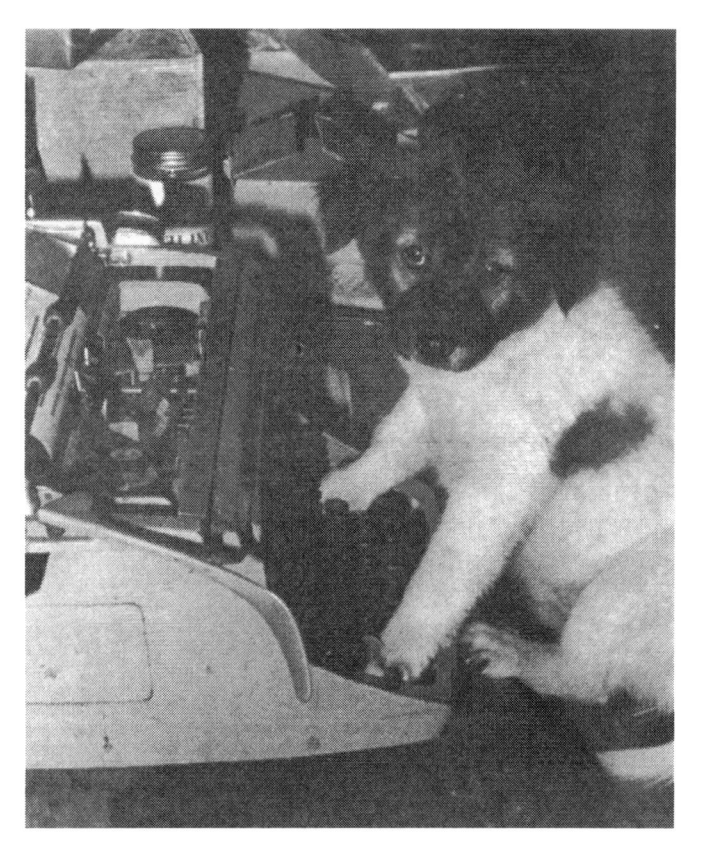

Epilogue 3

Some of my White House photos, on the left, President Nixon and Italian Prime Minister Emilio Colombo chat in the Oval Office. In the center, the President with West German Chancellor Willy Brandt pose on the south lawn. On the right, Prime Minister Harold Wilson of Great Britain reviews the troops with the President at a White House Full Honor Arrival Ceremony.

July 1970, Washington D.C.

After my first three months in D.C., Sally called to inform me our relationship was over. I was upset, but moved on. *Six months later I would meet my future wife, Nancy, a beautiful fashion show model.* I had photographed several assignments at the White House, the Pentagon, and many ceremonies and funerals at Arlington National Cemetery. I had made countless friends, and acquaintances in Vietnam, so I dreaded the thought of photographing the funeral of someone I knew.

I took pictures of dozens of funerals, some were Vietnam war KIAs. Sadly, I knew how randomly death struck in the chaos of war. Even though I didn't know any of them, it reminded me how lucky I was to have escaped my own close calls. Some of the memorial services were for long-retired generals who had nothing to do with the war. These featured a color guard, Blackjack, the riderless horse and the general's flag.

We heard the news that on July 7, 1st Cavalry Division Commanding General George Casey flew to Cam Ranh Bay to visit severely wounded skytroopers in the hospital. His Huey had to cross the highest mountains in Vietnam during poor weather. Division Chief of Staff, Col. E. C. "Shy" Meyer, and others tried to dissuade him from making the flight. As usual, CG Casey was determined. His Huey disappeared into a cloud as they neared the crest of the mountain range. The wreckage was found three days later, with no survivors. He did not have a photographer with him that day.

Also killed in the crash was Captain John Hottell, Casey's aide. Before he joined the general, he was Officer In Charge of the 14th Military History Detachment, located one building away from the Information Office. He helped our writers, and attended some of our parties. We knew him well.

I had worked with then Brig. Gen. Casey when he was 1st Cav Assistant Division Commander during September and October of 1969. I had taken the portrait of him in front of his Huey. It ran later in many U. S. newspapers along with the story of his death (photo at right). It was obvious to many that Maj. Gen. Casey was a gifted leader, and one day he would be Army Chief of Staff. Two of his immediate subordinates, Assistant Division Commander Brig. Gen. Robert Shoemaker and Division Chief of Staff Col. E. C. "Shy" Meyer later became four-star Generals. Ironically, General Casey's son, George, Jr., rose through the ranks and became Army Chief of Staff from 2007 to 2011.

The day of the funeral, July 23, rain and gloom covered Arlington National Cemetery. *Never mind the rain. There was no way I was going to cover the Cav patch on my uniform with a raincoat.* As the service at the Chapel concluded, the flag-draped casket was placed on the caisson. The 3rd Infantry Honor Guard started the procession through the rain to the gravesite. Honorary pall bearers included all five of the former 1st Cavalry Division Commanders. Directly behind the caisson were the pall bearers, the general's red two-star flag, and the symbolic riderless horse, Blackjack, famous from John F. Kennedy's funeral.

226   Epilogue

All five former 1st Cav Commanders are visible, (from right in order of rank) Lieutenant Generals Harry W. O. Kinnard, George I. Forsythe, John Tolson, John Norton, and Major General E. B. Roberts. Generals Forsythe and Roberts looked at me a few times and each gave me a subtle nod of recognition. I had worked with each of them for six months in Vietnam.

General Casey's casket was carried up to the gravesite, the flag and the generals followed, ahead of the large number of mourners.

The generals from right by rank, Lieutenant Generals Harry W. O. Kinnard, John Tolson, George Forsythe, and John Norton, Major Generals Charles Gettys and Elvy Roberts salute the flag draped casket.

The mourners gathered, some sat under the cover and several stood in the rain. The generals stood at attention and saluted their fallen comrade. These five generals represented the history of airmobile warfare in the U.S. Army. A huge Cav patch shaped floral wreath dominated the site.

It was a powerful, emotional scene of deep grief, but there was also intense pride. I was very proud to be a part of it, and never noticed the rain, because I felt I belonged.

About a month later, I was trying to find my way out of the Pentagon after a photo assignment. The enormity of the building was overwhelming, five sides, five rings, five floors. One floor of one side of one ring was a huge shopping mall. The route given to me to find my way out was blocked by a top secret area, so I had to improvise. Wandering through the halls, I saw a directory for that section. Prominent on the list was Chief of Plans, Major General Elvy B. Roberts, my former Commanding General. *What a coincidence!* I entered his office, told the receptionist who I was, and that I would like to speak to General Roberts. She buzzed him, and he responded, "Send him in."

He smiled broadly as I entered. "I saw you at General Casey's funeral," he said, remembering me from the countless times I worked with him. "The other generals noticed your Cav patch, General Forsythe remembered you too," he added.

We talked about how General Casey had been killed on his way to visit wounded skytroopers in a hospital. General Roberts and I had shared many memorable hospital tours, all uplifting experiences. "I was proud to have led those courageous warriors," he said. We both understood why it was so important for General Casey to visit the wounded that day.

My combat assault and Nighthawk photos were mentioned. He remembered they ran in several Army publications. I told him about my recon scout team flight, complete with enemy tracers, when I had only five days to go. He laughed.

"I bet you are enjoying your time here," he said, not surprised that my next duty station after Vietnam was here in D.C. We talked for fifteen or twenty minutes. He shook my hand again, patted me on the back as I left. It was satisfying to talk to him in a situation where he wasn't the commanding general and I wasn't the photographer and reminisce about the special times we shared. We saw events from totally different points of view, his omnipotent perspective, to my narrow window through my camera. However, we also saw some of them exactly the same way.

The receptionist kindly wrote out directions for me through the maze of the Pentagon to the entrance where I needed to go.

I felt much better after speaking with him. He was too nice to be a general, but he was an excellent one. The pride I had working with the great team under his command would remain with me forever.

ACKNOWLEDGEMENTS

Above all, I must thank my late mother for saving all 257 letters that I had sent home from Vietnam. She kept them in such a safe place they were only discovered three years ago. I was amazed reading all the details and quickly converted them into a rough journal.

Only a few months after we found the letters, my beloved wife of 43 years, Nancy, died suddenly of a cerebral hemorrhage, just as she had recovered from her latest Lupus flareup. Many people, including Kay, George, Allan, Kate, Mary, and Frank helped me through the grief to reinvent myself after many years as a reclusive caregiver. I then turned to seriously writing the journal as a sanctuary.

My brother, Dennis was in this from the beginning, offering help and support.

A few months later I showed the fledgling manuscript to a former teacher of mine, and author, the late Jim Downs. He liked it and encouraged me to expand it. He helped me as long as his health would allow and had many helpful suggestions, including the title.

I joined a writer's critique group, Writer's Bloc. Early sessions were brutal, but I learned so much. They helped make my manuscript much more professional, as I read, and they marked-up copies. As I was rewriting, many more memories returned to me, and the manuscript kept expanding.

In 2007, I built a website with a few of my stories and photos from Vietnam. Through the site I was contacted by hundreds of Vietnam veterans, mostly from the 1st Cav. One, Jason Holmes, had been a chaplain's assistant at Phuoc Vinh at the same time that I was there, and we had surely crossed paths. Now an English Professor, he encouraged me and helped improve my writing, especially the all important beginning.

Sally sent me over fifty photos that I thought had been lost forever.

My lady friend, Linda patiently supported me and helped with the line by line second and third rewrites.

A LRRP team member is ready as he scans the jungle ahead.

BIBLIOGRAPHY

Coleman, J. D., Pleiku, The Dawn of Helicopter Warfare in Vietnam. St. Martins Press, 1988.

Coleman, J. D., Incursion, From America's Chokehold on the NVA Lifelines to the Sacking of the Cambodian Sanctuaries. St. Martins Press, 1991.

Kelley, Michael P., Where We Were in Vietnam, A Comprehensive Guide to Firebases, Military Installations and Naval Vessels of the Vietnam War 1945-1975. Hellgate Press, 2002.

Stanton, Shelby L., Anatomy of a Division, 1st Cav in Vietnam. Presidio Press, 1987.

Stanton, Shelby L., Vietnam Order of Battle. U. S. News Books, 1981. Kraus Reprint 1986.

232   Epilogue

In the early evening, a guard watches the airstrip at LZ Carolyn.

Glossary

AAIB: Aircraft Accident Investigation Board, they investigated all aircraft accidents, which weren't always pilot error.

AHB: Assault Helicopter Battalion

ARA: Aerial Rocket Artillery

Arc Light: Name for a B-52 strike, spectacular chain of flashes at night, and could be felt ten miles away.

ARVN: Army of the Republic of South Vietnam, individual soldiers were referred to as ARVNs

Bangalore Torpedo: Long tubular explosive device used for breeching wire barriers.

Beehive: An artillery round containing steel dart-like flechettes, a massive shotgun shell.

Berm: Four foot high earthworks made by bulldozers, with built in defensive bunkers around the perimeter of a fire support base.

Bird Dog: Light "Piper Cub" aircraft, used as an artillery spotter.

Blackhat: Air traffic controllers, guided helicopter traffic at LZs

Blues: Rifle platoon of 1/9, responded quickly to hot spots, very well respected.

CA: Combat assault, troops brought in to an LZ by helicopter

C and C: Command and control aircraft, from which unit commanders directed their troops.

Caribou: C-7, a small twin-engine cargo plane, that could land on a very short runway, and held 19 passengers.

CG: Commanding General

Chieu Hoi: Program that encouraged NVA soldiers to defect.

Chinook: Large tandem rotor helicopter, could hold about twenty men or cargo. Often carried materials or equipment as a "Sling-out" hanging below. Also called "Hooks," or "Shithooks."

Claymore: Curved, directional, command detonated, antipersonnel mine, fired a 60 degree wide blast of steel balls with a kill zone up to 100 meters.

Cobra: AH-1G gunship, thin shark-like body, excellent view below, carried rockets, a 40 mm grenade launcher, and a minigun.

Concertina Wire: Coiled barbed or razor wire strung around a defensive perimeter as a barrier.

C-rations: Canned meals for use in the field. Each usually consisted of a can of some basic course, a can of fruit, a packet of dessert, powdered cocoa, sugar, powdered cream, coffee, a small pack of cigarettes, two pieces of chewing gum, and toilet paper.

Glossary

CS: Strong tear gas, also used for riot control in the USA, nasty stuff.

Daisy Cutter: Creating an LZ in the jungle with a 10,000 pound bomb, exploded above the ground. It created an open area where helicopters could deliver troops.

DEROS: Date of expected return from overseas, the day you finally went home.

Deuce-and-a-half: A two and a half ton truck

DRO: Dining room orderly, the best job on KP

Fire Support Base: Temporary artillery position secured by infantry to support field grunt units

Flak jacket: Thick fiberglass lined vest, worn for protection from shrapnel.

FNG: Fucking (Funny) New Guy, new arrivals were taken advantage of, and had pranks played on them

Foo Gas: Usually a 55 gallon drum of napalm and explosives used for perimeter defense.

Frag: Fragmentation grenade

Freedom Bird: The plane carrying soldiers back to the USA

Greenline: Defensive wire and bunker defensive ring around larger bases. It was one word to us.

Graves Registration: Unit for discrete out processing of American KIAs.

Grunt: Term for an infantryman, used proudly.

Hoi Chanh: South Vietnamese term for enemy soldier who defected.

Huey: Nickname of the Bell UH-1 utility helicopter, the workhorse, and a symbol of the Vietnam War. Also called a slick, it had a cruising speed of 127 MPH.

II Field Force: Area of responsibility was III Corps Tactical Zone, later renamed Military Region 3, which comprised eleven provinces surrounding Saigon, a component of the Military Assistance Command, Vietnam (MACV) headquartered at Bien Hoa and Long Binh.

Killer Junior: An high explosive artillery round fired horizontally with a short fuse to detonate just beyond the berm in fire support base defense.

Log Bird: Supply or logistics helicopter, usually a Huey bringing supplies to field units from fire support bases.

LOH: Light Observation Helicopter, OH-6a, pronounced: loach. The sports car of helicopters.

LRRP: Long Range Reconnaissance Patrol, elite teams of six men dropped out in the field to observe the NVA and avoid contact.

LZ: Landing zone, small area secured for bringing in troops or for resupply helicopters. The Cav called its fire support bases LZs

M-79: A 40 mm grenade launcher, like a large, very short, sawed-off shotgun filling the range between hand grenades and mortars. It fired high explosive rounds and canister, shotgun like rounds, handy for close jungle firefights.

MACV: Military Assistance Command, Vietnam, the highest American command in Vietnam. Headquarters near Tan Son Nhut in Saigon.

MARS: Military Affiliate Radio Station, soldiers could call home via Signal Corps and ham shortwave radio equipment.

Med Cap: Medical Civil Action Program, Medics went to villages and gave medical aid to civilians.

Medevac: 1st Cavalry term for medical evacuation by helicopter.

Minigun: Six barrel, rapid fire electronically controlled, machine gun, 3000 rounds or more a minute, mounted in a turret on Cobra gunships and others, when it fired at night, it looked like a red fire hose stream.

MOS: Military Occupational Specialty, the job description, 11B was an infantry rifleman, I was 84B, still photographer.

MPC: Military Payment Certificates: Our money while we were in Vietnam, small like monopoly money, with paper nickels and dimes.

Mule: Small motorized platform used for transporting supplies and personnel, mostly around fire support bases.

NCOIC: Noncommissioned officer in charge, a manager of enlisted men, usually a sergeant

NVA: North Vietnamese Army, soldiers also referred to as NVA.

P-38: Tiny folding can opener, came with C-rations.

Pink Team: 1/9 Scout team of a LOH low flying observation helicopter (white), and a high flying Cobra gunship (red). They were very successful finding NVA in the jungle and inflicting heavy casualities on the enemy.

PIO: Public information office, usually referred to as simply the information office.

Poncho Liner: Nylon insert to poncho, mainly used as a lightweight blanket.

PRC-25: Backpack FM radio, commonly used throughout the division.

PSP: Perforated steel plate, had many uses, airstrip surface, and bunker roofs, among others.

PSYOPS: Psychological operations

PV: 1st Cavalry Division base camp at Phuoc Vinh. Also called Camp Gorvad in honor of Lt. Col. Peter Gorvad, 2/12 Battalion Commander killed at LZ Grant March 8, 1969.

Recoilless Rifle: a type of lightweight tube artillery that is designed to allow some of the propellant gases to escape out the rear of the weapon at the moment of firing, creating forward thrust that heavily buffers its recoil. Light enough to be carried by infantry.

Recon: Reconnaissance

REMF: Rear Echelon Mother Fucker, label given soldiers serving in the rear by front line grunts. In reality, anyone further from the fighting than you were.

Rome Plow: Large bulldozer with protective cab, and a special tilted blade for cutting trees. It was very efficient in clearing dense jungle.

Sapper: Enemy soldier specially trained to penetrate perimeter wire defenses.

Satchel Charge: Backpack sized explosive charge carried by sappers.

Skycrane: Large, heavy lift helicopter, would sling out heavy loads, 155 howitzers or bulldozers.

Shadow: AC-119 The Air Force Flying Boxcar carried four miniguns, and an illumination flare launcher, an upgrade of Spooky with the same mission.

Sling out: Cargo attached with a sling like harness that dangled under a helicopter

Spooky: AC-47 A military version of the DC-3 that had been modified by mounting three miniguns to fire out of the left side. It also carried illumination flares. Flown by the Air Force, its primary function was close air support for troops on the ground.

Starlight Scope: Night vision scope used by base camp defenders to see in the dark, also called green eye because of its green image.

Sundry Pack: Hershey tropical chocolate bars, Hersheyettes, soap, gum, chuckles, tooth brushes, writing paper, envelopes, razors, shave cream and other things for field troops, that would normally be bought at a PX.

Tanglefoot: Single-strand barbed wire strung in a meshwork pattern at about ankle height to make it difficult for anyone to walk through it, part of greenline defenses along with concertina wire.

TOC: Tactical Operations Center

Tracer: Ammunition round that glows so its flight can be followed. American tracers were red, NVA tracers were green.

Trip Flare: ground flare triggered by a trip wire, used to catch the approach of the enemy.

Triple Canopy: dense jungle with three distinct layers of growth, usually sixty feet high.

USARV: United States Army, Vietnam, Headquartered at Long Binh. Pronounced: you-sar-vee

Printed in Germany
by Amazon Distribution
GmbH, Leipzig